# Pascal Programming Structures

## an introduction
## to systematic programming

# Pascal Programming Structures

## an introduction to systematic programming

### George W. Cherry

Reston Publishing Company, Inc.
A Prentice-Hall Company
Reston, Virginia

QA 76.73
P2C46

**Library of Congress Cataloging in Publication Data**

Cherry, George W.
    Pascal programming structures.

    Includes index.
    1. Pascal (Computer program language) I. Title.
QA76.73.P2C46        001.64'24         80-10107
ISBN 0-8359-5463-3

© 1980 by
Reston Publishing Company
A Prentice-Hall Company
Reston, Virginia

10  9  8  7  6  5  4  3

Printed in the United States of America

THIS BOOK IS DEDICATED TO

ALYCE F. CHERRY

# Contents

Contents

# Preface

Beginning students in programming have several kinds of difficulties in writing well constructed and correct programs:

1. Getting started
2. Finishing
3. Writing statements free of syntactical errors

A helpful textbook on programming assists the student in these three areas. This book was written in accordance with this idea. The book helps the student to get started by illustrating the top-down strategy of design. It helps the student to complete his design by illustrating step-wise refinement. And it helps the student to avoid syntactical errors by careful descriptions and illustrations of Pascal syntax. I believe the result will be that students using this book will write error-free and pleasing programs earlier in their courses.

The book emphasizes good reading and writing skills. One of my hopes is that the book's emphasis on clear style will infect the reader with an enthusiam for writing and reading well written computer programs. A bibliography tells the student where he can find many more well written Pascal programs.

I have chosen Pascal for this textbook because of its outstanding balance of data structuring facilities, control structures, and size. Pascal facilitates the objectives of an introductory programming course better than any other language I know. Pascal is a _practical_ as well as educationally significant language. _Efficient_ compilers for Pascal are available for virtually every contemporary computer. The present trickle of ads for programmers who know Pascal should grow steadily during the 1980s. Students who learn to program in Pascal according to the principles expounded in this book should write better BASIC, FORTRAN, and COBOL programs when their jobs require these older languages.

The first two chapters of the book are different in style and intent from the rest of the book. The purpose of these chapters is to introduce the rank beginner to simple program statements and simple, complete computer programs. It's beneficial for students to see and comprehend a handful of _whole_ programs before getting into details. This is by no means a new approach; but it's sound and sadly underused.

The student who already knows another programming language and wants to "pick up" Pascal could skip Chapter 1 completely and read Chapter 2 rapidly. This student may find the rest of book somewhat verbose; but it's my experience that students don't save time when an author leaves them half guessing at some syntactical point or semantic possibility.

The book starts at a level suitable for the rank novice; but it covers ground fairly rapidly as the student's knowledge grows. The book describes the <u>complete</u> Pascal language. It concludes with records (Chapter 8), dynamically created data structures (Chapter 9), files (Chapter 10), and sets (Chapter 11). (However, files in the context of the standard input and output operations are also covered in Chapter 4.) We leave sets until last because, while elegant, they are more peculiar to Pascal, and not essential.

I see the book's application in three settings:

**1.** A textbook for a one-semester course entitled something like "Introduction to Computer Programming." Such a course would probably assign the first seven chapters and thus cover all the simple data types, all the control structures, subprograms, and arrays. The order of the chapters on arrays (Chapter 6) and subprograms (Chapter 7) can be switched (by deferring the array examples in the chapter on subprograms). At any rate, we introduce the concept and some simple illustrations of subprograms long before the formal chapter on subprograms.

This would be a very respectable introductory course. It would give the students possession of a language approximately equal in power to BASIC and FORTRAN. The instructor might, of course, elect to omit the sections on recursive subprograms, procedures and functions as parameters, and any other section he deemed too advanced.

**2.** A second course in programming entitled "Data Structures" or "Information Structures." In this course the instructor would assign Chapters 6-11 and the students could use the earlier chapters for reference. Pascal is an exquisite language for teaching and learning data structures. For this course the instructor would no doubt want to augment this book with his own notes or one of the excellent books covering data structures (Professor Wirth's own "Algorithms + Data Structures = Programs" or Horowitz and Sahni's "Fundamentals of Data Structures," for example).

**3.** A self-study text for the computer professional or hobbyist who wants to learn Pascal for professional or cultural reasons.

I have taken very seriously the careful explication of Pascal's syntax. It's gratuitous frustration for a student to wrestle with a malfunctioning program because his textbook failed to elucidate some syntactical banana peel it's easy to slip on. I know of one student who spent three hours trying to debug a program because his textbook did not explain Pascal's peculiar behavior while reading numbers and looking for eof = true. Where there are ambiguities or disputes about a particular definition, I have appealed to the proposed BSI/ISO/ANSI* standard as well as Pascal's <u>de facto</u> standard, Jensen and Wirth, 1974.

All the major and many of the minor programming examples have been compiled and run on a computer.

The book requires very little mathematical knowledge of the student beyond elementary algebra.

I have taken illustrative problems from the fields of business, computer science, elementary chemistry, information theory, psychiatry, psychology, typesetting, word processing, and others.

Finally, for those who are interested in such things, I should like to say a little about the production of this book. The author prepared the text on his personal microcomputer and "set the type" himself with the same microcomputer, using a popular serial character printer. (The only type the author did not personally set was the Bauhaus Medium display type used for the title page and chapter titles.) This kind of composition system dissolves some of the technologically obsolete boundaries between author and copy editor, author and typesetter, author and proofreader. Therefore, I must bear fuller responsibility than usual, for better or for worse, for errors occurring in this book.

I am particularly pleased to acknowledge the expertness of Ellen Cherry, my wife and very fortunately my production editor at Reston Publishing Company. Ellen skillfully guided me through the many shoals of bookmaking.


* BSI: British Standards Institution
  ISO: International Standards Organization
  ANSI: American National Standards Institute


George W. Cherry
Reston, Virginia


PREFACE TO THE THIRD PRINTING


I am grateful to my publisher and readers for the opportunity to include in this printing several improvements and corrections. I especially want to express my gratitude to those thoughtful readers who found and reported errors or obscurities in the earlier printings.


January 1981                                      George W. Cherry

# 1. Introduction to Programming

A computer program is a sequence of instructions to a computer processor to perform useful actions on significant objects. The significant objects are often--but by no means always--numbers. For example, there are extremely useful computer programs for helping authors, secretaries, editors, and typesetters to create, prepare, edit, and typeset English text. In these cases the objects are letters, numbers, punctuation marks, words, sentences, and paragraphs; and the useful actions are insert, delete, move, justify (meaning to make the margins line up, as in the case of both margins of this book), paginate, and print. This book, for example, was composed, edited, and printed with the aid of such a computer program. There are several excellent word-processing and page-formatting programs written in the Pascal programming language.

The significant objects can also be lines, curves, characters, and other elements of figures; examples of the useful actions are position, scale-up (or scale-down), rotate, extend, change color, move, erase, connect, and print. Objects and actions like these are used in computer programs for computer-aided drafting, drawing, and design. An example of the output of such a program is Figure 1.1. A relatively short and simple Pascal program generated this intricate figure, called a Sierpinski curve.

Our final example of significant objects is records that are arranged in lists. The useful actions in this case are manipulations on the data in the records; this is called "list processing." An important example would be an insurance company's list of records of its policy holders. Useful actions would be to print the names of all policy holders who had more than three claims in the last five years; to print reminder notices to all policy holders whose premiums are 30 days overdue; to send information about life insurance to all policy holders who have fire insurance with the company and no life insurance; or to send information about automobile insurance to all the policy holders who have life insurance and no automobile insurance. Unlike the programming languages Fortran and BASIC, which are somewhat deficient in features that facilitate list processing, Pascal has language features allowing the full generality of list processing.

1

Figure 1.1  Sierpinski Curve


We call the significant objects on which the computer performs useful actions, _data_. We have seen that the family of data contains more types of objects than just numbers. (It also includes more than one type of number, as you will learn.) The first ingredient of a well written program is a thorough and careful description of the types of data on which your program acts. There are two kinds of data in a computer program: data whose values cannot change during the execution of the program, called, for obvious reasons, constants (such as the number of ounces in a quart, 32); and data whose values can change, called variables. Variables are, of course, where most of the program's action is. The value of a variable can change; but in the Pascal language _a variable's data type cannot change_. If a programmer defines a variable to hold a string of characters, he must not later treat that variable as though it held a number representing a component of the national debt. Therefore, every variable in a Pascal program has a distinct and unchanging _data type_ associated with it; and this data type determines both the values the variable can assume and the operations the program may perform upon it. An immediate advantage of this data type stability is that we may give every variable a meaningful name like Employee, HoursWorked, HourlyRate, CitationsInStock, OptionalEquipment, SalesToDate, and so on; and these meaningful names are more likely to stay meaningful during the existence of the variable.

A computer programming language is a formal means of describing the significant objects (the data) _and_ the useful actions that the computer processor should perform on the data. Since computers don't "think" the way we do, there is always some compromise when we human beings try to communicate with a computer. We prefer to speak in an abstract and problem-oriented natural language. We would like to say something to the computer like "Keep a record of the hours and hourly rate, overtime, and bonuses of each employee and print out their paychecks each month," or "Keep an inventory of all the new automobiles we have in stock and tell me right now how many air-conditioned, manual transmission, two-door Citations we have in stock," or "Keep a record of the sales of all salesman and print out their names and sales-to-date in descending order."

Unless you believe the movies in which space travelers carry on colloqial dialogues with talking computers, you probably already know there's a vast gulf between what we would like to say to the computer and what the computer can understand. The computer's objects, after all, are only strings of binary digits, or "bits," like 11010001, 00100101, 11100111, and so on, not the consequential objects (like Employee, HoursWorked, and HourlyRate) with which we associate names, meanings, and data types. And the computer's native actions are primitive and elementary, not related in any way we can readily see to the problem-solving actions we've been discussing. Furthermore, the computer hardware requires all its nondescript data and its primitive instructions to be expressed as strings of bits. If we didn't already know that computers are useful, we might despair that they ever could be. How do we bridge this vast gulf between the human problem and the computer's reliable and fast but simplistic mechanisms? One aid in bridging the gap is an appropriate programming language. Ideally, a programming language should make it easy for us to express our problem solutions; but the language should also be easy to translate into those machine language strings of ones and zeros.

Fortunately, since the installation of the first useful digital computers in the 1950s, the compromise in communication has been continually shifting in our--the human being's--favor. The reason is the successful effort of computer scientists to develop high-level, problem-oriented languages _and_ efficient computer programs to translate these languages into the strings of ones and zeros required by computer processors. Consequently, we don't have to worry about the ones and the zeros, the machine's internal language, and other esoteric matters like that. Someone must, of course, and you may want to learn about that kind of programming also--it's called machine-level or machine language programming. But this is a book about programming in a high-level, problem-oriented language. The computing community often uses one of the following abbreviations for this kind of programming: HLL (High-Level Language) or POL (Problem-Oriented Language) programming.

A computer program called the compiler (and sometimes the interpreter) makes the translation of your HLL program into the computer's internal language. Thus, the computer helps solve the

communication problem which it created. You use the computer to
translate your language into its language. Therefore, when you approach
the computer for the first time with your first Pascal program, you will
be meeting the compiler and asking it to compile (translate) your
program. A good compiler will do more than translate your program for
you. It will also rigorously check your program's adherence to Pascal's
data typing and syntax rules and make whatever checks it can of your
program's logical consistency. A good compiler is the HLL programmer's
best friend. Compilers make possible programming enterprises that would
probably be quite impossible without them. We will make frequent
reference to the compiler throughout this book. Here's a definition of
compiler from the 1977 edition of Webster's New Collegiate Dictionary:
"a computer program that translates instructions in a higher-level
symbolic language (as COBOL [Fortran, BASIC, PL/I, or Pascal]) into
machine language."


A COMPUTER PROGRAM IS LIKE A RECIPE...


    The recipe for a cake, the instructions for knitting a sweater, or
the directions for building a birdhouse or assembling an electronic kit
have a logical format. Consider the following recipe:


        BAKED ZITI (Serves 4)

        Ingredients:
        1  (8-ounce) package ziti
        2  cups Italian tomato sauce
        1  cup shredded mozzarella cheese

        Actions:
        1. Cook ziti according to
        spaghetti recipe on page 343.
        2. Prepare Italian tomato sauce
        according to recipe on page 186.
        3. Combine ziti, tomato sauce,
        and 1/2 cup shredded cheese in
        2-quart casserole.
        4. Sprinkle remainder of cheese
        on top of casserole.
        5. Heat casserole uncovered on
        full power for ten minutes or
        until cheese is melted and sauce
        is bubbly.


This recipe is a program for preparing a pasta casserole; it has many

parallels with a computer program. Like the recipe, a Pascal program
must start with a heading. Like the recipe a Pascal program must follow
the heading with a list of its "ingredients," the objects upon which the
program operates.

Notice that for the sake of compactness and readability the recipe
refers to subrecipes (or procedures) on other pages of the cook book:
the procedures for cooking the ziti and preparing the Italian tomato
sauce. Indeed, the procedure (for preparing the tomato sauce) on page
186 of the cookbook is actually longer than this recipe for Baked Ziti.
The single instruction in action 2 in the main recipe stands for the
many declarations and actions defined in the Italian tomato sauce
procedure on page 186. Many well organized cook books declare a set of
useful procedures, functions, and subrecipes which the author invokes
again and again. For example, procedures for drawing a bird and stuffing
and trussing a bird may appear at the beginning of the poultry section;
later in the cookbook, recipes for wild duck, turkey, and partridge
invoke these predefined procedures. The author will give gravy and sauce
subrecipes and then invoke them in main recipes by short-hand phrases
such as "White Sauce III, page 285." Pascal offers two forms of
subprograms (procedures and functions) which are analogous to these
subrecipes. They serve the same purpose: they make the main program more
compact, readable, and comprehensible.

A particularly useful kind of instruction in a recipe is one that
makes the actions of the cook contingent on the condition of the item
under preparation. Statement 5 above contains such an instruction: the
recipe instructs the cook to heat the casserole "until cheese is melted
and sauce is bubbly." There are many such contingent actions in cooking
recipes; they ensure repetition of an action (heating, in our example)
until a condition is achieved (melted cheese and bubbly sauce). Other
examples from a popular cookbook are: "simmer celery until tender";
"beat the batter until it is smooth"; "whip the egg whites until they
stand in peaks." Pascal has two kinds of instructions for controlling
contingent program repetitions (see Chapter 5 in Contents). Borrowing
the Pascal keywords they are:

```
while "the batter is lumpy" do
   "beat the batter."
```

and

```
repeat
   "simmer the celery"
until "the celery is tender."
```

The above is pidgin Pascal. Here's some real Pascal:

```
repeat
   X := X / 2
until X < 1
```

What does it do? First of all, every trade and profession has special jargon and symbols. Computing (and cookery!) is no exception. There's one of these special symbols in the above statement: ":="; it's called the assignment operator. The assignment operator enforces a two-stage process:

> **1.** Evaluate the expression on the right-hand side; i.e., find the value of X divided by 2.

> **2.** Assign this value to the variable whose name appears on the left-hand side.

How do you say "X := X / 2"? Programmers usually simply say "X equals X over two." Of course, this is not an accurate translation of the assignment operator; and it's sheer arithmetical nonsense unless X is zero. But you're invited to say it the easy way. Pascal will always try to remind you that the assignment operator is not the same as "=" or "equals"; that's precisely why Pascal uses ":=" for the assignment operator. If you wanted to be strictly correct (and sound rather pedantic and stiff!), you might say "replace the old value of X with the old value of X divided by two."

Let's go back to our original question: what does this **repeat-until** statement do? It repeatedly halves the value contained in the variable X until that value is less than one. If the initial value in X is 10, then the sequence of values generated by the **repeat...until** loop is: 10.0, 5.0, 2.5, 1.25, 0.625; and the final value assigned to X by this process is 0.625.

A simpler kind of repetition in a recipe is noncontingent: the action is repeated for a fixed number of times or for a given duration. Examples are: "stir mixture ten times"; "blend for six minutes"; "rinse in clear, cold water three times." Pascal has a control structure analogous to this. Here's some pidgin Pascal translating two of the above instructions.

```
for J := 1 to 10 do
    "stir the mixture";
```

```
for J := 1 to 3 do
    "rinse in cold, clear water";
```

And here's some real Pascal.

```
for J := 1 to 4 do
    writeln('This is a test.');
```

This Pascal instruction prints (writes a line) "This is a test." four times on the output device (printer or video console).

The nature of a cooking or programming problem may be such that, depending on the condition of the object, the cook or the processor should or should not take some action. From a recipe book we have: "pare apples only if the skins are very tough" and "if the caramel is sugary, add more cream and boil again." In pidgin Pascal these instructions would be:

```
if "skins are very tough" then
    "pare the apples";

if "caramel is sugary" then
    begin
        "add more cream";
        "boil again"
    end;
```

Note in the second example that we enclose the compound statement "add more cream; boil again" with **begin** and **end**. A compound statement is two or more consecutive statements. With only one exception, we use **begin** and **end** to bracket compound statements in Pascal. You will see that this bracketing, which allows us to aggregate many simple statements into a delimited unit, enhances the convenience and clarity of writing and reading Pascal programs.

Sometimes the nature of the problem is such that, depending on the condition of the object or the option selected, the processor must choose <u>one of two</u> different actions. From a candy recipe that offers the two-way choice of making old-fashioned fudge or penuche, we have the following structured control statement.

```
if "candy = old-fashioned fudge" then
    begin
        "combine 2 cups granulated sugar, 5 tablespoons cocoa,
        and one-quarter teaspoon salt in mixing bowl";
        "stir in thoroughly 1 tablespoon light corn syrup and
        1 cup milk"
    end
else {"candy = penuche, so"}
    begin
        "combine 1 cup granulated sugar, 1 cup brown sugar,
        and one-quarter teaspoon salt in mixing bowl";
        "stir in thoroughly 2 tablespoons light corn syrup and
        1 cup milk"
    end;
"Add 3 tablespoons butter";
"Cover";
for minutes := 1 to 5 do
    "microwave at high setting";
```

This control structure directs the processor to execute either the first compound statement or the second compound statement. In either case (fudge or penuche), the program directs the processor to execute the last three statements because these actions are common to the making of both fudge and penuche.

Sometimes a problem requires us to chain **if** statements together. From a recipe book we have: "if mixture is too thin, add more milk powder; if mixture is too thick, add more water." Using Pascal reserved words and syntax we have.

```
if "mixture is too thin" then
    "add more milk powder"
else if "mixture is too thick" then
    "add more water"
```

The chaining of if statements by the **else if** phrase is so common in programming, that the new Department of Defense programming language, Ada, proposes a reserved word **elsif**.

Some recipe books give menus for every day of the week or every day of the month. The problem here is to select, according to the value of the variable today, one of many actions. Pascal provides the **case** statement to deal concisely with this type of selection.

```
case today of
    Monday :
        "Prepare menu 1";
    Tuesday :
        "Prepare menu 2";
    Wednesday :
        "Prepare menu 3";
    Thursday :
        "Prepare menu 4";
    Friday :
        "Prepare menu 5";
    Saturday :
        "Prepare menu 6";
    Sunday :
        "Prepare menu 7"
end.
```

This control structure will cause the processor to: prepare menu 1 when today is Monday; prepare menu 2 when today is Tuesday; prepare menu 3 when today is Wednesday; and so on.

NEED FOR CARE AND PRECISION IN WRITING COMPUTER PROGRAMS

Although there's an analogy between a cooking recipe and a computer program, there are also distinct differences. Programs for computers tend to be much longer and more intricate than cooking recipes; and computer programs are processed by ignorant and rigid automata, whereas cooking recipes are usually processed by relatively perceptive, versatile, and knowledgeable human beings. Therefore, the author of a

computer program must exercise a great deal more care and precision in
the preparation of his instructions.

The cook, with his knowledge of cookery, the context, and the
probable intention of the recipe's author, can compensate for some vague
directions, ambiguities, and even downright errors. But the compiler,
which translates the high-level instructions into the computer
processor's language, and the processor itself, have a very restricted
"understanding"; they cannot compensate for the short-comings or
ambiguities of the careless programmer. Since the computer system cannot
really understand your intention (even though it might be patently clear
to any other human being), the system will translate and execute your
data descriptions and instructions in a robotic, literal way. The
compiler which translates your statements is also extremely fussy about
spellings and syntax. Like any functionary low in the cognitive
hierarchy, the compiler is very rule bound: it may reject a tightly
reasoned and beautifully structured program because of one missing
semicolon. You must quickly learn that the computing system is a dutiful
automatic servant but a terrible professional peer.

You also write programs for your professional peers who may have to
understand your program in order to modify it or correct an error that
crops up in it long after you've finished it. Since computer programs
can be very large and complex, you should take special pains to make
your program clear and readable to other programmers. Also, you may want
to understand your own programs six months or six years from the time
you write them. Many programmers cannot understand their own programs a
few months after they write them.

You write your programs for two kinds of "agents": human beings like
yourself who possess rationality and intuition but whose rationality is
limited and whose intuition is fallible; and the computer itself which
possesses a very high degree of responsiveness but a responsiveness that
is robotic, literal, and finicky.

These agents require that you write your programs with professional
care and precision.


NAMES (IDENTIFIERS) IN PASCAL


As an example of the programmer's writing for two audiences, we will
take the formation of names or identifiers in Pascal. The programmer
must form an identifier for every constant synonym, nonstandard data
type, variable, procedure, and function in his program. He must also
form a name for his program. How should he do this? First, he must
comply with Pascal's syntax rules for identifiers. Second, he should
obey the programming injunction to choose mnemonic names. A mnemonic
name conveys meaning; it reminds you of the thing it stands for. The
reader of your program is on a quest for meaning. Assist him!

Here's an example of a program that uses syntactically legal but
semantically uncertain identifiers. What does it mean? What does it do?

```
program Cherry4(input, output);
    var
       X, Y : real;

    begin
       read(X);
       Y := (4/3)*3.1416*X*X*X;
       write(Y)
    end.
```

Here's the same program with <u>meaningful</u> identifiers. (We've also added line numbers to which we'll refer later.)

```
1.      program FindVolumeOfSphere(input, output);
2.         const
3.            Pi = 3.1416;
4.         var
5.            Radius, Volume : real;

6.         begin
7.            read(Radius);
8.            Volume := (4/3)*Pi*Radius*Radius*Radius;
9.            write(Volume)
10.        end.
```

Both programs compute the volume of a sphere, given the radius of the sphere. The use of meaningful identifiers for the name of the program, the constant, and the two variables make the second version of the program <u>almost</u> self-explanatory. The lesson here should be clear to you.

Before we pass on to the syntax rules for Pascal identifiers, let's try to understand the second recipe. A recipe is (1) a list of ingredients and special utensils and (2) a statement of the actions to be followed in making an item of food or drink. What we want to "make" in the case of our <u>computer</u> recipe is some writing on the computer's output device which tells us the volume of a sphere whose radius we supply to the recipe by means of the computer's input device. Let's see how the program generates this writing.

Line 1 tells the computer that this is a "**program**" named "FindVolumeOfSphere" and that this program will use both the computer's "input" and "output" device.

Lines 2-5 provide a list of the ingredients and utensils. They are: one **const**ant, "Pi = 3.1416", and two **var**iables, "Radius, Volume", which are both "real" numbers.

Lines 6-10 prescribe the basic actions of the program. Line 6 indicates the prescribed actions "**begin**" in this section of the recipe. Line 7 "reads" the value of the radius from the computer's input device and stores this value in the variable named "Radius". Line 8 (right hand part) computes the volume with one division, "/", and four multiplications, "*". In line 8 (left hand part) the variable "Volume" receives, ":=", the result of the division and multiplications. Line 9

causes the computer to write the value placed in "Volume" on the output
device. Finally, line 10 signals that the program has come to its **"end."**
    The syntax rules for Pascal identifiers are conveniently given by the
syntax diagram in Figure 1.2. To use the chart, simply follow the arrows
through the chart. The chart offers many choices; but note that the
first character in every identifier must be a letter. Can identifiers
contain lowercase as well as uppercase letters? That depends on both
your terminal and your compiler. It's desirable to have a system that
permits both uppercase and lowercase letters (for reasons you'll see
later). In this book we'll freely use both. Even when your system
recognizes both uppercase and lowercase letters, it probably won't
distinguish between matching letters. That is, most systems regard X and
x as the same identifier. This is consistent with English and most
natural languages: we expect dog, Dog, and DOG to mean the same thing.

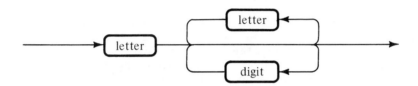

Figure 1.2   Syntax diagram for identifiers


    Notice that the syntax chart in Figure 1.2 can generate identifiers
of unlimited length (just keep traveling around the letter or the digit
loop). However, many Pascal compilers consider only the first eight
characters of an identifier and ignore the rest of the characters.
Sometimes this can be a great annoyance when you're trying to make up
meaningful identifiers; but you will just have to live with it.
    We can describe all of Pascal's syntax with diagrams like the one in
figure 1.2. Syntax diagrams are clear and rather neat; but they suffer
from one important disadvantage: they cannot be prepared on a typewriter
or typesetting equipment. The <u>Backus-Naur Formalism</u> (BNF) is a widely
used <u>metalanguage</u> for describing the syntax of programming and natural
languages. BNF descriptions can be typed on most typesetting systems and
many typewriters. We describe BNF in Appendix A of this book and also
give a BNF description of Pascal there. You should read the explanatory
information in Appendix A sometime before you read Chapter 3; and you no
doubt will want to refer to Appendix A whenever you can't recall the
exact syntax of a Pascal construct. You'll need such a reference quite a
lot in the beginning because syntax isn't something you can learn
overnight; and, as we said, you have to get the syntax of your programs
exactly right, not just "nearly right." To give you a taste of BNF,
here's the BNF desciption of a Pascal identifier:

    <identifier> ::= <letter> {<letter or digit>}
    <letter or digit> ::= <letter> | <digit>

Read "::=" as "may be composed of." The curly braces indicate the optional repetition of the enclosed symbols (i.e., the enclosed symbols may occur 0, 1, or more times). And the vertical bar means "or."

Here are some examples of legal (syntactically correct) identifiers along with some comments about their meaningfulness or advisability.

OLDSMOBILE98        See note just below.

OLDSMOBILE88        Both this identifier and the preceding one are legal but your compiler might not distinguish between them. It would be safer to use OLDS98 and OLDS88.

PRICEOFTUNEUP       Perhaps not as readable as PriceOfTuneUp.

A, B, C             These may be meaningful. But we doubt it!

Daphne              If Daphne is the name of your girl friend and you are using her name here to store the annual rainfall, then you might make points with Daphne but you won't impress other programmers. How about buying Daphne an ice-cream soda and changing your identifer to YearlyRainfall?

Here are some **illegal** identifiers.

1stTry              Identifiers must begin with a letter. Try FirstTry.

NAME_OF_JOB         Underscores are legal in identifiers in some languages, but not in Pascal.

NAME OF JOB         Embedded blanks are not permitted in Pascal, either. Try NameOfJob.

This&That           Use only letters and digits in Pascal identifiers.

RECORD              RECORD is a reserved word in Pascal.

There are 35 reserved words which have a fixed meaning in Pascal. You can't use any of these special symbols for any other purpose. If you study all of this book you'll learn the meaning of each of these symbols. At any rate, you must know about their existence so that you don't declare any of them as an identifier in your programs. In this book we'll use lowercase boldface type for reserved words:

| and   | div    | file     | in    | of        | record | type  |
|-------|--------|----------|-------|-----------|--------|-------|
| array | downto | for      | label | or        | repeat | until |
| begin | do     | function | mod   | packed    | set    | var   |
| case  | else   | goto     | nil   | procedure | then   | while |
| const | end    | if       | not   | program   | to     | with  |

EXERCISES

1. Rewrite the following instructions in the **case** statement form.
   Hint: see menu selection on page 8.

```
if Weather = Sunny then
    begin
        "walk to work";
        "make tennis date for this evening"
    end
else if Weather = Rainy then
    begin
        "take umbrella";
        "ride bus to work";
        "go to library this evening"
    end
else {Weather = Uncertain, so}
    begin
        "take umbrella";
        "walk to work";
        "wait until afternoon to plan evening"
    end
```

2. Rewrite the candy recipe (page 7) in the **case** statement form.

3. What does ":=" mean in Pascal? What do X and Y equal after each of
the following statements? What do the last three statements accomplish?

```
X := 13;
Y :=  7;
T := X;
X := Y;
Y := T
```

4. What is the effect of the following statements? (That is, after the
processor executes these statements, what value would you find in the
variable Sum?)  = 45

```
Sum := 0;
Count := 0;
repeat
    Count := Count + 1;
    Sum := Sum + Count
until Count = 10
```

5. Which of the following are legal <u>user</u> identifiers in Pascal?

|   |   |   |
|---|---|---|
| ✓ a. HoursWorked | ✓ b. HOURSWORKED | c. 2ndTrial |
| d. ValueIn$ | e. case | f. Part Number |
| ✓ g. xxx | ✓ h. Number8 | ✓ i. A1Sauce |

# 2. The General Structure
# of Pascal Programs

There are two general approaches we can take in studying Pascal, the part-whole approach and the whole-part approach. The part-whole approach would permit us to launch immediately into a rigorous definition of each isolated part (detail) of the language. Many advanced mathematics courses pursue this approach. The disadvantage of the part-whole approach is that it postpones your examining complete, working, goal-directed programs. It makes it difficult for you to see the overall effect of the program parts--how they fit together to form a purposeful whole.

The part-whole approach in language learning is like the bottom-up approach in problem solving. In the bottom-up approach one jumps immediately into the detailed solution of some subproblem or sub-subproblem. In programming we prefer the top-down approach to problem solving. In the top-down approach to problem solving we defer the working out of details, concentrating initially on formulating broad general statements which appear to solve the problem. Then we successively refine each broad statement into a more detailed statement, carrying on this process of successive refinement of each statement until we finally reach the stage of detailed implementation. Being advocates of the top-down approach and its cousin the whole-part approach, we will start by showing you several complete Pascal programs, looking for general understanding rather than detailed information, and then, after you have grasped the general idea and purpose of each program, we will discuss some of its essential details.

SOME SAMPLE PASCAL PROGRAMS

In this section we're going to show you five Pascal programs. Each program introduces a new semantic and/or syntactic idea. Do not feel anxious to understand every detail of every program; we'll get into the details in Chapter 3 and beyond. What we're trying to do in this section is to help you grasp the general idea of a Pascal program.

<u>Example 1</u>. (Addition; **program** heading; **const**ant and **var**iable declarations; action statements)

The first program we'll look at is named AddLegislators. The work that AddLegislators does for us is trivial; we could easily do the program's "computation" in our heads. But this simple example illustrates many of the structural features of a Pascal program. The line numbers on the left margin of AddLegislators are not part of the program; we added them for our discussion.

```
 1. program AddLegislators(input, output);

 2. const
 3.    NmbrOfSenators = 2; {For Number of Senators}
 4. var
 5.    NmbrOfRepresentatives, NmbrOfLegislators : 1..127;

 6. begin
 7.    read(NmbrOfRepresentatives);
 8.    NmbrOfLegislators := NmbrOfRepresentatives + NmbrOfSenators;
 9.    write(NmbrOfLegislators)
10. end.
```

If the input to this program is:

    2

the output, directly caused by line 9, is:

    4

In other words, the program adds 2 and 2 and prints out the sum, 4!
    Assuming that AddLegislators is more than an academic illustation, what is its goal? The program's goal is to write on the output device the total number of legislators from a state. The means to achieve this end are simple: add the number of senators from the state (always 2) to the number of representatives (always at least 1 and certainly less than 127) and write this sum on the output device. So that the program can be used to compute the number of legislators from any state, the program requests the number of representatives from an input file (this happens in line 7 of the program). Before looking at some of the details, let's look at the general structure. The program has three distinct parts.

line 1.      program heading, containing the program's name and identification of the program's interfaces with its environment (input, output)
lines 2-5.   definition and declaration of all the program's objects--its **const**ant and its **var**iables
lines 6-10.  statement part of the program, specifying the actions which the processor should perform upon the objects

Note also the structure of the action part of the program.

> line 7. Read the input data
> line 8. Calculate the solution
> line 9. Write the output (result, solution)

Many programs exhibit this problem-solving structure. In the top-down approach to program development, we often start with broad statements like the sequence in lines 7, 8, and 9. In our present simple problem, it's extremely easy to refine each of the broad statements (e.g., "calculate the solution") to its final detailed instruction to the processor:

> NmbrOfLegislators := NmbrOfRepresentatives + NmbrOfSenators

In this section we are going to be precise about distinguishing between the program's instructions to the compiler or the processor and the compiler's or processor's performance of those instructions. For example, you often hear programmers saying something like "the program does _____," when they mean "the compiler, while it's compiling the program, does _____," or "the processor, while it's executing the program, does _____." The purpose of our precision is to emphasize the relation between the static program text and the dynamic computing process. Obviously, the program text guides the computing process. (The way a recipe might guide a perfectly obedient robotic cook.) Since computers rarely make errors in executing programs, the dynamic computing process is what the static program really means. What other meaning could the program possibly have? It could have the meaning that we intended it to have when we wrote it or that we interpreted it to have when we read it. But the process is the final arbiter on this matter. If the process is unsatisfactory or surprising because it differs from what we intended or interpreted the program to mean, then we must be critical of our writing and reading abilities, not of the process. In the following pages we will try to sharpen our ability to read programs. As we go through AddLegislators line-by-line, we will interpret the program text in terms of the resulting compiler or processor activity as well as what the writer intended.

1. **"program"** is the first symbol in the program heading and the first symbol in every Pascal program. Line 1 is the program heading, an obligatory part of every Pascal program.

"AddLegislators" is the program's name. The compiler and the operating system require that every Pascal program have a name; but this name has no significance within the program.

"(input, output)" tells the system that the processor, while it's executing the program, may read input data and may write output data. While executing AddLegislators, the processor will read the value of the variable NmbrOfRepresentatives and it will write the value of the variable NmbrOfLegislators.

   ";" is the last symbol on this line. But this ; does not <u>belong</u> to
the heading; it is used to <u>separate</u> the heading from the ensuing
definition, declaration, or statement. You <u>must</u> understand the function
of ; in Pascal or you will have many vexing difficulties trying to
compile and run your programs. The essential idea is that ; is a
statement separator. We will illustrate its use as we go through this
program.

**2. "const"** indicates to the compiler that this is the <u>**const**ant
declaration part</u> of the program. Since **const** is not a statement, there
is no ; between line 2 and line 3.

**3.** "NmbrOfSenators = 2" asks the compiler to let us use the identifier
NmbrOfSenators as an alias or synonym for the **const**ant 2 (the number of
senators from a state). We prefer to use the identifier NmbrOfSenators
rather than the value 2 because the meaning of NmbrOfSenators is clearer
than the meaning of 2. Perhaps the meaning would be still clearer if we
used the identifier NumberOfSenators rather than the abbreviation
NmbrOfSenators. The problem with the identifiers NumberOfSenators,
NumberOfRepresentatives, and NumberOfLegislators is that many Pascal
compilers would not discriminate between these three identifiers
(because their first eight characters are the same).

   ";" is used at the end of this line to separate the **const**ant
definition from the **var**iable declaration which follows.

   "{For Number of Senators}" is a <u>comment</u>. Comments are for the benefit
of the human reader. The compiler and the processor completely ignore
comments.

**4. "var"** indicates to the compiler that **var**iable declarations will
follow. Since **var** is not a statement, there is no ; between line 4 and
line 5.

**5.** "NmbrOfRepresentatives, NmbrOfLegislators : 1..127" declares that
NmbrOfRepresentatives and NmbrOfLegislators will be used as variables in
the program. This declaration is a request to the compiler to set aside
two physical locations in the computer memory and to associate the name
NmbrOfRepresentatives with one of the locations and the name
NmbrOfLegislators with the other location. This declaration also tells
the compiler that the legal or acceptable range of values of each
variable is from 1 to 127, a subrange of the integers. Thus, if the
processor finds the value 200 when it tries to read a value for
NmbrOfRepresentatives, the processor would be able to detect that this
value is an input error.

   ";" is used at the end of this line to separate the variable
declaration from the statements that follow.

**6. "begin"** is a <u>delimiter</u> It denotes the end of the definition and declaration part of the program (the description of the "ingredients of the recipe") and the beginning of the description of the actions of the program. The program describes its actions in lines 7 through 9. The **begin** in line 6 and the **end** in line 10 act as brackets for the compound statement composed of these lines (7 through 9).

You must not think of the **begin** as a statement; it helps the compiler to compile the program and the reader to read the program; but it doesn't direct the processor to <u>do</u> anything. In some programming languages brackets are used for the functions that **begin** and **end** serve in Pascal. We suggest that you think of **begin** and **end** as "fat brackets."

Note that we have aligned the **begin** and **end** on the same margin and indented the components (lines 7 through 9) of the compound statement with respect to the **begin** and **end.** Pascal's syntax rules do not require this alignment and indention; but clarity and readability make both the alignment and the indention very desirable.

**7.** "read(NmbrOfRepresentatives)" instructs the processor to read the next value on the input file and assign this value to the variable named NmbrOfRepresentatives.

";" appears at the end of the line to separate the statement on this line from the statement which follows.

**8.** "NmbrOfLegislators := NmbrOfRepresentatives + NmbrOfSenators" is an <u>assignment statement</u>.

":=" is the assignment operator. It directs the processor to evaluate the expression on the right-hand side of the operator and assign the result of the evaluation to the variable named on the left-hand side of the operator. The overall effect is to replace whatever value was stored in NmbrOfLegislators with the sum of the constant NmbrOfSenators and the value stored in NmbrOfRepresentatives. This operation does not alter the value stored in NmbrOfRepresentatives or, of course, the value represented by NmbrOfSenators.

";" separates the assignment statement on this line from the write statement in the next line.

**9.** "write(NmbrOfLegislators)" writes the value stored in NmbrOfLegislators on the standard output medium (probably a printer or a video display). There is no ; after this statement because no further statements follow in the program.

**10. "end."** indicates the end of the compound statement and the end of the program AddLegislators. Because there can be many compound statements in a program, there can be many **begin...end** pairs in a program. However, in each program there is one and only one **end** which we follow with a period. This combination of symbols, **end.,** always indicates the end of the program.

Example 2. (Deterministic Repetition)

AddLegislators is obviously an unrealistic program. One would never write a computer program to add two numbers, and two small whole numbers at that. (Unless you take seriously the joke which asks "how many WASPs does it take to add 2 and 2." Answer: "Five. One to write the program, one to debug it, one to punch the cards, one to run the computer, and one to interpret the results.") Most realistic or practical computer programs repeat sequences of instructions over and over again. The computer is good at repetitious operations. In fact, a program without any repetitions is likely to run for only a second or so since most computers can execute about one million instructions per second. So let's look next at a problem which invites the kind of repetition of actions that is the digital computer's forte.

The problem we will look at is the computation of the number of electors in the electoral college of the United States, the body which officially elects the president and vice-president of the U.S. If we were to make this computation on the basis of census data, it would indeed be a problem for the digital computer. But we don't want to get embroiled in computational details; we simply want to illustrate the handling of repetition in a computer program. Therefore, we will assume that the number of electors from each state (50) and the District of Columbia are available on, say, 51 punched cards. (To simplify the notation, we will consider the District of Columbia to be a state.) Here's the pattern for the computation.

1. Start with a variable named Sum which has zero stored in it.
2. Read the number of electors from the 1st state from card #1.
3. Add this number to Sum.
4. Read the number of electors from the 2nd state from card #2.
5. Add this number to Sum.
6. Read the number of electors from the 3rd state from card #3.
7. Add this number to Sum.
.........................
.........................
.........................
100. Read the number of electors from the 50th state from card #50.
101. Add this number to Sum.
102. Read the number of electors from the 51st state from card #51.
103. Add this number to Sum.
104. Print out the Grand Sum of the electors from the 51 states.

The following program follows exactly this pattern; but it avoids the tedium (and the possibility of error!) involved in writing out 102 statements that merely say,

```
read(Electors);
Sum := Sum + Electors
```

over and over (51 times).

```
1.  program AddUpElectors(input, output),

2.  var
3.     Electors, Sum   : integer;
4.     State           : 1..51;

5.  begin
6.     Sum := 0;
7.     for State := 1 to 51 do
8.        begin
9.           read(Electors);
10.          Sum := Sum + Electors
11.       end;
12.    writeln('There are ', Sum, ' members in the electoral college.')
13. end.
```

Figure 2.1 is a flowgraph of the actions of this program. The dashed lines enclose the representaton of the **for** loop--lines 7 through 11 in the program. (The exact mechanization of a **for** loop depends on the compiler. We intend that Figure 2.1 merely capture the _principle_ of the **for** loop.) Notice that the **for** loop generates 51 repetitions of statements 9 and 10. We will call statements 9 and 10 the body of the **for** loop.

"State" is the **for-loop** control variable. The processor keeps track of ("controls") the number of repetitions by means of its control variable. (Every **for** loop has a control variable.) When the processor enters the **for** loop it sets the value of State equal to 1 (**for** State := 1 ...). After each execution of the body of the **for** loop, the processor increments by one the value of State. Then the processor checks the value of State. If the value of State is less than or equal to 51, the processor executes the statements in the body again; but if the value of State would exceed 51 then the processor exits the **for** loop. By this means, the processor executes the body of the **for** loop exactly 51 times.

After the processor executes the **for** loop the required number of times it executes the writeln statement, line 12. The output of this program is:

There are 538 members in the Electoral College.

Note that the writeln statement prints out strings of alphabetical characters as well as the value of Sum. In general, write or writeln will print out any series of characters enclosed by single quotes (but without the quotes). Thus

writeln('Hello, programmer.');

would print the following message on the output device:

Hello, programmer.

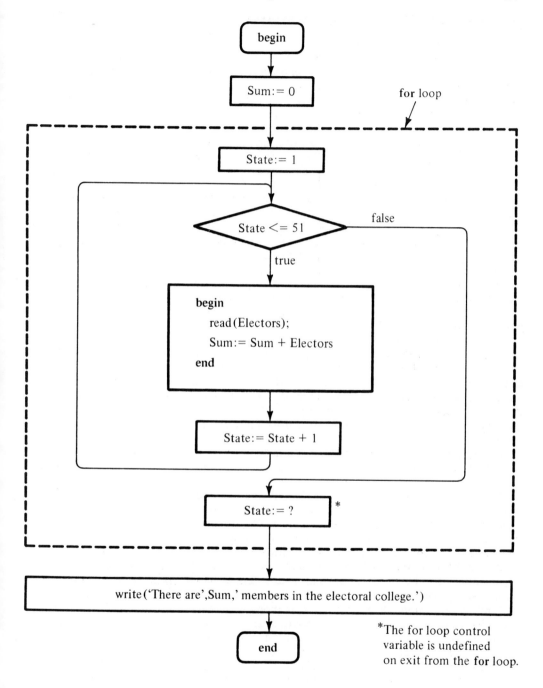

**Figure 2.1** Flowgraph of AddUpElectors

Example 3. (Deterministic Repetition with Exit for Invalid Data, **label** declarations)

In this section we're laying the groundwork for showing you the general structure of a Pascal program. In the general structure there are six different categories of definitions and declarations that can appear before the action statements of the program. So far we've met two of them, **const** and **var**. Now we're going to show you a modification of AddUpElectors which uses a third, the **label** declaration. The **label** declaration is actually the least useful and least used of all the declarations and definitions. You only have to declare a label when you use a **goto** statement. A goto statement is an unstructured control statement indicating that processing should continue not at the next statement in the text but at some other part of the text, namely at the statement prefixed by the label. We call the labelled statement the target of the goto. It's always possible to write programs without goto statements and consequently without labels. However, this is a convenient opportunity to introduce label declarations and goto statements.

We'll consider a modification of AddUpElectors which allows the new program to make a limited amount of checking of the validity of the input data to the program. (While our example isn't very useful, the principle can be.) We know that every state has at least three electors because every state has two senators and at least one representative. Therefore, any input to the program which is less than three would be an invalid input. We'll deal with the detection of an error by writing an error message identifying the number of the state for which the error occurs and then transferring control to the end of the program so that the program can conclude gracefully. (There's no point in continuing the addition of inputs because we know the final value of Sum will be wrong.)

Do not be dismayed by the length of the new program. If you understood AddUpElectors, you'll easily understand our modification of it.

Before we look at the details of AddAndCheckElectors, let's look at the heart of the change, which appears in lines 14 through 18. Lines 14 through 18 constitute an **if** statement, one of Pascal's conditional control structures. After reading a value for Electors in line 13, the processor determines (line 14) whether this value is less than MinNmbrOfElectors. If the condition of the if statement is satisfied (Electors < MinNmbrOfElectors is true) then the processor executes the statement immediately following the **then**. The statement immediately following the then is a compound statement (lines 15 through 18); and so the processor executes each statement in the sequence: line 16, line 17. First (line 16) the processor prints out the error message; then (line 17) the processor transfers control to the statement to which the programmer attached the label 13.

The target statement of the goto instruction is curious (if you haven't found it yet, it's in line 22). We find the label (followed by an obligatory :) but that's all! We call the void or blank spaces following "13:" the "null" or "empty" statement. The processor does not have to do anything when it encounters an empty statement; it merely goes on to the next statement, if any, in the sequence. The programmer did not provide a statement of substance following 13: because nothing remains to be done. Since the empty statement occurs at the end of the program, the effect of transferring control to 13 is simply to end the program.

```pascal
1.   program AddAndCheckElectors(input, output);
2.   label
3.       13; {For exit if input datum too small}
4.   const
5.       MinNmbrOfElectors = 3; {2 senators + 1 representative}
6.   var
7.       Electors, Sum : integer;
8.       State         : 1..51;

9.   begin
10.     Sum := 0;
11.     for State := 1 to 51 do
12.         begin
13.             read(Electors);
14.             if Electors < MinNmbrOfElectors then
15.                 begin
16.                     writeln('Too few electors for state ', State);
17.                     goto 13 {to terminate program}
18.                 end;
19.             Sum := Sum + Electors
20.         end; {of the for loop}
21.     write('There are ', Sum, ' members in the electoral college.');
22.     13:
23.   end.
```

Now let's return to line 14 in the program text and assume that the current value of Electors is equal to or greater than three. In that event the condition of the **if** statement is _not_ true (Electors < MinNmbrOfElectors is false); the processor will not execute the compound statement immediately following the **then.** For this case of "valid data" (Electors >= 3), the processor skips lines 15 through 18 in the text and begins processing the statement in line 19. As long as the data is "valid" (Electors >= 3), the modified program produces the same results as the first program.

Finally, let's look at the label declaration part of AddAnd-CheckElectors.

**2. "label"** indicates that this is the label declaration part of the program.

**3. "13"** is the actual label declaration. You can only declare a positive integer of four digits or less as a label.

";" separates the label declaration from the statements that follow.

"{For exit if input datum too small}" is a <u>comment</u>. The compiler ignores comments. The careful programmer includes them to help readers of his program understand the program. Enclose comments with { and } or, if your system doesn't provide braces, (* and *). If you don't enclose your comments with these special symbols, the compiler will try to translate your comments as though they were regular text and become quite confused. Other comments occur in this program (lines 5, 17, and 20).

If the input to AddAndCheckElectors is:

    6    3    12    2      et cetera

the output is

        Too few electors for state          4


<u>Example 4</u>. (Euclid's Algorithm; Conditional Repetition; Decision; **type** declarations)
    In our next sample program we introduce three new ideas.

   **1.** A program is an implementation of an algorithm.
   **2.** We can define new data types that may help us.
   **3.** We may have to provide for an unpredictable number of repetitions.

    First, let's consider a famous and ancient algorithm called Euclid's algorithm. An algorithm is an unambiguous series of instructions, frequently involving repetition of an operation, that solves a problem in a finite number of steps. Euclid's algorithm solves the problem of finding the greatest common factor (or GCF) of two positive integers. It works by repeatedly applying an operation for an <u>a priori</u> unknown but finite number of times. Why not try processing Euclid's algorithm? Pick a pair of integers (336 and 480 will do) and execute the following statements in the given order. Follow all the directions. (In other words, be an obedient processor!)

                         Euclid's Algorithm

   **1.** If the two integers are equal, you're finished; either one of the equal integers is the GCF.
   **2.** If the two integers are not equal, subtract the smaller integer from the larger and henceforth work with what <u>was</u> the smaller integer and the <u>new</u> integer that resulted from the subtraction. In other words, replace the larger integer with the result of subtracting the smaller integer from the larger integer.
   **3.** Go back to statement 1.

Did you get 48? The algorithm yields 48 after 5 subtractions. Therefore, 48 is the GCF of 336 and 480.

If you process the algorithm with 203 and 91, after 8 repetitions of the algorithm you'll find both numbers equal to 7. Therefore, 7 is the GCF of 203 and 91. To demonstrate this, let's create the variables J and K, store the original integers 203 and 91 in J and K repectively, and follow the algorithm.

| J | K | Algorithmic Action |
|---|---|---|
| 203 | 91 | Replace J with J - K |
| 112 | 91 | Replace J with J - K. |
| 21 | 91 | Replace K with K - J. |
| 21 | 70 | Replace K with K - J. |
| 21 | 49 | Replace K with K - J. |
| 21 | 28 | Replace K with K - J. |
| 21 | 7 | Replace J with J - K. |
| 14 | 7 | Replace J with J - K. |
| 7 | 7 | J = K; therefore the GCF = 7. |

Now let's consider how to translate this algorithm into Pascal. First, consider the input data. We want to be able to find the GCF for any pair of positive integers that are not too big for the computer. Pascal provides a predefined constant, maxint, equal to the largest integer representable on the computer. Therefore, the upper bound on acceptable inputs is maxint. The lower bound on acceptable inputs is one (1). Using these constraints, we define a valid input type:

```
type
    ValidInteger = 1..Maxint
```

and then declare the variables to belong to this type,

```
var
    J, K : ValidInteger
```

Now let's consider the algorithmic actions. The conditional subtraction of integers in statement 2 of the natural language version of the algorithm strongly suggests a Pascal **if-then-else** structure. It should look like this.

```
if J > K then
    J := J - K
else
    K := K - J
```

The algorithm is repetitive. While J does not equal K, the algorithm should repeat the operation of subtracting the smaller integer from the larger. But we don't know how many times the processor will have to repeat the subtraction and replacement operation. How can we translate

this nondeterministic repetition into a Pascal control structure?
Obviously, a for-do loop will not work because it's deterministic (the
programmer must know __a priori__ how many repetitions he wants). The Pascal
while-do statement is the appropriate control structure. We must control
the repetition of the above if statement with a Pascal while structure.
Here's the way it looks in text.

```
while J <> K do
   if J > K then
      J := J - K
   else {K > J, so}
      K := K - J
```

Why does "**while** J <> K **do**" mean "while J does not equal K do?" The
symbol "<>" means "less than or greater than" which is equivalent to
"does not equal." When you see "<>" in a Pascal statement, read it as
"does not equal."
   We have developed the data types and the main algorithmic control
structures. All that remains is to provide the program heading, the
input statements (read), and the output statements (write). It's usually
good programming practice to print the input data; let's also do that.
Here's the complete program.

```
program FindTheGCF(input, output);

type
   ValidInteger = 1..Maxint; {Subrange of integer}
var
   J, K : ValidInteger;

begin
   read(J, K);
   write('The GCF of', J, ' and', K, ' is');
   while J <> K do
      if J > K then
         J := J - K
      else
         K := K - J;
   write(J) {J = K, so J = GCF}
end.
```

If the input to this program is

```
      7344    4224
```

the output is

```
      The GCF of      7344 and       4224 is     48
```

Example 5. (char data type; the eoln and eof functions; **procedures**)

Our last sample program operates on alphanumeric characters rather than numbers. Every computing system has a set of alphanumeric characters for communication between computers and human beings. Because of the importance of text editing and text formatting the character processing capabilities of computers have an intrinsic interest as well. This simple example of text formatting should suggest to you that computers are not limited to numerical applications. The computer's abilities to store, manipulate, and display millions of characters at electronic speeds make it an ideal symbol processor.

A variable that can store a character is distinctly different from a Boolean variable or an integer variable. The values which a character variable can assume are constants like 'A', '4', ';', ')', '<', '0', 'c', and ' '. These are printable characters except for the last one: the blank character. We shall consider the blank character, ' ', to be a "printable" character as well; after all, you can see and even count blanks. Pascal's predefined symbol for the character data type is char. In line 3 of RemoveIndention, we declare a variable named "Ch" to be of data type char. The variable Ch can store one character value at a time.

Our sample text-formatting program, RemoveIndention, does just what its name suggests: it removes the leading blanks at the beginning of every line of input text. It does this by copying the input file of characters onto the output file; however, it does not copy the leading blanks of the input lines onto the output lines. If the input to RemoveIndention were the while statement at the top of page 26, the resulting output would be:

```
while J <> K do
if J > K then
J := J - K
else {K > J, so}
K := K - J
```

This left-hand justified version of the while statement is equivalent to the first version as far as the compiler is concerned; in fact, the compiler ignores leading blanks (and other extra blanks) while translating a Pascal program into object code.

There may actually be practical applications for RemoveIndention. The resultant source program requires less storage because each blank character usually requires one byte of storage. Of course, indented programs are usually easier to read, and so we generally prefer logically indented programs to unindented ones.

How does RemoveIndention work? If we deleted line 14 from the program, then its main statement (i.e., lines 12-22 minus line 14) would exactly copy the input file to the output file. If you turn to page 75 you will see a program very similar to RemoveIndention. The program on page 75 exactly copies an input file to an output file. (Incidentally, RemoveIndention and the program on page 75 are not intended to work with an interactive system where the standard input file is a keyboard and

the standard output file is an associated video display. If you want to
run RemoveIndention on such a system, you can do so by using a
nonstandard input file--see the program on page 74.)

The copying of the input file to the output file is under the control
of two nested while loops. The outer while loop repeats its body (lines
13-22) while "**not** eof" remains true. Eof (e̲nd o̲f f̲ile) is a built-in
function in Pascal that's false as long as there are more characters on
the input file; it becomes true as soon as the processor reads the last
character on the input file. The inner while loop repeats i̲t̲s̲ body
(lines 16-19) while "**not** eoln" remains true. Eoln (e̲nd o̲f l̲i̲n̲e̲) is a
built-in function in Pascal that's false as long as there are more
characters on the current line; it becomes true as soon as the processor
reads the last character on the current line.

After the inner while loop copies all the characters on a line, the
"readln" in line 20 moves the file input index to the beginning of the
next line. Then the "writeln" in line 21 puts an end-of-line marker on
the output file, preserving on the output file the line structure that
existed on the input file.

The effect of the statement in line 14 is to strip off the leading
blanks occurring at the beginning of each line. The statement in line 14
gobbles leading blanks by invoking a **procedure**. The name of the
procedure is GobbleBlanks. (A more dignified name for GobbleBlanks would
be SkipBlanks.) What causes GobbleBlanks to act? The appearance of its
n̲a̲m̲e̲, GobbleBlanks, in the statement part of the main program.
GobbleBlanks is like a sleeping goblin which can only awake when someone
utters its name. The main program utters GobbleBlanks' name in line 14.
Upon this utterance--officially called a subprogram invocation--the
processor initializes GobbleBlanks and begins executing GobbleBlanks'
first statement (on line 6).

Notice--and this is a most significant point--that you don't have to
read the details of GobbleBlanks to get a good idea of how Remove-
Indention works. If you take on faith that GobbleBlanks does what its
name implies, then you can read the main program without being
distracted by the details of the procedure.

The name "GobbleBlanks" answers our question "w̲h̲a̲t̲ does this
procedure do?" We may not want to know any more than this. In case we
do, the p̲r̲o̲c̲e̲d̲u̲r̲e̲ d̲e̲c̲l̲a̲r̲a̲t̲i̲o̲n̲ in lines 4-10 answers the question "h̲o̲w̲
does the procedure gobble blanks?" (To understand the gist of the
program, you don't have to ask the "how?" question.) The easiest way to
gobble blanks is to read them without writing them. That's exactly what
the repeat statement in lines 6-8 does. GobbleBlanks does not consume
n̲o̲n̲b̲l̲a̲n̲k̲s̲; as soon as it finds a nonblank, it dutifully passes it on to
the output file (write(Ch) in line 9); then Gobbleblanks returns control
to line 15, the line following its invocation in the main program.

Note that the program d̲e̲c̲l̲a̲r̲e̲s̲ the procedure GobbleBlanks in lines
4-10 and i̲n̲v̲o̲k̲e̲s̲ the procedure in line 14. If we deleted the invocation
of GobbleBlanks from the main program (line 14), the processor would
never execute GobbleBlanks. The declaration of a procedure does not
cause its execution; similarly, the declaration of a variable does not
cause its initialization with a value assignment.

```
1.  program RemoveIndention(input, output);
2.  var
3.     Ch : char;

4.  procedure GobbleBlanks;
5.     begin
6.        repeat
7.           read(Ch)
8.        until (Ch <> ' ') or eoln or eof;
9.        write(Ch)
10.    end {GobbleBlanks};

11. begin {RemoveIndention}
12.    while not eof do
13.       begin
14.          GobbleBlanks;
15.          while not eoln do
16.             begin
17.                read(Ch);
18.                write(Ch)
19.             end {inner while};
20.          readln;
21.          writeln
22.       end {outer while}
23. end.
```

## THE SKELETON OF A PASCAL PROGRAM


So far we've examined only five Pascal programs and seen only some of the data structures and algorithmic actions which Pascal provides. But you may have induced already that there's a prescribed order for defining and declaring data structures and prescribing algorithmic actions. It is time to formalize that order. All Pascal programs must be constructed on the following skeleton.

```
program <identifier>(<program parameters>);

label
   <labels>;
const
   <constant definitions>;
type
   <type definitions>;
var
   <variable declarations>;
```

```
    procedure <identifier>(<parameter list>);
       <procedure block>;
    function <identifier>(<parameter list>) : <result type>;
       <function block>;

    begin
       Statement #1;
       Statement #2;
       Statement #3;
       ............;
       Statement #N
    end.
```

**Note:** Procedures and functions are both <u>subprograms</u>. Note that the declaration of subprograms occurs after all other definitions and declarations and just before the main statement. **End of note.**

Not all of the above parts are required in every program. The program heading and the statement part (between the main **begin** and **end.**) <u>are</u> required. If a program didn't have a heading we could neither refer to the program nor know how to communicate with it. If the program didn't have a statement part, it wouldn't do anything. None of the declarations or definitions is required; but it's hard to conceive of a useful program that did not declare and manipulate at least one variable. Here's a program that has only a heading and a statement part.

```
    program NoVariables(output);

    begin
       writeln('I have no variables.')
    end.
```

But this minimum "program" doesn't do anything very interesting. Here's a slightly more interesting program which still doesn't contain an explicitly declared variable.

```
    program PowerOfTwo(output);

    begin
       writeln('The sixth power of two =', (2*2*2*2*2*2))
    end.
```

In general, though, you will declare at least one variable in every program you write. The economic justification of the activities of programming and the building and operation of computers is <u>repetition</u>, the repetitive execution of the same program with varying inputs or the iterative execution of the same lines of code in a loop or subprogram. Repetition is impossible without variables.

There's some more terminology you ought to know. We call the definition and declaration parts plus the statement part of a Pascal program a <u>block</u>. Thus we have:

```
<program> ::= <program heading>;
              <block>.
```

And we have:

```
<block> ::= [<label declaration part>]
            [<constant definition part>]
            [<type definition part>]
            [<variable definition part>]
            [<procedure declaration part>]
            [<function declaration part>]
            <statement part>.
```

where the square brackets indicate that the part is optional (can occur zero or one time). While the occurrence of a bracketed part is optional, its position in the list when it does occur is not. You must either remember the order of the declarations and definitions or you must look the order up each time you write a program. Here's a mnemonic device that makes remembering the order easy: "let's construct the very perfect function."

The order of the block's parts is not arbitrary. First of all, the definitions and declarations, which describe the data and the subprograms, must come before the statements, which describe the operations on the data and invoke the subprograms. Similarly, constants may occur in type definitions; user-defined types may occur in variable declarations; constants, types, and variables may occur in procedure and function declarations; and procedure and function invocations may occur in the main statements of the program. Thus the order is logical; it permits each successive part to define itself in terms of a well-defined preceding part. The following program fragment illustrates this building on what preceded.

```
const
   LowerBound =    0;
   UpperBound = 600;
   StallSpeed = 120;
   MaxSpeed   = 500;
type
   SpeedType = LowerBound..UpperBound;
var
   AirSpeed : SpeedType;

procedure CheckAirSpeed;
   begin
      if AirSpeed < StallSpeed
         then writeln('IN STALL')
      else if AirSpeed > MaxSpeed
         then writeln('MAXIMUM SAFE SPEED EXCEEDED')
   end;
```

```
        begin
           read(AirSpeed);
           CheckAirSpeed;
                 .
                 .
                 .
        end.
```

Notice that this skeleton or schema ensures that the processor can read the program in sequence, from beginning to end, without ever encountering an undefined or undeclared entity. Pascal's sequential declarative structure helps Pascal compilers to translate source code into machine code in a single pass through the source text.

There's no syntactical need for the processor to look ahead in the program text in order to translate it, but the human reader usually understands a program faster by carefully reading all the comments at the beginning of the program, skimming over the constant and variable declarations, and then reading the main actions of the program, saving the reading of the details of procedure and function declarations until later. The programmer can help the reader follow the program by providing comments when a declaration, definition, or statement would be puzzling until its use or effect occurs later in the program.

THE LAYOUT AND TYPESTYLE OF PASCAL PROGRAMS

Pascal programs are intelligent and meaningful concatenations of lexical tokens. Do not be alarmed by this pedantic definition. Here's a "concatenation of lexical tokens:"

```
        if Symbol = Blank then GobbleBlanks
```

The "lexical tokens" are if, then, =, Symbol, Blank, and GobbleBlanks; and we have concatenated (linked together in a chain) these tokens to form the above if statement. How you concatenate Pascal's tokens to solve a problem is one of the main subjects of this book. In this section we are mainly concerned with a semantic consideration: the arrangement of tokens on the page so that the resulting text reveals its meaning readily. But first we take up a few topics concerning the syntax of token arrangements.

The syntactical topics are simple: they mainly involve the use of comments, spaces, and ends of lines as token separators and the use of semicolons as statement separators. You must observe these few rules. If you don't, you may expect the compiler to reject your program or to badly misconstrue it.

There will be considerably more choice in the "semantic rules" we propose later. Our semantic rules involve the typestyle and layout of Pascal programs. Understanding these topics is crucial if you want to produce professional-looking and readable programs. However, Pascal imposes very few rules concerning typestyle and layout. In fact, Pascal compilers accept programs written in a "free format." Careful consideration of the last part of this chapter will help you use that freedom responsibly.

Before examining the rules, let's survey Pascal's lexical tokens. Pascal provides the following categories of lexical tokens.

## Lexical Tokens in Pascal

special symbols:  + - * / = < > [ ] { } . , : ; ^

compound special symbols:  (*  *)  <>  <=  >=  :=  ..

reserved words: **and  array  begin  case**  (See page 12 for all 35)

identifiers (predefined):  maxint  boolean  char  integer  et cetera

identifiers (user-selected):  PriceOfGas  PartNumber  UnionDues

numbers (integers):  -349  0  32000  54  et cetera

numbers (real): 6.0  3.14159  6.29E-23  1E9 et cetera

labels:  13    99    1  et cetera

character strings:  'Hello'  '***'  'A'  '7'  'What''s up?'

'What''s up' means What's up. Since a single quote terminates a string, how do you print a single quote, an apostrophe, on the output? Pascal interprets two single quotes as "please print one single quote."

Comments, spaces, and ends of lines serve as token separators. There are two strict rules for separating tokens:

**1.** There must be at least one separator between any consecutive pair of tokens made up of identifiers, reserved words, or numbers.

**2.** Separators must not occur within tokens (with the sole exception of blanks in character strings).

Here are some violations of the the first rule:

**if** I = 0**then**                  --No separator between 0 and **then**
     write('Solution found')

**program**Edit(input, output)    --No separator between **program** and Edit

**if not**Found **then**            --No separator between **not** and Found
     write('No solution')

Here are some violations of the second rule:

6.29 E+12                    --There's a space between 6.29 and E

**if** Ch < > '*' **then**     --There's a space within the compound token <>
    ReadALine

**type**
    Score = 1. .100     --There's a blank within the compound token ..

The above rules are minimally restrictive in laying out a Pascal program. In fact, because Pascal permits an arbitrary number (as long as rule 1 above is satisfied) of separators between any two consecutive tokens, programmers may write their programs in a "free format." Furthermore, comments and ends of lines, as well as blank characters, may be used for token separators. Consequently, both of the following examples are legal; both compile to produce the same result.

**if** X<0 **then begin** Y:=-X; write('Sign of input X has been changed') **end**
**else** Y:=X

```
        if
        X
        <
        0
        then
        begin
        Y
        :=
        -X
        ;
        et cetera
```

Our preference is to use the format freedom to produce as readable code as possible. For example, we prefer to write the above as

```
        if X < 0 then
            begin
                Y := -X;
                write('Sign of input X has been changed')
            end
        else {X >= 0}
            Y := X
```

This layout emphasizes the structure of the **if-then-else** statement, clearly indicating (by indention) what the processor should do if X < 0 and what the processor should do if X >= 0.
    The following is a summary of the "rules." As you read them, you may want to refer to an example. TakeOutExtraBlanks on page 29 exhibits many of the rules in an actual program.

**1.** For programs, align the reserved words **program, label, const, type, var, procedure, function,** the first (main) **begin,** and the final **end,** on the same margin.

**2.** For procedures and functions, align and <u>indent</u> the reserved words **label, const, type, var, procedure, function,** the first (main) **begin,** and the last **end,** on the same margin. See TakeOutExtraBlanks for an example of both rules 1 and 2.

**3.** Indent and subordinate all definitions and declarations with respect to the reserved words **label, const, type,** and **var.**

```
label
    99;
const
    Star = '*';
type
    WordType = array[1..20] of char;
var
    Ch   : char;
    Word : WordType
```

**4.** Do not put more than one statement on a line.

```
Not:  Z := 1; U := X; E := Y
```

```
But:
      Z := 1;
      U := X;
      E := Y
```

**5.** Lay out compound statements this way:

```
begin
    statement#1;
    statement#2;
    ...........
    statement"N
end
```

Note: In the rest of the rules, S, S1, S2, and so on, stand for simple <u>or</u> compound statements.

**6.** Lay out **if-then-else** statements this way:

```
if expression then
    S1
else
    S2
```

Some authors prefer:

```
if expression
    then
        S1
    else
        S2
```

We do not like this alternative. It creates another level of indention, makes the **then** too prominent, and becomes rather messy on chained **if** statements.

**7.** Lay out chained if statements this way:

```
if expression#1 then
    S1
else if expression#2 then
    S2
else if expression#3 then
    S3
else
    S4
```

**8.** Lay out **while-do** statements this way:

```
while condition do
    statement(s)
```

**9.** Lay out **repeat-until** statements this way:

```
repeat
    S1;
    S2;
    ...
    SN
until condition (becomes true)
```

**10.** Lay out **for-do** statements this way:

```
for Control := lowerlimit to upperlimit do
    statement(s)
```

**11.** Lay out **case** statements this way:

```
case Variable of
    Value1: S1;
    Value2: S2;
    ...
    ValueN: SN
end
```

Note particularly that the rules vertically align **begin** with its corresponding **end, if** with its corresponding **else** (if there's one **else**), **repeat** with its corresponding **until**, and **case** with its corresponding **end**. The rules clearly emphasize the "signpost" tokens **label, const, type,** and so on, and the "control-of-action" tokens **if, else, while, for,** and so on.

We want to emphasize that these "rules" are to some degree our personal preference although they are consistent with common practices. If you have an alternative format that you like, which is clear, and which isn't too unconventional, then by all means use it.

The following question arises when laying out a program: how many spaces (columns) should you indent? We prefer to indent by three columns. This seems to be a _de facto_ standard among Pascal programmers. Deeper indentions increase the danger of "running off the page" when writing programs with many loop nestings or long statements. We believe that an indention of less than two is hard to read.

Our final topic bearing on program readability is typestyle. Unfortunately, on many computers you may not even have a choice of lowercase and uppercase characters. In that case, programs must be written in monotonous rows of capital letters. The good news is that the situation is beginning to change. Some video terminals and printers provide boldface characters and underlining as well as uppercase and lowercase letters. In this book we shall make free use of lowercase and uppercase letters as well as boldface characters. We shall reserve capital letters for a special function: the initial character of a user-defined identifier and the first character of an embedded word in a user-defined identifier. We believe that this use of uppercase (capital) letters increases the readability and comprehensibility of the text. The reader can spot user-defined constants, types, variables, procedures, and functions quickly. The reader can also perceive embedded words readily. The case of letters in a literal string will be the same as that of normal English prose.

Here's a summary of the typestyle "rules" we will use.

reserved words: (boldface lowercase letters) **program, if, begin, end,** etc.

predefined identifiers: (lowercase letters) integer, char, write, read etc.

user-defined identifiers: (uppercase letters for initial character of identifier and initial character of an embedded word) I, J, K, BigLetter, TaxDeduction, JustifyMargin, SkipBlanks, DateOfInduction, etc.

literal strings: (ordinary English) 'To be, or not to be? That is the question.'

Note that the rules for identifiers give a distinct type style for each of the three kinds of identifiers. Some authors capitalize reserved words, italicize predefined identifiers, and lowercase all user-defined identifiers. Another popular style uses underscored lowercase letters for reserved words. The objective is to use some kind of convention so that your reader can quickly distinguish among the different categories.

EXERCISES

**1.** What does the following "mystery" program do?

```pascal
program Mystery(output);
var
    I, S : integer;
begin
    I := 0;
    S := 0;
    while I < 100 do
        begin
            I := I + 1;
            S := S + I
        end;
    writeln('The mysterious value is ', S)
end.
```

Hint: Trace the program for a few cycles to figure out what it's doing.
    After you figure out what the program is doing, give it an appropriate name and give the variables new names which fit their functions in the program. What should the literal phrase in the output command be changed to? Is there a simpler, faster way to do the same thing Mystery does?

**2.** The following program has two errors. What are they?

```pascal
program AddAPair(input, output);
var
    X,Y : integer;
begin
    read(X);
    read(Y);
    Z := X + Y;
    writeln('The inputs are: ', X, ' and ', Y)
    writeln('The answer is: ', Z)
end.
```

**3.** Format the following program according to the rules on pages 35 and 36.

```pascal
program FindAverage(input, output); var I, N : integer; Average, Sum,
Number : real; begin read(N); Sum := 0; for I := 1 to N do begin
read(Number); Sum := Sum + Number end; Average := Sum/N; writeln('The
average of the', N , ' numbers is', Average) end.
```

**4.** What output does the program in exercise 3 produce for the following inputs:

**a.** 2   2   2
**b.** 5   1   2   3   4   5
**c.** 5   1   2   3   4   5   6   {Hint: does the program read the six?}

**5.** Format the following program according to the rules on pages 35 and 36. Explain what the program does after you've formatted it.

**program** From1ToMonday(input, output); **var** Day : 1..7; **begin** read(Day); **case** Day **of** 1: write('Monday'); 2: write('Tuesday'); 3: write('Wednesday'); 4: write('Thursday'); 5: write('Friday'); 6: write('Saturday'); 7: write('Sunday') **end end.**

**6.** Format the following program according to the rules on pages 35 and 36.

**program** CommentOnScore(input, output); **var** Score : 0..100; **begin** read(Score); **if** Score > 90 **then** write('Excellent') **else if** (Score > 80) **and** (Score <= 90) **then** write('Good') **else if** (Score > 70) **and** (Score <= 80) **then** write('Fair') **else** write('Mediocre') **end.**

**7.** For what range of scores does the program in exercise 6 write "Mediocre?"

# 3. Declaring and Operating

# on

# Simple (Unstructured) Variables

Data are things given or granted and made the basis of inference or calculation. This broad definition includes last Friday night's prize fight. What complex data that is! It exhilarated some viewers and depressed others. The fight might inspire Norman Mailer to write a book, the novelist's form of "inference and calculation." Into the record books go some <u>abstract</u> attributes of the fight: the names of the fighters (strings of alphabetic characters), their heights, weights, reaches (real numbers), previous fights won and lost (integer numbers), whether they fought as amateurs (true or false), if true, their records as amateurs, the number of knockdowns and rounds in this fight (integer numbers), whether the fight was won by a knockout (true or false), the judges scoring of the rounds (integer numbers), the name of the winner (string of alphabetic characters). If you believe the latter type of data are meaningful, then good; for they are the way computers represent the world. No matter how sophisticated the program's data abstractions, their ultimate components are simple (or unstructured) data types like integers, decimal numbers, alphanumeric characters, or the Boolean values true and false.

When we say that the integer data type is "unstructured" we do <u>not</u> mean that the set of integer <u>values</u> has no structure. Of course, the set of values belonging to the integer data type has "structure." For example, the sequence 0, 1, 2, 3, 4, 5, 6, 7 has structure: the operators less than, equal to, and greater than have a well-defined meaning for every pair of integer values because the integer values are ordered and therefore "structured." What we do mean when we say that the integer data type is "unstructured" is that a variable of type integer cannot be decomposed or subdivided into <u>other</u> <u>meaningful</u> <u>variables</u>.

In this chapter we will formally and thoroughly cover all the unstructured data types, which are the "atoms" of Pascal data structures. Just like chemical atoms (e.g., aluminum, carbon, hydrogen, oxygen) the atomic data types have great intrinsic interest and utility. Carrying this analogy further, this chapter is like a chart of chemical elements or those chapters in a chemistry book which describe the properties and applications of the chemical elements. You may not want to read such a chart or chapter thoroughly the first time you encounter it; you surely will need to refer to it again and again.

VARIABLES IN COMPUTING


A computer program is a sequence of instructions to a computer processor to manipulate a set of values or symbols. However, the instructions rarely refer <u>directly</u> to the values or symbols. Instead, the instructions refer to "variables." A variable
> 1. is a physical location in the computer memory,
> 2. will store values or symbols of <u>one</u> data type,
> 3. has an identifier (name) associated with it.

(We will refer to the physical location by several near synonyms: "memory cell," "storage location," or just "location.") There is a great advantage in referring to variables rather than values. Consider the following two programs. Both programs add together a pair of integers.

```
program Adder1(output);

var
   Z : integer;

begin
   Z := 1929 + 51;
   writeln(Z)
end.
```

```
program Adder2(input, output);

var
   X, Y, Z : integer;

begin
   read(X, Y);
   Z := X + Y;
   writeln(Z)
end.
```

The first program has little utility because it deals with an extremely limited set of values. Its limitation stems from the fact that it refers <u>directly</u> to the values of its augend and addend, 1929 and 51. The second program is of much more general use because it refers to two flexible variables, X and Y. The variables X and Y name two storage locations in the computer memory to which any (well, not quite <u>any</u>) integer values may be assigned. The read statement in the program assigns user-selected values to these variables. The difference between Adder1 and Adder2 is analogous to the difference between arithmetic and algebra. By referring to variables rather than explicit values we produce programs and procedures that may be applied to whole sets of values and whole sets of symbols. The virtue of a variable is that we can use it to store <u>any</u> value from its declared data type.

The compiler allows us to create a variable, i.e., to give a name to a particular physical location in the computer's memory. The computer processor cannot refer to storage locations by the convenient names we think up. The processor must refer to memory locations by their <u>numerical</u> addresses, much the way the post office finds your friend's, Jack Smith's, mailbox--by referring to his address, 182 Oak Street, Boston, MA, 01960. One of the chores of the compiler is to translate the convenient English-like names you think up for your variables into the rather meaningless (to us) numerical addresses which the computer processor uses.

The numerical address of Jack Smith's current mailbox is invariant, permanent; whereas "Jack Smith" on the mailbox is semipermanent; it is put there when Jack moves to 182 Oak Street and lasts until a new owner buys or leases the house at 182 Oak Street. Most transient of all is the current contents of Jack's mailbox; these contents change daily. Similarly, the numerical address of a location in the computer memory is permanent; the name the compiler allows you to associate with that location is semipermanent--it exists from the time the processor starts executing the block in which you declared the variable until the processor finishes execution of that block. Least permanent of all--in fact, at times extremely transient--is the value stored in the location, which is analogous to the contents of the mailbox. The value in a variable may change thousands of times during the execution of a block; but at any given instant the variable contains a single, specific value, which we call the <u>current value</u> of the variable. Consider Adder2 a moment; just before the execution of read(X, Y), the current values of X and Y are undefined; right after the execution of read(X, Y) the current value of X is the first value found on the input file and the current value of Y is the second value on the input file.

There is one aspect of value assignment that the mailbox analogy overlooks. The mailman can stuff any kind of mail into your mailbox; but the processor cannot stuff any kind of value into a variable. Variable boxes cannot store just any value--the values must be of the right data type. It's as though every variable box had a specified particular shape. The processor will deposit only those values whose shape matches the shape of the box.

It is important that you understand the difference between asking the compiler to associate a given name and data type with a memory cell and asking the processor to assign a value to that cell. The former happens only once for each variable; the latter may happen over and over again. It's analogous to the difference between your painting your name on a mailbox, and the mailman's depositing some mail in your mailbox. In the first case you stake out a claim on a physical location; in the latter case the processor deposits a value in the staked-out location.

In Pascal, "declaring a variable" is the way we ask the compiler to associate a given name and data type with a physical location in memory; writing an "assignment statement" is the way we ask the processor to assign a value to the physical location. The third line in Adder2 declares the variables X, Y, and Z; the fifth line assigns values to the variables X and Y; and the sixth line assigns a value to the variable Z.

In the next section we discuss the details of variable declarations; in later sections we discuss the details of assignment statements.


DECLARING VARIABLES


It is very important that the programmer understand (and communicate this understanding to the compiler) the <u>type</u> of data on which his program acts. Just as the master chef must understand the ingredients which he chops, kneads, salts, minces, broils, or boils, the competent programmer must understand the data which he **and**s, **or**s, **\***s, **div**s, or **pack**s. The programmer who adds a Boolean data type to an integer data type has acted just as stupidly as the cook who adds Tobasco sauce to the melted butter in his cake batter. Your Pascal compiler will catch your obvious data clashes because Pascal <u>requires</u> you to declare your understanding of the types of <u>all</u> of your data.

Some language compilers--and this includes some of the most popular languages like FORTRAN and BASIC--have data type "defaults." A default is a permissive device that allows you to omit saying what data type a variable is. The computer then decides for you. Since the computer can't read your mind it may only be shooting in the dark. When the compiler shoots in the dark the result can be fatal--to your program. Pascal believes that an ounce of prevention is worth a pound of cure. There are no data type defaults in Pascal. Therefore, Pascal is characterized as a "strongly typed language." <u>It is mandatory that you declare all your variables and their data types in your Pascal programs.</u> Your instructor will not have to enforce this rule because your Pascal compiler will. (When I studied FORTRAN in a university my professor decreed that the students should declare all the variables in our programs; he decreed this because he knew that it was good programming practice and discipline. He had to police his decree himself because he didn't have a compiler to act as his teaching aid for the enforcement of strong typing.) Pascal's strong typing will help you find logical and typographical errors in your programs long before you try to run them.

As we have said, when you declare a variable you accomplish two things: you associate a name with that variable and you state the data type of the variable (i.e., you define the set of values which the processor can assign to the variable and the operations which the processor can perform on the variable). Here are several examples from the variable-declaration part of a program:

```
var
    Ownshome        :  boolean;
    MiddleInitial   :  char;
    SickLeaveTaken  :  integer;
    GrossWeight     :  real
```

These four variables are examples of the four simple, scalar, standard types--boolean, char, integer, and real. Because they are standard data types, the compiler recognizes boolean, char, integer, and real without your defining these data types in the program. The word <u>scalar</u> signifies that the variable can assume a value from a well-defined set of <u>ordered</u> values. For example, OwnsHome can assume a value from the well-defined, ordered set (false, true); and SickLeaveTaken can assume a value from the set (-maxint, -maxint + 1,..., -1, 0, +1,..., maxint - 1, maxint) where maxint is the largest integer available on the computer. An important property of the scalar data type is that if X and Y are both of the same scalar type, then the following expressions are all well-defined:

```
X < Y;  {X is less than Y}
X <= Y; {X is less than or equal to Y}
X = Y;  {X is equal to Y}
X > Y;  {X is greater than Y}
X >= Y; {X is greater than or equal to Y}
X <> Y; {X is not equal to Y}
```

The <u>cardinality</u> of a data type is the number of distinct values that you can assign to a variable that belongs to the data type. Thus the cardinality of the Boolean data type is two; the cardinality of the integer data type is 2maxint+1. The cardinality of the real data type is denumerable but very large. The cardinality of the character data type (type char) depends on the computer you're using; but a typical cardinality is 128, the size of the character and control set defined by the American Standard Code for Information Interchange (ASCII). The ASCII set of values includes the alphabet (upper <u>and</u> lower case letters), the ten digits (0, 1, 2, 3, 4, 5, 6, 7, 8, 9), the punctuation symbols and other special symbols (like <, =, >), and special control characters for communication and control between computers and their peripheral devices. We shall discuss the scalar, standard types in the order of their increasing cardinality: boolean, char, integer, and real. We will also discuss Pascal's two extensions of the scalar data types: the user-defined scalar and subrange data types.

## BOOLEAN: THE TRUE/FALSE DATA TYPE

Boolean expressions are important and therefore omnipresent in computer programs. For example, there's a Boolean expression in line 14 of the sample program on page 23:

Electors < MinNmbrOfElectors

This expression has the value true when the value stored in Electors is less than the value stored in MinNmbrOfElectors; the expression has the value false otherwise. The value of this Boolean expression provides the basis for the decision in line 14 of the sample program.

There are two Boolean expressions in the program on page 26: J <> K and J > K. They control a while loop and an if statement.

There are three Boolean expressions in the program on page 29. The expression, **not** eof, controls the outer while statement; it ensures the reading of the entire input file. The expression, **not** eoln, controls the inner while statement; it ensures the copying of all the characters on a line. The compound Boolean expression in GobbleBlanks,

(Ch <> ' ') **or** eoln **or** eof

controls the termination of the repeat loop. As long as this Boolean expression is false, GobbleBlanks reads character values without printing them, resulting in the skipping of leading blanks.

As you see from these examples, Boolean expressions provide the basis for much of the variation in programs' actions. Indeed, three major control constructs base their contingent actions on Boolean expressions:

**if** \<Boolean expression\> **then**
    \<statement\>

**while** \<Boolean expression\> **do**
    \<statement\>

**repeat**
    \<statement\>
**until** \<Boolean expression\>

where, in BNF notation,

\<Boolean expression\> ::=
    \<simple expression\> \<relational operator\> \<simple expression\> |
    \<Boolean term\> { **or** \<Boolean term\> }

where

\<relational operator\> ::=
    = | \<\> | \< | \<= | \>= | \> | **in**

and

\<Boolean term\> ::= \<Boolean factor\> { **and** \<Boolean factor\> }
\<Boolean factor\> ::= \<Boolean variable\> | \<Boolean constant\> |
    \<Boolean function designator\> | ( \<Boolean expression\> ) |
    **not** \<Boolean factor\>

(If you still haven't read Appendix A on the Backus-Naur Form, we suggest that you read at least the introductory parts of that appendix now.)

With respect to the number of values belonging to its data type, the

Boolean type is the simplest of all the types: it's cardinality is only
two. A Boolean variable can assume either the value true or the value
false. If Finished is a Boolean variable and your program prints this
variable (on your CRT or on a line printer), the value printed will be
"true" or "false." The Boolean variable is a scalar data type, which
means that its values are ordered. The order is (false, true); i.e,
false is "less than " true. Because of the ordering of the Boolean
values, we can apply the relational operators to Boolean variables. We
rarely use this feature of the Boolean data type; but you ought to know
about it.

Boolean values usually arise from the evaluation of expressions that
involve comparisons. For example, the following declarations and
assignment statements illustrate how Boolean values might arise:

```
var
    P, Q, R : boolean;
    Ch      : char;
    I, J    : integer;
    X       : real;

begin
    Ch := 'A';
    I := 0;
    J := 3;
    X := 0.0001;
    P := Ch = ' ';
    Q := I < J;
    R := X > 0;
        .
        .
        .
```

After execution of these statements, P is false, Q is true, and R is
true. P is false because the first action of the program assigns the
value 'A' to Ch and therefore Ch = ' ' is false (i.e., the value of Ch
is not the blank symbol). Q is true because the second action of the
program assigns 0 to I and the third action of the program assigns 3 to
J; therefore I < J is true. R is true because the fourth action of the
program assigns 0.0001 to X and therefore X > 0.

This is a good opportunity to make sure that you understand the
difference between the assignment operator, :=, and the equality symbol,
=. Consider the following assignment statement:

```
    R := X = 0
```

**Note:** It is perhaps clearer to write this as R := (X = 0) **End of note.**
This assignment statement is an instruction to perform two distinct
actions: first, <u>evaluate</u> the expression on the right-hand side of :=
and, second, <u>assign</u> the resulting value to the variable R. Note the
asymmetry of an assignment statement: the right-hand side must be an

expression; the left-hand side must be a variable to which the processor will assign the value of the expression. An assignment statement is not commutative. For example, the following commutation of the above statement is nonsense.

    X = 0 := R; {THIS VIOLATES THE SYNTAX AND SEMANTICS OF PASCAL.}

Now consider the right-hand side of the correct statement (the expression X = 0). Here we use the equality symbol, =. This expression is a <u>statement of fact</u> (which may be true or false); after the processor evaluates the <u>truth value</u> of the expression, the processor assigns this value to the variable R.

In general (for all the data types) the assignment statement has this form:

    <variable> := <expression>;

where an expression is any entity which has a determinable value that belongs to the data type of the variable. Considering the previous declarations, we can form the following valid and invalid assignment statements:

    P := X;      {NONSENSE: X has a determinable value but it's not a
                 Boolean value.}
    Q := false;  {VALID: you can assign the values true or false directly
                 to a Boolean variable.}
    R := P;      {VALID, assuming P has already been assigned a value}

As the BNF description of Boolean expressions shows, a Boolean expression can be as simple as a single Boolean constant, variable, or function designator or as complicated as many Boolean terms connected by **or** operators and containing Boolean factors connected by **and** operators and modified by **not** operators.

How does the processor evaluate an expression containing many elements and operators? There must be well-defined rules for evaluating complicated and possibly ambiguous expressions. These are the rules of <u>precedence,</u> so-called because they state which operator precedes which in the order of evaluation. The precedence of the operators is:

( )  --used for grouping terms or factors; has greatest precedence.

**not**  --used for negation; has greater precedence than **and.**

**and**  --used for conjunction; has greater precedence than **or.**

**or**   --used for disjunction; has greater precedence than the
         relational operators: <, <=, =, >, >=, <>.

Assuming that P and Q are Boolean variables, we define the meaning of these operators as follows:

not P    is false if P is true; is true if P is false
P **and** Q is true if <u>both</u> P and Q are true; is false otherwise
P **or** Q  is false if <u>both</u> P and Q are false; is true otherwise
P = Q    is true if P and Q have same value; is false otherwise
P <= Q   is false if P is true and Q is false; is true otherwise
P <> Q   is true if P and Q have different values; is false otherwise

    P <> Q is equivalent to **not**(P = Q); but we prefer the former because it's simpler. Similarly, we prefer P > Q to **not**(P <= Q). Because of the rules of precedence (the processor considers **not**, then **and**, then **or**, and then the relational operators), we have the consequence that

       **not** P **or** Q    is equivalent to    (**not** P) **or** Q
       P **or** Q **and** R    is equivalent to    P **or** (Q **and** R)

You can override the rules of precedence by using parentheses because the processor evaluates every expression within parentheses <u>before</u> it applies the rules of precedence. Thus you can write (P **or** Q) **and** R to force the **or** operation to be performed before the **and** operation. To avoid ambiguity or uncertainty in complex statements, use parentheses to clarify your intention.
    There are times when you <u>must</u> use parentheses to avoid a syntax error; for example, consider

```
var
    I, J : integer;
    X, Y : real;
    Q    : Boolean;
begin
    X < Y and I = J and Q   {THE COMPILER CANNOT DECIPHER THIS.}
```

This expression is meaningless because by the laws of precedence the processor would have to evaluate Y **and** I first and then J **and** Q. In other words, the processor would have to form the logical **and** of a real variable and an integer variable as well as the **and** of an integer variable and a Boolean variable.
    The compiler recognizes this as a syntax error: the syntax of Pascal insists that Boolean operators (like **and**) operate only on Boolean variables. Remember: Pascal is a strongly typed language. In this case, the strong typing feature results in the compiler's warning you that you have made a programming error. The correct version of the expression is

    (X < Y) **and** (I = J) **and** Q

    There are several predeclared functions in Pascal which yield a Boolean result. One of these functions is named odd. Odd must be supplied with an integer argument; it yields the value true if the argument is odd and the value false if the argument is even. We will use this function in the short program below.
    A very important Boolean-valued function is eof. Eof requires the

name of a file for its argument; however, if the program does not supply
a file name for the argument, the compiler assumes that the programmer
intended to use the default file, input. Eof is true when the processor
reaches the end of the designated input file.

The programmer can also define his own Boolean-valued functions. In
the program that follows we've defined a Boolean-valued function named
Positive which accepts an integer argument and yields a Boolean value.
This program illustrates many of the concepts we've discussed in this
chapter. It also illustrates again the most important use of Boolean
expressions--the basis of decision.

Although we've been discussing Boolean variables, in practice we
often write Boolean expressions whose values we never assign to Boolean
variables. This is because programs often use Boolean values in their
internal processes and do not need to preserve the Boolean values for
later use or output.

The mnemonic identifiers and the comment in the program should be
sufficient information for you to understand what the program does and
how it does it.

```
1.      program PrintsOddPosInts(input, output);

2.      {This program reads a list of integers and
3.         prints out all the odd, positive integers.}

4.      var
5.         I : integer;

6.      function Positive(I : integer) : Boolean;
7.         begin
8.            Positive := (I >= 0)
9.         end;

10.     begin
11.        read(I);
12.        while not eof do
13.           begin
14.              if Positive(I) and odd(I) then
15.                 writeln(I);
16.              read(I)
17.           end
18.     end.
```

Note that even though we declared no Boolean variables in this program,
we used two anonymous Boolean expressions. We used the Boolean
expression "not eof" in line 12 to decide whether or not to start or
continue the while loop. And we used the expression "Positive(I) and
odd(I)" in line 14 to decide whether or not to print out the current
value of I.

Pay particular attention to the function declaration in lines 6-9;
line 6 declares the argument of Positive to be of type integer and the

function itself to be of type Boolean. In a sense, we did declare a Boolean variable with the identifier "Positive." Note that in line 8 we actually assign a Boolean value to this identifier. Note also that the processor does not execute the function until the main program invokes it in line 14. The earnest student should assume a set of integers (negative and positive, odd and even) and trace the program starting at its first executable statement in line 11.

There may be occasions when you would like to supply a Boolean value as an input to a program in order to control a repetition or a choice. You can't do this directly because the read procedure does not accept a Boolean argument. However, you can provide some lines of code that will interpret the input character F as false and the character T as true.

```
var
    Condition : boolean;
    Ch : char;
        .
        .
        .
begin
    read(Ch);
    if (Ch = 'F') or (Ch = 'T') then
        Condition := (Ch = 'T')
    else
        writeln('INPUT ERROR: T OR F expected')
```

If you don't thoroughly understand this program now, look at it again after you read the next section.


CHAR: THE PRINTABLE CHARACTERS DATA TYPE


The printable characters are of data type char. They're important because they permit communication between computers and other computers and between computers and human beings. All the data inside the digital computer are in binary form, strings (hardly comprehensible to us) of 1s and 0s. The printable characters allow us to communicate with the computer in symbols we understand. Those symbols are the elements of data type char.

We declare a variable V to be of type char in the usual way.

```
var
    V : char;
```

We denote a constant or literal of type char by enclosing the character in single quotes.

'Y'        represents the letter Y

    '4'        represents the numeral--<u>not the number</u>--4
    ' '        represents the character blank
    ''''       represents the single quote '

Thus

    V := 'N'

assigns the character value 'N' to the variable V.

    Unfortunately, there's no universally accepted standard for the set
of printable characters and the way they're coded inside the computer.
The American Standard Code for Information Interchange (ASCII) is quite
close to being a standard. Most of the video consoles, printers, and
telecommunications equipment for minicomputers and microcomputers
communicate according to the ASCII system or a subset of that system.
It's desirable to have the full ASCII character set because it supports
word processing and automated composition which are important
applications of microcomputers and minicomputers. In this book we've
assumed the computer we're using supports the full ASCII character set.
This assumption implies that:

    1. '0' < '1' < ... < '8' < '9'
    2. 'A' < 'B' < ... < 'Y' < 'Z'
    3. 'a' < 'b' < ... < 'y' < 'z'

Almost every computer provides at least the 26 capital letters and the
10 digits, ordered as shown above in 1 and 2. Since most of our
character-processing examples depend only on the 1st and 2nd
implications of the ASCII set we do not surrender generality by our
assumption.
    The character set is represented inside the computer by binary
numbers. In the case of the ASCII system they are seven bit binary
numbers. For example, in ASCII we have:

| Character | Binary Code | Decimal Code |
|-----------|-------------|--------------|
| '0' | 0110000 | 48 |
| '1' | 0110001 | 49 |
| '2' | 0110010 | 50 |
| '3' | 0110011 | 51 |
| . | . | . |
| . | . | . |
| 'A' | 1000001 | 65 |
| 'B' | 1000010 | 66 |
| 'C' | 1000011 | 67 |
| . | ....... | .. |

Appendix B exhibits the complete ASCII coding chart.
    The characters have the same order (sometimes called the "collating"
or "enumeration" sequence) as their integer representations. In fact, as
you might guess, 'A' "is less than" 'B' because 'A' is represented by 65

and 'B' is represented by 66. Now that you have seen this chart you should never confuse '0' and 0. Indeed, '0' is represented by 0110000 (decimal 48)!

A word of warning: never write a program on the basis of particular details of the ASCII codes! This could jeopardize the portability of your program. That is, your program could work well on an ASCII machine and then fail utterly on a machine that used the EBCDIC system (used by IBM). If you do find a pressing reason to exploit the details of a particular character coding system, document this dependency conspicuously.

Because of their ordering you can use the comparison operators (<, =, >, and so on) on variables of type char. (But these are the only operators that you can use on char variables.) Of course, these operators yield a Boolean result.

The following program copies all the lines of text on an input file to an output file, replacing the digits with asterisks. (This program could be used to suppress sensitive numbers on memoranda that will be distributed to personnel not authorized to see the numbers.) The program illustrates many of the ideas we've been discussing.

The program also introduces the Boolean function eoln; eoln is true when the processor has read all of the characters on a line (including its trailing blanks); eoln is false otherwise. The standard input files, "input" and "output," are textfiles; i.e., files whose components are characters. The author of a textfile can arrange it in lines. This line structure can be quite meaningful, as in tabular material and typeset natural language. CensorDigits faithfully transmits the line structure of the input file to the output file.

```
program CensorDigits(input, output);

const
    Star = '*';
var
    Ch : char;

begin
    while not eof do
        begin
            while not eoln do {copy the line.}
                begin
                    read(Ch);
                    if ('0' <= Ch) and (Ch <= '9') then
                        write(Star)
                    else
                        write(Ch)
                end;
            readln; {Prepare to read next line in input file.}
            writeln {Put line separator on the output file.}
        end
end.
```

If the input to this program is:

>     Ms. Mary Clover Jone's total
> remuneration including bonus is $78,940.
> Mr. James Watson's total remuneration
> including bonus and lease fee for
> company car privately used is $57,734.

the output is:

>     Ms. Mary Clover Jone's total
> remuneration including bonus is $**,***.
> Mr. James Watson's total remuneration
> including bonus and lease fee for
> company car privately used is $**,***.

There are several comments worth making about the Boolean expression in the **if-then** statement. First, we used the collating assumption ('0' < '1' <...< '8' < '9') to write the condition that Ch currently stores the representation of a digit. Second, in mathematical notation you often see this kind of statement

'0' <= Ch <= '9'

which we expressed in the longer, equivalent form

('0' <= Ch) **and** (Ch <= '9')

You can't use the shorter notation in Pascal; you must accept the slight inconvenience of writing the compound condition as the conjunction of two simple conditions.

Pascal provides several standard functions that are useful in manipulating char variables.

ord  This function transforms a character value into the <u>ordinal number</u> (the integer) that represents the character. ( An ordinal number is a number that designates the place--0th, 1st,..., 126th, 127th--occupied by an item in an ordered sequence.) Assuming ASCII coding we have: ord('=') has the value 63; ord('0') has the value 48; ord('X') has the value 88; and so on.

chr  This function is the inverse of ord; it transforms an ordinal number from the enumeration sequence into the corresponding character value. In ASCII coding, chr(57), for example, has the value '9'.

Note this important consequence of our definitions: if we want to transform a digit character ('0', '1', '2', ..., '9') into the corresponding integer (0, 1, 2, ..., 9) we must use the expression in the assignment statement of the following code.

```
type
    DigitChar = '0'..'9'; {This is a subrange data type}
var
    Digit : DigitChar;
    N     : integer;
begin
    ...........................
    N := ord(Digit) - ord('0');
    ...........................
end
```

This formulation is necessary because, for most computers, ord('0') does not equal zero.

If you want to make the inverse tranformation--i.e., find the character, 'N', that corresponds to the integer N--then you must use the expression chr(N + ord('0')). This expression is valid, of course, only for (N >= 0) **and** (N <= 9).

This is a good time to emphasize that char variables can hold only a single character. Literal expressions like '1979', '1776', 'JONES', and 'HELLO, USER' cannot be assigned to a char variable. These multi-character constants belong to the data type _string_. We will discuss the string data type later.

Using the ord and chr functions we can write a statement that changes any lowercase letter to its corresponding uppercase letter.

```
if ('a' <= Ch) and (Ch <= 'z') then
    Ch := chr(ord(Ch) - 32);
    {CAUTION: WORKS IN ASCII ONLY!}
```

If you examine the ASCII coding table in appendix A you should see why this is true. (The ordinal numbers for the small letters are 32 larger than the ordinal numbers for the capital letters.)

We can make our programs more or less portable, that is more or less able to run on a variety of computers. For example, we can concoct a statement which converts lowercase letters to uppercase letters in any character set for which the following relationships are true.

```
ord('A') = ord('a') + C
ord('B') = ord('b') + C
.....................
ord('Z') = ord('z') + C
```

that is, in any character set in which the ordinal values of all the uppercase letters differ from the ordinal values of all the corresponding lowercase letters by exactly the same constant. This is true for most character sets that have both uppercase and lowercase letters. The more portable statement is:

```
if (Ch >= 'a') and (Ch <= 'z') then
    Ch := chr(ord(Ch) + ord('A') - ord('a'))
```

The Boolean expression in the if statement of the above code assumes that every character between 'a' and 'z' is a lowercase letter. This assumption is true in most character sets. It is true in ASCII, for example. But it is not strictly true in EBCDIC because certain control characters may occur in the gap between 'i' and 'j' and the gap between 'r' and 's' (See Appendix B). However, these control characters are not likely to appear in normal data; therefore, our assumption is a reasonable one, and we shall continue to make it throughout this book.

There are two more standard functions that are sometimes useful when working with char variables.

pred    This function yields the predecessor of the argument--_if one exists_. Thus pred('5') is '4' and pred('B') is 'A'. But beware: in the ASCII character set, pred('0') is '/'!

succ    This function yields the successor of the argument--_if one exists_. Thus succ('2') is '3' and succ('W') is 'X'. Again, a strange character may crop up at the end of a sequence; for example, succ('9') is ':'.

Here's a program fragment that helps test an ASCII printer by printing 95 lines of output. Each line starts at a different point in the ASCII enumeration sequence, and all 95 printable characters (including ' ') appear on each line. Furthermore, each ASCII character appears once on each column of the output. The first for-loop prints each ASCII character in the order of the enumeration sequence. The second for-loop controls the starting point of each subsequent line. The first inner for-loop prints all the ASCII characters between FirstCh and '~'; and then the second inner for-loop prints the remaining ASCII characters from ' ' to the predecessor of FirstCh.

```
for Ch := ' ' to '~' do
   write(Ch);
writeln;
for FirstCh:= succ(' ') to '~' do
   begin
      for Ch:= FirstCh to '~' do
         write(Ch);
      for Ch:= ' ' to pred(FirstCh) do
         write(Ch);
      writeln
   end
```

The output (partial) of this code is:

```
 !"#$%&'()*+,-./0123456789:;<=>?@ABCDEFGHIJKLMNOPQRSTUVWXYZ[\]^_`abcdefg
!"#$%&'()*+,-./0123456789:;<=>?@ABCDEFGHIJKLMNOPQRSTUVWXYZ[\]^_`abcdefgh
"#$%&'()*+,-.o/0123456789:;<=>?@ABCDEFGHIJKLMNOPQRSTUVWXYZ[\]^_`abcdefghi
#$%&'()*+,-./0123456789:;<=>?@ABCDEFGHIJKLMNOPQRSTUVWXYZ[\]^_`abcdefghij
$%&'()*+,-./0123456789:;<=>?@ABCDEFGHIJKLMNOPQRSTUVWXYZ[\]^_`abcdefghijk
```

## USER-DEFINED SCALAR DATA TYPE

The user-defined scalar data type allows you to make up a scalar type appropriate to your problem. You are allowed to define

1. the number of values belonging to the type,
2. the identifier associated with each value,
3. the order of the values.

Since the programmer determines the number of values belonging to the type, the cardinality of this type is variable. In practice, the cardinality of the user-defined scalar is usually greater than the cardinality of the Boolean type and smaller than the cardinality of the char type.

You define this type by simply providing an _ordered_ list of the values belonging to the type. Thus the type definition

**type**
    TemperType = (Cringing, Placating, Inhibited, Harmless, Peaceable,
    EvenTempered, Hotblooded, Combative, Destructive, Assaultive,
    Murderous);

states that a variable of the type TemperType may assume any one of the eleven values listed, and no other values. You declare a variable of the type TemperType in the usual way.

**var**
    Temper : TemperType;

And you may assign a value to the variable Temper in the usual way.

    Temper := Destructive;

The following ordering relationships follow directly from the order of the values in the type definition.

    Cringing < Placating < Inhibited < Harmless < Peaceable <
    EvenTempered < Hotblooded < Combative < Destructive < Assaultive <
    Murderous

You may use all of the relational operators with scalar variables (but no other operators). As usual, the relational operators yield a Boolean result.

    if (Temper >= Harmless) **and** (Temper < Hotblooded) **then**
        writeln('Patient's Temper is within normal range.');

    if Temper <= Inhibited **then**
        writeln('Enroll patient in assertiveness training program.');

```
if Temper >= Combative then
   writeln('Start patient in self-control program.');
```

The predeclared functions pred and succ are available for user-defined scalar data types. For example

```
succ(Inhibited) is equal to Harmless
pred(Peaceable) is equal to Harmless
```

You must never go beyond the ends of the enumeration sequence. For example, succ(Murderous) and pred(Cringing) are both undefined.

The Boolean data type is similar to the user-defined scalar data type; however, the Pascal system predefines the Boolean type. It also provides special operators for Boolean variables which are not available for user-defined scalar variables (**not, and, or**). The following type definition is implicit for the Boolean data type.

```
type
   Boolean = (false, true);
```

There's another similarity between the Boolean and the user-defined scalar data type: you can't read the scalar values of either data type directly. In addition, you can't write the value of a user-defined scalar variable. By the use of the function ord and other mechanisms you can work around these limitations.

The ordinal number of the first value of a user-defined scalar data type is 0. Therefore

```
ord(Cringing)   is  0
ord(Placating)  is  1
ord(Inhibited)  is  2
      .      .      .
ord(Assaultive) is  9
ord(Murderous)  is 10
```

The following program illustrates many of the concepts of this section. This program assumes an input file of ratings by many mental health professionals of the same psychiatric patient. Each professional rates the patient's temperament by assigning a number from 0 to 10 with 0 meaning Cringing, 1 meaning Placating, 2 meaning Inhibited, and so on. The program reads, counts, and averages the ratings; finds the scalar value of Temper corresponding to this average; and prints out the value of Temper along with appropriate diagnostic or prescriptive messages.

Don't confuse the _values_ of a user-defined variable with _variables_. The identifiers Cringing, Placating, and so on, are _constants_ of the variable Temper and the type TemperType. You can't assign a value to a constant; therefore Cringing and the other constants of TemperType can't appear on the left-hand side of an assignment statement. Cringing and Placating have the same sort of relationship to the variable Temper that false and true have to a Boolean variable.

```
program EstimateTemper(input, output);

type
   RatingType = 0..10; {This is a subrange data type}
   TemperType = (Cringing, Placating, Inhibited, Harmless, Peaceable,
                 EvenTempered, Hotblooded, Combative, Destructive,
                 Assaultive, Murderous);
var
   Rating          : RatingType;
   AverageRating   : RatingType;
   Temper          : TemperType;
   NmbrOfRaters    : integer; {To accumulate number of Raters};
   SumOfRatings    : integer;

begin
   SumOfRatings := 0;
   NmbrOfRaters := 0;
   while not eof do
      begin
         readln(Rating);
         SumOfRatings := SumOfRatings + Rating;
         NmbrOfRaters := NmbrOfRaters + 1;
      end;
   AverageRating := round(SumOfRatings / NmbrOfRaters);

   Temper := Cringing;
   while ord(Temper) <> AverageRating do
      Temper := succ(Temper);

   case Temper of
      Cringing: writeln('Cringing: try assertiveness training.');
      Placating: writeln('Placating: try assertiveness training.');
      Inhibited: writeln('Inhibited: try assertiveness training.');
      Harmless: writeln('Harmless: assertiveness training?');
      Peaceable: writeln('Peaceable: temper in normal range.');
      EvenTempered: writeln('EvenTempered: temper in normal range.');
      Hotblooded: writeln('Hotblooded: self-control program?');
      Combative: writeln('Combative: try self-control program.');
      Destructive: writeln('Destructive: try self-control program.');
      Assaultive: writeln('Assaultive: try self-control program.');
      Murderous: writeln('Murderous: try self-control program.')
   end;

   if Temper > Combative then
      begin
         writeln('Patient may be VERY dangerous.');
         writeln('Consider: major tranquillizers and a locked ward.');
         writeln('Use restraints or seclusion when necessary.')
      end
end.
```

## INTEGER: THE WHOLE NUMBERS DATA TYPE

An integer is any of the natural numbers, the negatives of these numbers, or zero. Thus 4945, 0, and -32767 are all integers. Since computers have memory cells of finite bit length, any computer can represent only a finite number of the integers. Pascal provides an identifier, maxint, to refer to the largest integer available on the computer. If you want to find out what this number is on your computer, use the instruction write(maxint), which will print it on the computer's output device. Microcomputers usually have 16-bit data cells, resulting in a maxint of 32,767 (unless the hardware or software makes special provisions for longer integers). Many minicomputers have 32-bit data cells, resulting in the much larger maxint of 2,147,483,647. At any rate, your computer will handle all operations on arguments of type integer so long as the result of an operation falls between the limits -maxint and maxint. If an operation would produce a result lying outside the representable range, -maxint..maxint, the computing system has the responsibility to terminate the computation and provide an "overflow" signal.

The integer data type satisfies the need for a data type providing <u>exact</u> operations and values. In certain problems--accounting, record-keeping, exact counting, exact census, and so on--approximation and rounding-off are not permissible. Aside from the condition of overflow, all operations on variables of type integer are exact.

The cardinality of the integer data type is 2*maxint + 1.

There are five arithmetic operators for integers. They come in two levels of precedence: higher precedence (**\***, **div**, and **mod**) and lower precedence (+, -). The operator **\*** stands for multiplication in Pascal; the use of **\*** for multiplication is traditional in computer languages. **div** stands for integer division; it gives a truncated integer for the quotient. Thus

        21 **div** 4  is 5
        12 **div** 10 is 1
        10 **div** 11 is 0

Particularly note the last result; programmers sometimes forget that N **div** (N + 1) is zero for all N > 0.

If you wanted to know how much has been truncated from the quotient when you perform integer division, you could use the **mod** operator which gives the integer division remainder. Thus

        21 **mod** 4  is 1
        12 **mod** 10 is 2
        10 **mod** 11 is 10

and the truncation error in performing M **div** N is

        (M **mod** N)/N

One of the important uses of the **mod** function is to determine whether one integer divides another one exactly. If N divides M exactly then M **mod** N is zero. The following lines print out all the integers between FirstInteger and LastInteger that are exactly divisible by three and four.

```
For I := FirstInteger to LastInteger do
    if (I mod 3 = 0) and (I mod 4 = 0) then
        write(I, ' is exactly divisible by 3 and 4')
```

Whereas **div** is used for integer division, / is used for "real" division. By "real" division we mean that / does not truncate the fractional part of the decimal quotient. You may use the operator / with integer operands; however, the result is a real number--not an integer number. So, even though I and J are both integers, you may not assign (I / J) to an integer variable. If you want to assign the result of (I / J) to an integer variable, you can use the Pascal standard functions trunc or round which transform a real argument into an integer value. The function trunc accomplishes the conversion by truncating the fractional part of its argument; round converts its argument by rounding it to the nearest integer. The use of trunc to convert (I / J) is wasteful and foolish because

trunc(I / J) is equal to I **div** J

and we might as well have used **div** rather than / to begin with. The use of round(I / J) is useful because it gives a rounded result whereas integer division, I **div** J, gives a truncated result. This is exactly why we used the expression

round(SumOfRatings / NmbrOfRaters);

to compute AverageRating in the program EstimateTemper.

The processor applies the rules of precedence during the evaluation of an expression. When two or more operators of the same precedence follow each other in an expression, the processor applies the operators in the order in which the compiler encounters them, parsing from left to right. Thus

```
I * J div K  =  (I * J) div K (Apply from left to right)
I - J div K  =  I - (J div K) (Apply div before -)
I * J + K    =  (I * J) + K (Apply * before +)
I - J * K + L  =  (I - (J * K)) + L (Apply * before -)
J + K < L      =  (J + K) < L  (Apply + before <)
```

There are many standard functions in Pascal that accept an integer value for their arguments, yield an integer value for their results, or both accept and yield an integer value. Here's a summary. The functions abs and sqr and all the functions in the third group (sin through sqrt) will also accept real arguments.

| Standard Function | Argument | Value | Rule |
|---|---|---|---|
| pred | integer | integer | pred(I) is I - 1 |
| succ | integer | integer | succ(I) is I + 1 |
| abs | integer | integer | if I < 0, abs(I) = -I, else abs(I) = +I |
| sqr | integer | integer | sqr(I) is I*I |
| ord | boolean | integer | ord(false) is 0; ord(true) is 1 |
| ord | char | integer | ord(Ch) is ordinal number of Ch |
| sin | integer | real | trigonometric sine |
| cos | integer | real | trigonometric cosine |
| arctan | integer | real | trigonometric arctangent |
| ln | integer | real | natural logarithm |
| exp | integer | real | exponential function |
| sqrt | integer | real | square root |
| odd | integer | boolean | odd(I)=true for odd I, false for even I |
| chr | integer | char | chr(I)=character whose ordinal value is I |
| trunc | real | integer | trunc(X)=integer part of X |
| round | real | integer | round(X)=integer closest to X |

Integer values must be written without commas and without decimal points; that is, they must be sequences of digits. You may, of course, prefix the sequence of digits with a + or - sign. If an integer is positive, the + sign is optional.

The standard procedures, read and readln, read integers written in the correct format. If I and J are declared integers, then

    read(I, J)

will read the next two integers on the input file. But if any other symbols occur on the input file before the next integer or between the next and following integer, the processor will signal a read (type) error. Thus

    -31825    17896

would be acceptable on the input file. The processor would read the six characters "-31825" as a single group, convert the corresponding integer to the computer's internal representation of integers (a binary form), and store this internal representation of -31825 in the variable I. Then the processor would automatically skip the blanks between the first and second sets of characters, read the group 17896, convert it to internal form, and assign this value to the variable J. But if the input appeared as

    -31,825    17,896

the processor would find a comma where it expects a digit and abort its attempt to read the rest of the integer. (Some implementations might assign -31 to I and 825 to J. We'll explain why in the next chapter.) Other characters like "$" and '.' could also give rise to read errors.

Is there any way the program could read, say, integers which have embedded commas? The answer is "Yes": one can write a special procedure that reads integers formatted with commas. The input data would look like this:

    96,345    1,230    3,462,230

These numbers are clearly more readable than integers without commas; and this could be the motivation for preparing them this way. Or someone could have prepared a great deal of input data without knowing the standard format for integers. At any rate, let's write a procedure that converts input data in this form to legal integer forms so that the program can process the input data.

First, it should be clear that we have to process the data a character at a time, ignoring or skipping the commas and converting the numerical characters to an integer number. The algorithm might look like this:

1. Skip blanks.
2. If the first nonblank character is a sign (+, -) then
        store this sign and read next character;
    otherwise, assume sign is positive.
3. While the current character is not a blank, execute this loop:
    a. Process numerical character to form integer.
    b. Ignore comma.
    c. Read another character.
4. Attach the correct sign to the resulting integer.

Here's a realization of this algorithm. We've written it as a procedure with a _variable parameter,_ Number. (For now consider Number to be like any other variable in the procedure; we'll explain the variable parameter in a moment.)

```
    procedure ReadPuncInt(var Number : integer);
       {Read Punctuated Integer}

       var
          Ch          : char;
          NegativeSign : Boolean;

       begin {ReadPuncInt}
          Number := 0; {Integer will be returned in Number}

          repeat {to skip blanks}
             read(Ch)
          until (Ch <> ' ') or eof;
```

```
      if (Ch = '+') or (Ch = '-') then
         begin
            NegativeSign := Ch = '-';
            read(Ch) {Get the first digit}
         end
      else {the first character is a digit}
         NegativeSign := false;

      while (Ch <> ' ') and not eof do {process characters}
         begin
            case Ch of
               '0': Number:= 10*Number + 0;
               '1': Number:= 10*Number + 1;
               '2': Number:= 10*Number + 2;
               '3': Number:= 10*Number + 3;
               '4': Number:= 10*Number + 4;
               '5': Number:= 10*Number + 5;
               '6': Number:= 10*Number + 6;
               '7': Number:= 10*Number + 7;
               '8': Number:= 10*Number + 8;
               '9': Number:= 10*Number + 9;
               ',': {empty statement}
            end; {case statement}
            read(Ch)
         end; {while loop}
      if NegativeSign then
         Number := -1*Number
   end; {ReadPuncInt}
```

We can <u>invoke</u> (call) this procedure by simply writing

```
   ReadPuncInt(Number)
```

or

```
   ReadPuncInt(Datum)
```

or

```
   ReadPuncInt(SomeIntegerVar)
```

The identifiers Number, Datum, and SomeIntegerVar are <u>actual parameters</u>. (They must all be of type integer, of course.) In the first call the procedure stores an integer in Number; in the second call it stores the integer in Datum; in the third call it stores the integer in SomeIntegerVar. This flexibility of ReadPuncInt's action derives from its <u>variable parameter</u>. The **var** preceding Number in the procedure <u>heading</u>,

```
   procedure ReadPuncInt(var Number : integer);
```

indicates that Number is a variable formal parameter--which means that you should regard this formal parameter as a synonym for the actual parameter in the calling statement. Thus, when the procedure stores values in Number, it also stores them in the corresponding actual parameter.

If you don't understand

```
'1': Number:= 10*Number + 1;
```

then assume a two or three digit integer and trace the procedure. You'll catch on right away.


SUBRANGE DATA TYPE


The programmer may define a type as the subrange of any other already defined scalar type (except real), which we will call the host scalar type. The most useful host scalar data types are char, integer, and a user-defined scalar. As we indicated, the real data type cannot be the host for a subrange data type. Here are some examples of subrange data type definitions followed by the corresponding variable declarations.

```
type
    LetterType = 'A'..'Z'; {Host is char.}
    DigitType  = '0'..'9'; {Host is char.}
var
    Letter : LetterType;
    Digit  : DigitType;
```

However, you may--when it's convenient and clear--combine the subrange type definition and the variable declaration in one statement.

```
var
    Letter : 'A'..'Z'; {Host is char.}
    Digit  : '0'..'9'; {Host is char.}
```

There are, of course, an infinite number of integers. Therefore the integer data type is itself a subrange of the infinite sequence of integers. In effect, your computer system makes the following type definition whether you like it or not.

```
type
    integer = -maxint..maxint;
```

If your problem cannot be encompassed by these limits, then you must find another computer on which to run your program. In most cases these limits will be more than ample, however.

We often use integer variables for counters, indexes, or the ordinal numbers of small ordered sets. In these cases we should follow the good programming practice of defining the subject variable as a subrange of the host type integer. The resulting reduction in the cardinality of the data type may save thousands of bytes of storage in some problems on some computers. There is another reason for communicating subrange information to your compiler: your Pascal compiler can automatically include run-time checks in your program to verify that all assignments to subrange variables comply with your definitions and declarations. This automatic run-time checking can help you to "debug" (find the errors in) your program or data.

```
type
     CtrType = 0..99; {Host is integer.}
     Index   = 1..64; {Host is integer.}
     AgeType = 1..120; {Host is integer.}
var
     Ctr  : CtrType;
     I, J : Index;
     age  : AgeType;
```

We could also declare the above variables without the explicit type definitions.

```
var
     Ctr  : 0..99;
     I, J : 1..64;
     age  : 1..120;
```

Either one of the above forms of declaration is acceptable. Use the form that is most readable and clear for your application.

We can also define a subrange of a user-defined scalar data type.

```
type
     DayType = (Monday, Tuesday, Wednesday, Thursday, Friday,
               Saturday, Sunday);
var
     Day     : DayType;
     WorkDay : Monday..Friday; {Host is DayType}
     Weekend : Saturday..Sunday; {Host is DayType}
```

An attempt to assign any of the values in the range Monday..Friday to the variable Weekend would result in a run-time error and error message. Similarly, an attempt to assign the values Saturday or Sunday to the variable WorkDay would result in a run-time error.

Subrange data types possess all the attributes of their host data types except their range. Thus any operation or function defined on the host is available to the subtype--so long as the result does not violate the subrange limits.

REAL: THE DECIMAL NUMBERS DATA TYPE

   Real variables are essential to engineering and scientific applications. There are a variety of forms for representing a real value. In fact, there are 24 different paths through the syntax diagram for real numbers, although many paths differ only by the sign of the mantissa or the sign of the exponent.

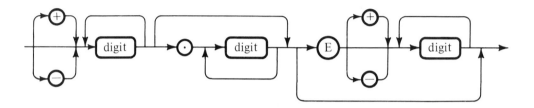

Note that the representation employing scientific notation (the path with E in it) is optional: there's an alternate path in the syntax graph. (When you encounter E within a number, read it as "times ten to the power of" or "times ten to the....") When should you use the E (Exponential) notation? It's useful for writing very large and very small numbers. Compare writing a very large number, Avogadro's number, without and with the E notation,

        602486000000000000000000000 = 6.02486E+26

or a very small number, Planck's constant, without and with the E notation.

        .000000000000000000000000000000000662517 = 6.62517E-34

In English, Planck's constant is "six point six two five one seven, times ten to the minus thirty-fourth." The use of the E notation reduces both your labor and your chances of making a mistake when you're writing very small or very large numbers.
   The following are examples of <u>valid real values</u>.

        75993    (a valid real <u>or</u> integer value)
        3.1416
        -78.0
        1E6      (same as 1000000)
        -25E-6   (same as 0.000025)

The student should check these values against the real number syntax graph to verify that they're valid constants (values).

The following are <u>invalid real values</u>.

```
3.27 E -12   (Pascal doesn't permit embedded blanks)
1,937,573    (Pascal doesn't permit commas)
56983.       (Pascal requires a digit after a decimal point)
.00378       (Pascal requires a digit before a decimal point)
4.7E-3.8     (Exponents must be integers)
```

Real values must be stored in physical locations in the computer's memory. Since these physical locations have finite length (i.e., a limited number of bits) there's obviously a limit to how many digits the computer can represent. Furthermore, the internal representation of real numbers is not in decimal form--it's in binary form, the form which is most reliable and convenient for the computer hardware. When writing a computer program in a high-order language like Pascal, you can usually forget about the details and idiosyncracies of the hardware which runs your program. In fact, buffering the programmer from these details and idiosyncracies is one of the main reasons that computer scientists developed high-order languages. In general, therefore, you can forget about the hardware. But in the case of the finite representation of the real numbers you may have to be aware of the computer's limitations.

The <u>real</u> real numbers are dense, so dense that they form a continuum. Between any two real numbers there are an infinite number of real numbers. An infinite number of the real numbers have an infinite number of digits. For example

$$1/3 = 0.3333333333333333333333333333333333....(forever)$$

Obviously, your computer cannot represent this decimal exactly. Therefore

$$1/3 + 1/3 + 1/3 = 1$$

<u>would not be true on your computer</u>. Let's make sure you understand this statement, which follows from the fact that your computer uses finite representations for non-terminating decimals. Assume that your computer uses only 8 binary digits (bits) to represent the mantissas of real numbers. This assumption is almost certainly worse than the actual case of your computer (which may represent mantissas with anywhere between 16 and 65 bits); but the assumption serves to make our point. The four contiguous 8-bit binary fractions closest to 1/3 are

```
.01010100 = 0.328125
.01010101 = 0.33203125
.01010110 = 0.3359375
.01010111 = 0.33984375
```

So while the real numbers are a continuum with an infinite number of real numbers between any two real numbers, this 8-bit representation of the reals is very granular indeed. In this granular representation

        1/3 "=" 0.33203125 or
        1/3 "=" 0.3359375

and therefore

        1/3 + 1/3 + 1/3 "="  0.99609375 or
        1/3 + 1/3 + 1/3 "="  1.0078125

depending on which representation of 1/3 the division operation yields. Consequently,

        1/3 + 1/3 + 1/3 <> 1 (!!!!!!!!)

in our granular real representation. This leads to one of the rules for operations with real numbers: Never check for exact equality between two real numbers when the processor has had to compute one of the numbers. Instead, check to see whether the computed value is "close enough" to the target value and accept that more tolerant criterion in place of exact equality. For example

```
    const
        Epsilon = 0.01; {Depends on computer word length}
    var
        X, Y, Z : real
    begin

        {Compute X, Y, and Z}

        if abs((X + Y + Z) - 1.0) <= Epsilon then
            writeln('X + Y + Z = 1.0');
```

would be one way to handle the problem we have been discussing. Obviously, the greater the number of bits in your computer's representation of the mantissa, the smaller you can make Epsilon.
    There are other implications of the granularity of the real data type. This granularity implies, of course, that there's a many-to-one mapping of the real numbers onto the computer's representations of the real numbers. That is, if x and y are real numbers and very close together, they may both be mapped onto the same value Y. This happens whenever the computer does not have enough bits to distinguish between x and y. If the computer value X represents the real number x, and the computer value Y represents the real number y, then X and Y may not be different, even though x and y are different. This means that although x < y, we can't be sure that X < Y--because x and y may be so close together that X = Y. Therefore, we <u>may</u> have to make the following translation when applying inequality checks.

        x < y may have to be translated into  X <= Y

In general, whenever two numbers differ by less than the least significant bit in the computer's data word, then the hardware will force these two numbers to have the same representation in the computer.

The limitation we have been discussing is a limitation in the precision or accuracy of the computer's representation of a real number. This limitation stems from the finite number of binary places (bits) in the computer word that stores the mantissa of a real value, which in turn limits the number of decimal digits the computer can represent. But the computer represents numbers in floating point format, a mantissa times 2 (usually) raised to some integral power, called the exponent of the floating point number. Just as there is a limit to the number of bits available to represent the mantissa, there's a limit to the number of bits available to represent the exponent. This latter limitation restricts the range of the real values. The restricted range limits both the number of trailing zeros (remember Avogadro's number) and the number of leading zeros (remember Planck's constant), and thus limits both how large and how small a number your computer can represent. But you can always count on there being an exact representation of zero on your computer. (However, you can't always count on computations yielding an exact zero even though they theoretically should. Remember the limited precision due to the finite mantissa.)

To sum up this discussion, the computer represents the continuum of the real numbers with the granular values of the real data type, the best it can do. (Don't get the wrong idea; it's usually good enough.) The real data type can't represent numbers that are too large or too small (because of its finite exponent); and it can't exactly represent a lot of the numbers in between (because of its finite mantissa).

There are many standard functions in Pascal that accept a real value for their arguments, yield a real value for their results, or both accept and yield a real value. Here's a summary.

| standard function | argument | value | rule |
|---|---|---|---|
| abs | real | real | if X < 0, abs(X) = -X, else abs(X) = +X |
| sqr | real | real | sqr(X) is X*X |
| sin | real | real | trigonometric sine |
| cos | real | real | trigonometric cosine |
| arctan | real | real | trigonometric arctangent |
| ln | real | real | natural logarithm |
| exp | real | real | exponential function |
| sqrt | real | real | square root |
| trunc | real | integer | trunc(X)=integer part of X |
| round | real | integer | round(X)=integer closest to X |

The following program illustrates the use of some of these functions. There's a common problem in surveying of finding the distance between two points when these points are separated by uncrossable terrain.

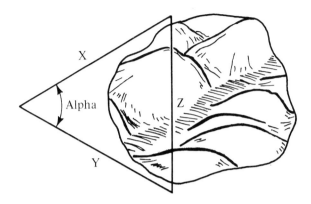

    If we identify this unknown distance as Z, the surveyor can calculate Z by measuring X and Y and their included angle, Alpha, and then applying the following formula.

        Z = sqrt(X*X + Y*Y -2*X*Y*cosine(Alpha))

Here's the program performing this calculation.

```pascal
program FindSideZ(input, output);

var
   X, Y, Z : real;
   Alpha   : real; {angle in radians}

begin
   read(X, Y, Alpha);
   Z := sqrt(sqr(X) + sqr(Y) - 2*X*Y*cos(Alpha));
   writeln('The unknown distance is', Z)
end.
```

In the expression for Z we used the integer 2 as a factor. Since the expression involves all real terms and factors, is it correct to use 2 rather than 2.0 or 2E0? The answer is yes. In general, Pascal will accept an integer value (which it has to translate into a real representation) even though it expects a real value. This is logical: the integers form a proper subset of the real numbers. However, sometimes it doesn't make sense to find an integer when you're looking for a real value. For example, the functions trunc and round are provided to truncate or round real values to integer values. If Pascal finds an integer value for the argument of either one of these functions, it will show its strong typing colors by calling this type confusion an error (which it is likely to be).

EXERCISES

**1.** Give the data type and the proper form for each of the following values or constants:

a. The letter A
b. The character 3
c. The number 3
d. 10,000,000
e. 6/12
f. .0000000000000000012487

**2.** Give the data type and value for each of the following expressions:

a. (3 <= 4) **and** (5 <> 6)
b. **not**(4 = 0) **and** true
c. chr(ord(succ('0')) - ord('0'))
d. 17 **div** 3
e. 17 / 3
f. trunc(17 / 3)
g. round(17 / 3)
h. sqr(ord('2') - ord('0'))
i. sqrt(ord('2') - ord('0'))

**3.** Declare a variable named State that can assume the values KeyAbsent, KeyFound, Searching.

**4.** Define a data type Color that can assume the values red, brown, pink, or gray.

**5.** Declare a variable Caps that can assume the capital letters (but no other character value).

**6.** Declare the variable I. (Assume that it's only used in the following statements.)

```
I := 1;
Sum := 0;
while (I <= N) and not eof do
   begin
      readln(Number);
      Sum := Sum + Number;
      I := I + 1
   end
```

**7.** Declare a variable named Sum that can hold values like -345.78 and 0.00094387.

**8.** Declare the variables H and J. (Assume that they only occur in the following statements.)

```
H := 0;
for J := 10 downto 1 do
   H := H + 1 / J;
writeln(H)
```

**9.** The following code converts lowercase letters to uppercase letters in a computer that employs either ASCII character codes or EBCDIC character codes. In case the host computer's character code is neither ASCII or EBCDIC, the code prints out an appropriate announcement. What advantages (if any) does this code offer over the simpler conversion statement on page 20.

```
        const
            ZeroASCII  =  48; {ord('0') = 48 in ASCII}
            LtoUASCII  = -32; {Conversion term for ASCII}
            ZeroEBCDIC = 240; {ord('0') = 240 in EBCDIC}
            LtoUEBCDIC =  64; {Conversion term for EBCDIC}

        begin{initialization}
            if ord('0') = ZeroASCII then
               LtoU = LtoUASCII
            else if ord('0') = ZeroEBCDIC then
               LtoU := LtoUEBCDIC
            else
               begin
                  write('Character set is neither ASCII nor EBCDIC.');
                  writeln('Prodedure cannot provide case conversion.')
               end;
            {Other initialization statements}
            ...
        end;{initialization}

        if (Ch >= 'a') and (Ch <= 'z') then
            Ch := chr(ord(Ch) + LtoU)
```

# 4. Introduction to Input and Output

Input and output instructions are essential in a programming language. Without an **input** instruction, a program could operate only on data defined inside the computer program. Obviously, a program that had to be rewritten for each new set of data would be very inconvenient. Without an **output** instruction, programs could not communicate their results to their users; the data would be "hidden" inside the computer in its storage locations, remote from human scrutiny. Furthermore, this data would be in the computer's internal language. Finally, there would be no way to save or archive any of the program's results. There wouldn't even be a record that the program had ever run.

Pascal provides the procedures **read** and **readln** for reading data and the procedures **write** and **writeln** for saving and displaying data. Before we discuss the details of the four individual procedures, we will introduce some general notions and terminology.

In computer jargon we talk about "input files" and "output files." An "input file" is just a name for the source of input data. We say that the procedures read and readln "read input data from an input file." The physical source of the input data could be a magnetic disc, a reel of tape, a deck of punched cards, or a keyboard. Similarly, "output file" is a name for the destination of the output data, and we say that the procedures write and writeln "write output data on an output file." The physical destination of the output data could be a magnetic disc, a reel of tape, a high-speed line printer, a low-speed character printer, a phototypesetter, or a video screen. There's some more terminology you should know: these external files are also called program parameters.

In most computing facilities, there are many possibilities for the source and destination of data. Therefore, the programmer must identify the specific input and output files (the program parameters) his program uses. The programmer does this by identifying the program parameters in the program's heading and then declaring them in the variable declaration part of the program. The program parameters appear in the program heading following the name of the program.

```
<program heading> ::= <identifier> [(<program parameters>)]
<program parameters> ::= <identifier list>
```

Notice that program parameters are optional; however, it will be a rare program that does not name and communicate with entities that exist outside the program. The programmer must also declare these external entities (usually files) as variables, set them up for reading or writing with special procedures, and refer to them explicitly in all the input or output statements. Here's an example of what's required in a program that makes an exact copy of a textfile named F. The copy file is named G. Remember that a textfile is a file of characters that are structured into lines by line markers. Pascal predefines the identifier "text" to denote the textfile data type. The standard procedures readln and writeln are used only on textfiles.

```pascal
program CopyText(F, G);

var
   F, G : text;
   Ch   : char;

begin
   reset(F); {Initialize F for reading}
   rewrite(G); {Prepare G to be written upon}
   while not eof(F) do
      begin
         while not eoln(F) do
            begin
               read(F, Ch);
               write(G, Ch)
            end;
         readln(F);
         writeln(G)
      end
end.
```

Notice how often we explicitly referred to the program parameters. This example may puzzle you because in previous examples we simply wrote read(Ch), write(Ch), and so on, rather than read(<program parameter>, Ch), write(<program parameter>, Ch), and so on. Also, in the previous examples in this book we did not declare program parameters. How did we get away without all these explicit references to external files?

Every computing facility has <u>standard</u> input and output devices, the devices the average user employs for communication with the computer. Pascal simplifies programming input and output operations for these devices by designating two standard files with the identifiers "input" and "output." If you want to use either one of these files, you must list it in the program heading as a program parameter; but you don't have to declare a standard file explicitly (in fact, you definitely must not declare a standard file) in the variable declaration part of the program, and you don't have to use the identifier "input" in the read and readln procedure or the identifier "output" in the write and writeln procedure. The compiler also automatically generates reset(input) for the input file and rewrite(output) for the output file. Finally, the files input and output are, of course, textfiles. (If they weren't, you wouldn't use the standard procedures readln and writeln on them.) Let's see what this simplification does for us when we write a program that copies the input file to the output file. (A program that makes a file copy is not an academic exercise. Such programs are very useful. We make file copies in order to "back-up" important files or to make a copy of a program or data for another facility. Pascal programs are stored as textfiles. If you wanted to give someone a copy of one of your Pascal programs, you would make a file copy of the program.)

```
program CopyText(input, output);

    var
        Ch    : char;

    begin
        while not eof do
            begin
                while not eoln do
                    begin
                        read(Ch);
                        write(Ch)
                    end;
                readln;
                writeln
            end
    end.
```

Obviously, it's simpler to write programs for standard textfiles. Incidentally, it's not unusual for a program to use "input" as well as a nonstandard input file and "output" as well as a nonstandard output file. For example, a computerized phototypesetting system might take certain editing and composition commands from the standard input file, take the text to be typeset from a nonstandard textfile, print system diagnostic and status messages on the standard output file, and send the formatted output text to the phototypesetter.

The inputting procedures read and readln have two modes of operation: a character-reading mode, and a number-reading mode. Since these modes are so different, we will discuss them separately.

INPUTTING NUMERICAL DATA: THE READ PROCEDURE

The simplest numerical read statement is

        read(Number1)

where Number1 may be of type integer or of type real. This statement
causes the processor to scan forward through the input file until it
finds the first nonblank character. If the first nonblank character is a
digit, the processor reads the number of which this digit is a part,
converts this number to the appropriate internal representation, and
assigns the result to the variable named Number1.

All the data type rules apply in this procedure of reading,
converting, and assigning. If the first nonblank character which the
processor finds in its forward scan is not a digit (or + or -), then the
processor announces something like "type error in read." Finding an
element that isn't part of a number is not the only way the processor
will detect a type error: the input number must be of the correct
numerical type. If Number1 is an integer type, then the number on the
input file must also be an integer--i.e., it must obey the syntax rules
for integers. If Number1 is a real data type, then the number on the
input file may be either real or integer.

If the programmer wants to read a series of numbers, then it is
inconvenient for him to write

```
        read(N1);
        read(N2);
        read(N3);
        read(N4);
        read(N5);
        read(N6)
```

Instead, Pascal permits him to write

```
        read(N1, N2, N3, N4, N5, N6)
```

which is exactly equivalent to the six separate read statements with
single parameters. (We sometimes call the names of the variables
appearing in a read statement, parameters or arguments. The motivation
for this terminology will be clearer when we cover prodecures.)

The question arises: how do we arrange for the processor to assign
numbers on an input file to the variables for which they are intended?
Pascal, like most languages, relies on the notion of positional
correspondence for correct assignment. The positions of the data on the
input file must correspond to the positions of the variables in the read
statements. Here is an example of positional correspondence. Suppose we
have the following declarations:

```
        var
           I, J, K : integer;
           X, Y    : real;
```

and want to make the following assignments by reading input data.

```
        X <-- 2E6
        Y <-- 2.7564
```

```
        I <-- 4
        J <-- 10
        K <-- 26
```

These read statements

```
        read(I, J, K);
        . . .
        read(X, Y)
```

coupled with this positional arrangement of input data

```
        4    10    26
        2E6    2.7564
```

results in correct assignments. But many other arrangements of the input
data would also result in correct assignments. For example,

```
        4
        10
        26
        2E6
        2.7564
```

and

```
        4 10   26    2E6     2.7564
```

would also result in correct assignments.
    It should be evident from these examples that the read procedure--in
the number mode--searches forward through the input file, skipping
blanks and ends-of-lines, until it finds the next datum. The read
procedure searches for a required value by examining every column in the
input file until it finds a datum or the end of the file. Read
automatically begins reading a new line of data (if the data file is
arranged in lines), when it doesn't find the required datum on the
current line.
    Often a programmer doesn't know how much data his program will have
to process; i.e, he doesn't know how long the input file is. In this
case he might put a test for a "sentinel symbol" after the read
statement, and require that the program user put a sentinel symbol at
the end of his data. Sometimes it's difficult to define an appropriate
sentinel symbol. The sentinel symbol must be legal, that is, it must
belong to the data type of the read parameter; but it must also have a
value that can't possibly occur as a valid input, so that the sentinel
test can distinguish it from valid data. For example, if valid values
for a variable were positive integers, then the sentinel symbol could be
any negative integer. But the sentinel symbol could not be, for example,
an asterisk, because reading * when the read procedure's parameter is an
integer data type, results in a "type error in read." There's also a

problem with using an "impossible" value for the sentinel. Careful programmers use subrange data types. If the programmer knows that only natural integer values are valid for a variable, he may declare the variable this way.

```
var
    Number2 : 1..maxint
```

With this declaration, negative values in the input file for Number2 would result in a "type error in read."

Because of the nuisance involved in finding a sentinel symbol and because program users frequently forget the sentinel anyway, Pascal provides a Boolean function, eof, which signals the end-of-file condition. The function eof takes as argument the identifier of the input file.

```
if eof(TapeDrive3) then
    <statement>
```

But if the eof test refers to the standard file input, the programmer may omit the argument.

```
if eof then {Reference is to file input by default.}
    <statement>
```

The function eof becomes true when the processor contacts the end of the file while trying to read the file; the function is false before the processor contacts the end of the file. It is sometimes useful to think of the eof function as a <u>flag</u> that the processor sets from false to true when it contacts the end of the file. To use the eof flag successfully, the programmer must understand precisely when the flag becomes true and what value the processor reads at that time. Failure to understand these points can lead to incorrect programs. Before explaining these points, we must introduce another Boolean function, eoln.

The processor sets the eoln flag to true when it contacts a line marker; when the processor executes the next read instruction, it resets the eoln flag to false. Data is often naturally arranged in lines. For example, data on punched cards is arranged in 80 column lines.

To understand precisely when the eof flag becomes true and what value the processor reads at that time, let's consider an example. Assume that a programmer writes the following **while** statement to read and sum an unknown number of integers.

```
Sum := 0;
while not eof do {WARNING: Read analysis of this loop.}
    begin
        read(Number);
        Sum := Sum + Number
    end
```

Assume further that the input data to this program appear this way:

```
45      574     54      9       8       284<-
75      956     825     736     88      902<-
end of file
```

When the processor reads the last number, 902, in the input file it contacts a line marker (indicated by <- in our representation) and sets the eoln flag to true. However, and this is the important point, the processor <u>does not contact the end of the file immediately after reading the last available input datum</u>. In fact, the processor does not contact the file end until it tries to read one more number <u>after</u> it reads the last number, 902.

Let's consider what happens in the while loop as a consequence of this delayed discovery of the file end. After the processor reads the last number, it adds this number to the accumulated sum of numbers. The variable Sum now has the correct answer to the problem, the sum of all the integers. However, the processor has not set the eof flag to true. Consequently, the Boolean condition for the **while** loop, **not** eof, is still true and the while logic causes another iteration of its body. When the processor reads the input file on this last (but one too many!) iteration, it contacts the file end and sets the eof flag. However, the processor has no value to assign to Number; and so Number is undefined. When the processor adds the undefined value in Number to Sum it "spoils" the value in Sum. (The sum of a correct value and an undefined value is, unfortunately, an undefined value.) After this final (fatal!) iteration, the while logic stops the loop. But the damage to the contents of Sum has already been done.

There are several ways to correct the problem in the above coding. One way is to use the readln procedure; we will explain that method in the next section. The other way is to execute the read statement just before the while loop's continuation test and execute the addition just after the while loop's continuation test. Here's the code for this approach.

```
Sum := 0;
read(Number);
while not eof do
    begin
        Sum := Sum + Number;
        Read(Number)
    end
```

This code avoids the problems of the first code.

INPUTTING NUMERICAL DATA· THE READLN PROCEDURE


Now that you've understood how the read procedure and the eof and eoln functions operate, you are in a position to understand the readln procedure. The readln procedure is like the read procedure in every respect except one: after the processor reads the number for the last argument in a readln statement, the processor skips over all the rest of the current line <u>including the line marker</u>. Consequently, when the processor executes the next read or readln instruction, it will begin reading in column one of the next input line. The readln procedure also resets the eoln flag.

We can use readln to solve the problem we discussed in the last section. If we replace read with readln in the original malfunctioning code, we have another way to avoid assigning an undefined value to Number.

```
        Sum := 0;
        while not eof do
            begin {Input must be arranged with one number per line}
                readln(Number);
                Sum := Sum + Number
            end
```

However, this solution requires that the input data be arranged with one number per line.

The readln function is particularly useful if you have data at the end of a line that you don't want the processor to try to read. For example, recall program EstimateTemper in Chapter 3. A desirable way to prepare input for that program is to give each rater a deck of 10 punched cards prepared as follows.

| | |
|---|---|
| 10 | Murderous |
| 9 | Assaultive |
| 8 | Destructive |
| 7 | Combative |
| . | .    . |
| 1 | Placating |
| 0 | Cringing |

The rater then selects the card that he believes best describes the patient, referring for his choice to the meaningful adjectives on the cards and his observations of the patient. The ordinal values (0, 1, 2,...) of the scalar constants (Cringing, Placating, Inhibited, ...) are, of course, the data that the program requires. The readln instruction will cause the processor to scan each card forward until it locates and reads the numeric value; then the processor will skip the rest of that card, setting up the next card for the next readln instruction. Thus the readln statement totally ignores the trailing adjectives. If we prepared input data in this form and used a read instruction rather than the readln instruction, the second execution of a read statement in the program would result in a type error when the processor found alphabetic characters where it expects an integer.

All our examples have had single arguments for the readln procedure, but you must not conclude that readln can't have multiple arguments. The readln procedure can have just as many arguments as you want; and it will function just like a read instruction, skipping over blanks and ends of lines to find data to match each of its arguments. The only difference is that when the processor has found a value for the last argument, it will discard all the rest of the data on that line. Consider the following statements

```
readln(A, B, C);
readln(D, E, F);
read(G, H)
```

operating on the following arrangement of input data.

```
234      746      9320     836
6435     550
801      402
142
329
```

This combination will result in the following assignments.

```
A <-- 234
B <-- 746
C <-- 9320
D <-- 6435
E <-- 550
F <-- 801
G <-- 142
H <-- 329
```

You may use readln without a variable argument in order to skip the rest of a current line and reset the eoln flag. Thus

```
readln(V1, V2,..., Vn)
```

is equivalent to

```
begin
    read(V1, V2,..., Vn);
    readln {causes a skip to the beginning of the next line}
end
```

INPUTTING CHARACTER DATA: READ AND READLN

If Ch is a char variable, the statement

    read(Ch)

reads a **single** character from the input file and stores that character in Ch.

The instructions read(Ch) and read(Number) appear superficially alike; but the operation of reading character data is quite different from the operation of reading numeric data. Therefore, we have elected to treat the topics separately.

Recall that the form of **numeric** values and constants is the same for internal and external assignment. For example, the programmer can internally assign 1 million to a variable, Debt, by writing

    Debt := 1E6

or he can externally assign this value to Debt by writing

    read(Debt)

and then placing the same form, 1E6, in the appropriate position on the input file.

But the form of **character** values and constants is not the same for internal and external assignments. Recall that for internal assignment of the character constant T to a variable Ch you write

    Ch := 'T'

enclosing the value in apostrophes. But for external assignment, you do not use the apostrophes. The combination of

    read(Ch)

in your program and

    T

on your input file will also assign the value 'T' to the variable Ch. In fact, the combination of

    read(Ch)

in your program and

    'T'

on your input file would assign an apostrophe to Ch. (Because the read statement reads the first character in the input file, which is '.)

This difference in the form of character constants for internal and external assignments may seem arbitrary to you. But it's actually very much to the programmer's and user's advantage. It would be extremely inconvenient to place apostrophes around every character in your input data. With such a requirement, how could you ever use the computer to process words, one of the useful functions of a digital computer? So why not eliminate apostrophes from the internal representation of character constants? This would lead to great confusion for the reader and the compiler. One could not easily tell the difference between a char constant 'X' and a variable named X. Nor could one tell the difference between the char constant '1' and the numeric constant 1.

Another difference between read(Number) and read(Ch) is that the former will skip blanks and ends of lines; but the latter will not. The instruction

        read(Number)

where Number is of data type real or integer will cause the processor to scan the input file until it comes to a nonblank character. In fact, read(Number) could cause the processor to skip dozens of empty lines or blank cards.

But the instruction

        read(Ch)

never skips a blank column in the input file. The instruction read(Ch) requires the processor to read the current column in the input file, blank or not. Indeed, the blank character is just another value in the char set of values. When reading character data, the read procedure does not and should not assume that blanks are insignificant.

Assuming these variable declarations

        NotInWord      : boolean;
        Ch             : char;
        NmbrOfBlanks   : integer;
        NmbrOfWords    : integer

the following code reads one complete line of input text and counts the words and blanks on that line. For the purpose of this program fragment, we define a word as a sequence of characters that contains neither a blank nor a line marker; i.e., blanks and line markers are word delimiters.

        NmbrOfWords  := 0;
        NmbrOfBlanks := 0;
        NotInWord := true;
        read(Ch);

```
while not eoln do
   begin
      if Ch = ' ' then
         begin
            NmbrOfBlanks := NmbrOfBlanks + 1;
            NotInWord := true
         end;
      if (Ch <> ' ') and NotInWord then
         begin {We've just entered a new word; count it.}
            NmbrOfWords := NmbrOfWords + 1;
            NotInWord := false
         end;
      read(Ch)
   end
```

## INPUTTING MIXED NUMERIC AND CHARACTER DATA

   You may mix numeric and char variables in a read or readln instruction; but you must--as always--carefully synchronize your parameters and input data.
   Suppose that someone had prepared the following input file of dates

      3/8/39  Author is born.
      12/7/41 Japanese attack Pearl Harbor
      1/1/80  First day of new decade
      . . .
      3/8/80  author's 41st birthday

and that you wanted to write a program that would read and process these dates one at a time. How could you do this? The following code shows how. We use the char variable "Slash" to read and store the /s; but the code does not use the contents of this variable.

```
var
   Month : 1..12;
   Day   : 1..31;
   Year  : 1..2080;
   Slash : char;

begin
   while not eof do
      begin
         readln(Month, Slash, Day, Slash, Year);
         ProcessDates
      end
end
```

   You may be surprised that this code works correctly to read an input

like 12/7/41 or 3/8/80. Why doesn't the processor, when it's reading the
value for Month, balk at the / that immediately follows the last digit?
The processor, while reading integer or real data, ceases reading as
soon as it detects that the next character does not form part of a
number (of the correct data type). Normally, the next character that
does not form part of a number, is the blank character; but it need not
be, as this example shows.

  Note, incidentally, that this code would not work if we had used read
instead of readln. Can you see why?

  Here is one more example of reading mixed character and numeric data.
This code checks--to the extent that it can--that the input data is in
the right order. Here is an example of the input data

        X = 5.463, Y = 4.57389E-8, Z = 8.8165

and here is the code that reads and checks this data

```
        var
          X, Y, Z        : real;
          XCh, YCh, ZCh  : char;
          Equals, Blank  : char;
          Comma          : char;

        begin
          read(XCh, Blank, Equals, Blank, X);
          read(Comma, Blank, YCh, Blank, Equals, Blank, Y);
          read(Comma, Blank, ZCh, Blank, Equals, Blank, Z);
          if (XCh <> 'X') or (YCh <> 'Y') or (ZCh <> 'Z') then
              write('Input data not in right order.')
```

Obviously, this is a great deal more complicated than coding

        read(X, Y, Z)

and preparing input data this way

        5.463   4.57389E-8   8.8165

Whether the strict syntactic and labelling requirements of the first
code improve the chances of preparing and interpreting input data
correctly, is a question to which I know no rigorous answer. At any
rate, if you thoroughly understand this example, you know a great deal
about reading input data.

The basic form of the write statement is

        write(item1, item2,..., itemN)

where the items can be expressions of arbitrary complexity or strings of
characters enclosed by apostrophes. Here's an example:

```
program SumProductQuotient(input, output);

var
   M, N : integer;

begin
   read(M, N);
   writeln('The sum and product of', M, ' and', N, ' are');
   writeln(M + N, ' and', M*N, ', repectively.');
   writeln('The quotient of', M, ' divided by', N, ' is', M/N, '.')
end.
```

If the input to this program is

    300     200

then the output, written directly on the standard output medium, is

    The sum and product of      300 and      200 are
          500 and    60000, respectively.
    The quotient of      300 divided by      200 is  1.5000000000000E+00.

Note the following in this example:

   **0.** There are unsightly gaps in the output because we didn't control
the field widths in which numbers were printed. Be assured that we'll
introduce tools later for creating tidy output.
   **1.** We enclosed character strings in apostrophes in the writeln
instructions; but the strings appeared in the output without the
apostrophes.
   **2.** The writeln instructions honored leading, embedded, or trailing
blanks in character strings. For example, ' and' prints "and" with one
leading blank.
   **3.** Data appeared in the writeln instructions as simple variables (M,
N) or as expressions involving simple variables (M + N, M*N, M/N).
   **4.** The processor printed the variables and expressions in their
proper forms; i.e., according to their data types. Thus the processor
printed M, N, and M*N as integers and M/N as a real.
   **5.** The processor printed the numerical data in fixed <u>field widths</u>,
about ten columns for integers and about 20 columns for the real value.

It printed the integer value <u>flush</u> <u>right</u> in its field, supplying leading blanks as necessary. It printed the real value with trailing (insignificant) zeros to fill up the field. The field widths for integers and reals depend on the computing system. Later, we'll show you how to control the field width of numerical output.

6. Each writeln instruction printed its last parameter and then transmitted a line marker (equivalent to a carriage return or cursor return). Consequently, each subsequent writeln instruction began writing at the beginning of the next line. In general, writeln(F) appends a <u>line marker</u> to the file F. If F is an output device, say a line printer, the "line marker" causes a carriage return. The line marker is <u>not</u> one of the constants of the standard data type char; the only way to generate a line marker is to execute the writeln procedure.

In order to provide flexibility in formatting output data, Pascal provides the write instruction which works exactly like the writeln instruction except write does not generate line markers. Consequently, successive write instructions print their outputs on the same line. Obviously, when using a series of write statements one must be careful not to exceed the maximum width of the output medium.

The following program uses write and writeln constructively. This program prints out, in two columns, the computer's internal codes for all the characters between 'A' and 'Z.' The program also demonstrates field-width parameters, our next subject.

```
program PrintOrdValues(output);
var
    Ch : char;
begin
    writeln(' ':10, 'CH', ' ':6, 'CODE', ' ':9, 'CH', ' ':6, 'CODE');
    writeln; {generate blank line for space between headings and data}
    for Ch := 'A' to 'Z' do
        begin
            write(' ':10, Ch, ' ':7, ord(Ch):3);
            if not odd(ord(Ch)) then writeln
        end;
    writeln
end.
```

Output: (assuming the ASCII character set)

| CH | CODE | CH | CODE |
|----|------|----|------|
| A | 65 | B | 66 |
| C | 67 | D | 68 |
| E | 69 | F | 70 |
| G | 71 | H | 72 |
| . | . | . | . |
| U | 85 | V | 86 |
| W | 87 | X | 88 |
| Y | 89 | Z | 90 |

The first writeln statement supplies the table headings. Note the first parameter in this statement: ' ':10. The first part of this parameter represents a single blank character, ' '. Normally, constants of type char are printed in a single column with no leading or trailing blanks; i.e., the processor prints them in a field width of one. But in this case the field-width parameter ":10" follows ' '. The value of this field-width parameter causes the processor to write ' ' in a field width of exactly 10 characters. The processor does this by supplying nine blank spaces to the left of ' '.

In general, the effect of "E:m" is to cause the processor to write exactly m characters with an appropriate number of blank spaces to the left of E's representation. By means of the field-width parameters we can avoid the unsightly gaps that some of our output has exhibited. We can format neat output displays.

Strings of length n are normally written in n columns. If the write statement looks like this, however,

    write('<string>':m)

the string will be written in m columns with m-n leading blanks. (If m is less than n, then the processor truncates the string to m characters by not writing the appropriate number of the leading characters.) The following statement is equivalent to the first statement in the above program.

    writeln('CH':12, 'CODE':10, 'CH':11, 'CODE':10)

And this write statement

    write(Ch:11, ord(Ch):10)

is equivalent to the write statement in the for loop. Note that we have specified a field width of 10 for the integer, ord(Ch). Some implementations use this field width for integers, anyway. Should you specify a field width when it's the same as your system's default field width? If the appearance of your output is critical, you may want to. When you specify field widths rather than rely on default values, you make your program more portable and make your intention clearer. It's part of thorough program documentation to specify a critical field width, even when it's equal to the data type's default field width.

**Suggestion:** We suggest that when you design an output format that you lay out your design on grid paper. Graph paper with quarter inch squares does very nicely. That way you can count blanks easily and clearly visualize the layout. **End of suggestion.**

What happens when the value of a field-width parameter does not accommodate all the characters required to represent an expression's numeric value? In that case, Pascal takes the sensible approach that the numeric value is more important than the specified appearance of the output: the processor will write the smallest number of characters still consistent with the representation of the expression. In the case of integers, the processor will always print all the significant digits no matter what the field-width parameter specifies. For example, if we had written

```
write(Ch:11, ord(Ch):1)
```

in the for loop of the above program, the processor would have written all the values of ord(Ch) in a field width of two.

We have one final topic on the subject of write parameters: floating point versus fixed point representation of real data types. Some people find floating point representation very unpleasant. Nonscientists may have a special aversion to the exponential form of representation. Certainly, the left exhibit is inapt for these data.

| YEAR-TO-DATE | | YEAR-TO-DATE | |
|---|---|---|---|
| GROSS | 8.806060E+03 | GROSS | 8806.06 |
| F.I.C.A. | 5.397600E+02 | F.I.C.A | 539.76 |
| FED. | 5.529600E+02 | FED. | 552.96 |
| STATE | 2.120600E+02 | STATE | 212.06 |

Pascal provides a field-width parameter that causes the processor to write fixed-point representations of real variables, the kind of representations you see in the exhibit on the right. The following writeln statements produced the exhibit on the right.

```
writeln('   YEAR-TO-DATE');
writeln;
writeln('GROSS   ', GrossPay:11:2);
writeln('F.I.C.A.', FICA   :11:2);
writeln('FED.    ', FedTax :11:2);
writeln('STATE   ', StTax  :11:2)
```

The general form of the fixed-point write parameter is:

```
<write parameter> ::=
    <real expression>:<integer expression>:<integer expression>
```

or, more briefly, E:m:n. The integer value m denotes the total field width the processor will devote to E; the integer value n denotes the number of digits that follow the decimal point. Pascal has rather complex rules for how it prints a real number when your specification doesn't leave room for all the digits preceding the decimal point. If you always leave room for the leading digits you won't cause the processor to invoke these rules (don't forget to leave room for the sign, too!). The philosophy is to show you the significant part of the value if your specification doesn't accommodate the numeric value.

EXERCISES


1. Joe wrote a program that contained the following assignment statements:

```
Credit := 104.27;
Debit  := -45.28
```

Write a read statement and a list of input data that assigns the same values to Credit and Debit.

2. Joe wrote another program with this list of input data:

3  6  9  12  15  18  21

Joe's first read statement was:

read(X1, X2, X2, X3, X2, X1)

What values does this read statement assign to X1, X2, X3? Improve Joe's program by writing a shorter read statement and input file that assigns exactly the same values to the three variables.

3. Mary wrote a program that declares a variable Color:

**type**
    ColorType = (Red, Blue, Green, Yellow, Orange);
**var**
    Color : ColorType

Assume that you want to use Mary's program. Write an input procedure that permits you to submit input as

**a.** A file of letters: R  G  Y  B  O  G  B  O  R  Y

**b.** A file of color names: Blue   Green   Orange   Yellow   Red

Hint: The program reads and processes one color value at a time. Think of using a case statement in your procedure.

4. Joe has prepared a large file of real numbers for input to a program. However, Joe prepared the numbers in this form:

-4.725*100   5.8155*-1000   8.6110*1   -9.315*100   6.1936*-10

that is, as

{<real number>*<signed integer>}

Each number is represented by a real number multiplied by an integer. Write a procedure which will read numbers on Joe's file and convert them to normal real values.
Hint: Will the following statement help you?

```
read(RealValue, Ch, IntegerValue);
```

**5.** Joe wrote a program that finds the number, average, minimum, and maximum of a file of integers. He reports his results with the following statements:

```
write(Number);
write(Average);
writeln(Min, Max)
```

Write a **single** statement that yields the same output.

**6.** Write some code that copies the input file to the output file with:
    **a.** all the vowels <u>deleted</u>.
    **b.** all the vowels <u>replaced</u> with asterisks.
Retain the line structure of the input file in both a and b.

**7.** Write code that prints the name and address of your best friend in the same format that you would use to address a letter.

**8.** Pascal provides a procedure <u>page(F)</u> which causes printing to skip to the top of a new page when writing the textfile F. Write a program which copies textfile F to textfile G with the following specifications:

**1.)** Double space the lines on textfile G
**2.)** Place 27 printed lines on each page of G
**3.)** Write the page number on each page of G
      **a.)** Put page number at bottom of page
      **b.)** Center page number on 80 character line
      **c.)** Skip two lines between last printed line and page number
      **d.)** Use this format for page number: -xx-

# 5. Structuring Program Actions

In Chapter 3 we formally discussed simple variables, laying the groundwork for describing structured variables in Chapters 6 and 8-11. We defined simple variables as variables of which no part constitutes another variable. By analogy, there are simple algorithmic actions; we express them as simple statements. In Chapter 3 we discussed a common form of simple statement, the assignment statement; and in Chapter 4 we discussed two other forms of simple statements, the read and write statements. In Chapter 2, we briefly alluded to the **goto** statement, which is another form of simple or unstructured statement. Simple statements are statements of which no part constitutes another statement. Structured statements, on the other hand, have constituent parts which are in turn statements; but "structure" implies more than having components: the structured statement organizes its components in a systematic, problem-solving pattern.

In this chapter we discuss structuring program statements or actions. We have already informally discussed structured statements (**if-then-else, while-do, repeat-until,** etc.) because it's almost impossible to convey the significance and power of the computer without invoking these concepts. In this chapter our treatment of these constructs will be more formal and more detailed.

There are four basic categories of structured statements:

the sequence:
```
   begin
      read(X, Y, Z);
      W := sqrt(sqr(X) + sqr(Y) + sqr(Z));
      writeln(W)
   end
```

the decision:
```
   if M > N then
      M := M - N
   else
      N := N - M
```

the repetition:
```
repeat
   read(Ch)
until Ch <> ' '
```

Notice in the above examples that each of the structured statements has component simple statements. The fourth basic structure <u>appears</u> not to share this attribute:

the procedure:
```
Swap(X, Y)
```

The procedure statement appears to be a simple statement: we cannot decompose it into other simple statements. However, the procedure is a very powerful structuring concept: the procedure statement allows a simple statement to stand for a structured statement of arbitrary complexity. For example, Swap(X, Y) stands for

```
begin
   Temp := X;
   X := Y;
   Y := Temp
end
```

which is a very simple example of a procedure's implementing actions. The procedure statement, Swap(X, Y), states <u>what</u> the procedure does, while we hide somewhere else the procedure's declaration describing <u>how</u> the procedure works. By hiding Swap's internal statements we prevent their details from distracting us from the meaning of Swap's action. We will discuss procedures formally in Chapter 7. However, we have so written Chapter 7 that you can read it immediately after this chapter. And in the meanwhile, we will make informal references to procedures.

   The decision structure and the repetition structure are especially important in programming. It is obvious that a program's statements act on and influence its data. But this type of influence is true of desk calculators as well as digital computers. In digital computing we want the program's data to be able to act on and influence the program's sequence of instructions. The decision and repetition structures allow this influence.


## BEGIN...END: CONCATENATING PROGRAM ACTIONS


   The simplest structuring of actions is a sequence (concatenation) of statements without decisions, repetitions, or invocations of procedures. We indicate the concatenation of statements in Pascal with the **begin** and **end** symbols bracketing the sequence and indicating the order in which the processor should execute the actions.

```
   begin
      Statement 1;
      Statement 2;
      Statement 3;


      Statement N
   end;
```

An example of a simple sequence is the following code for computing the distance between two points (X1, Y1) and (X2, Y2) in a Cartesian coordinate system.

```
   begin
      readln(X1, Y1);
      readln(X2, Y2);
      Distance := sqrt(sqr(X2 - X1) + sqr(Y2 - Y1));
      writeln('The Distance between the points is', Distance)
   end.
```

It's hard to believe that a problem of sufficient size or complexity to justify the use of a digital computer could be solved completely by a simple sequence of calculations. If the digital computer is going to function as more than a super-fast calculating machine, then the processor must, at various points in the program, make a choice to repeat a sequence of steps or to take some step other than the immediately following step. But in the simple sequence the processor executes each successive instruction once and only once; it neither skips nor repeats an instruction.

## FOR...DO: REPETITION FOR A KNOWN NUMBER OF TIMES

If the user of the program for finding the distance between two points told us that he was going to have **two** pairs of points on most occasions in the future, we could take one of three approaches:

**1.** We could tell him to run the program once for the first pair of points and then rerun the program for the second pair of points. (We would not appear very helpful to him.)

**2.** We could modify the program to handle the second pair of points (X3, Y3) and (X4, Y4), keeping the control structure of a simple sequence of actions:

```
   begin
      readln(X1, Y1);
      readln(X2, Y2);
      Distance := sqrt(sqr(X2 - X1) + sqr(Y2 - Y1));
      writeln('The Distance between the 1st pair is', Distance);
```

```
      readln(X1, Y1);
      readln(X2, Y2);
      Distance := sqrt(sqr(X2 - X1) + sqr(Y2 - Y1))
      writeln('The Distance between the 2nd pair is', Distance)
   end;
```

(When we programmed this illustration, we used the fact that after we calculated the distance between the first pair of points, the variables we used in the first calculation were free to be used in the second calculation. We didn't have to define new variables for (X3, Y3) and (X4, Y4) and the distance between them. This saving of memory suggests an even greater saving: if we can use the same variables for the first and second calculations, why can't we also use the same instructions over again? We can, of course, and that brings us to the third way of dealing with our client's request to help him find the distance between two pairs of points.)

**3.** We can modify the program to repeat the calculations as many times as the user requires.

```
program ComputeDistances(input, output);

var
   N          : integer; {number of pairs of points to follow}
   J          : integer; {index for loop}
   X1, Y1     : real; {first point of a pair}
   X2, Y2     : real; {second point of a pair}
   Distance   : real; {distance between pair of points}

begin
   readln(N);
   for J := 1 to N do
      begin
         readln(X1, Y1);
         readln(X2, Y2);
         Distance := sqrt(sqr(X2 - X1) + sqr(Y2 - Y1));
         writeln('Distance between pair', J: 2, ' =', Distance: 4:2)
      end
end.
```

Assuming the following input data:

```
   3                     number of pairs to follow
16.3      4.7           1st pair, point 1
 3.2      2.4           1st pair, point 2
10.0      5.0           2nd pair, point 1
 0.0      0.0           2nd pair, point 2
 3.0      2.0           3rd pair, point 1
 7.0      5.0           3rd pair, point 2
```

the output of ComputeDistances is:

Distance between pair 1 = 13.30

Distance between pair 2 = 11.18

Distance between pair 3 =  5.00

Solution 3 is better than 1 or 2 because it's more general (but only slightly more complex).
The general form of the for statement is:

```
<for statement> ::=
    for <control variable> := <initial value> to <final value> do
        <statement>
```

where

```
<control variable> ::= <entire variable>
<initial value> ::= <expression>
<final value> ::= <expression>
```

The definition of the for statement signifies that the processor should assign the following progression of values to the control variable:

initial-value, succ(initial-value), succ(succ(initial-value)),...,
final value

and execute the statement once for each successive value in the progression. The following rules and mechanisms hold for the for statement.

**1.** The programmer must declare <control variable>, just as he would any other variable.
**2.** <control variable> may belong to any ordinal data type: it cannot be a real variable.
**3.** <control variable> must be an <entire variable>. (This simply means that <control variable> may not be a component of a structured variable or a variable referenced by a pointer variable.)
**4.** The expressions for <initial value> and <final value> must yield values consistent with the data type of <control variable>. That is, <initial value> and <final value> must belong to the same ordinal data type as <control variable>.
**5.** The processor evaluates <initial value> and <final value> once, when it commences the for loop.
**6.** If <initial value> is greater than <final value>, the processor will not execute <statement>.
**7.** <statement> may be simple or compound.
**8.** <statement> may or may not <u>refer</u> to <control variable> in its computations.
**9.** <statement> <u>must not modify</u> (assign a value to) <control variable>.

**10.** The processor leaves the value of <control variable> undefined when it finishes executing the for loop.

The following example illustrates the useful structure of nesting one for statement inside another for statement.

```
program TruthTable(output);

var
    P, Q : Boolean;
begin
    write('  P        ',
         '  Q        ',
         'P or Q     ',
         'P and Q    ',
         'not P      ');
    writeln;
    for P := false to true do
        for Q := false to true do
            writeln(  P      , '  ':5,
                      Q      , '  ':5,
                    P or Q , '  ':5,
                    P and Q, '  ':5,
                    not P  , '  ':5)
end.
```

This program produces the following output, a truth table for the three Boolean operators.

| P | Q | P or Q | P and Q | not P |
|---|---|--------|---------|-------|
| false | false | false | false | true |
| false | true | true | false | true |
| true | false | true | false | false |
| true | true | true | true | false |

Study this program carefully and produce the output table by tracing the program. Note the sequence of processor actions in the nested for loops; this sequence is equivalent to the following compound statement.

```
P := false;
Q := false;
writeln(...);
Q := true;
writeln(...);
P := true;
Q := false;
writeln(...);
Q := true;
writeln(...)
```

There's another form of the for statement which allows the loop to "count down."

**for** <control variable> := <initial value> **downto** <final value> **do**
    <statement>

which signifies that the processor should assign the following progression of values to the control variable

initial-value, pred(initial-value),..., final-value

Here's an example using this structure.

```
program CountDown(output);
var
    J : 0..10;
begin
    writeln('Counting down from T minus 10...')
    for J := 10 downto 0 do
        begin
            write(J:2,'...');
            OneSecondDelay
        end
end.
```

This program produces the following output

Counting down from T minus 10...
10... 9... 8... 7... 6... 5... 4... 3... 2... 1... 0...

with one second elapsing between the printing of each digit.

The second example of a decrementing **for** loop sums N terms of the harmonic series.

```
program SumHarmonicSeries(input, output);
{Compute: Sum = 1 + 1/2 + 1/3 + ... + 1/N}
{Add smallest terms first so that they contribute to the sum.}

var
    J, N : integer;
    Sum  : real;

begin
    read(N);
    Sum := 0;
    for J := N downto 1 do
        Sum := Sum + 1/J;
    writeln('The sum for', N : 3, ' terms is', Sum)
end.
```

In the following sections we'll cover two more repetition control structures, the repeat-until and while-do statements. When should you use the for loop rather than one of the other available structures? The answer is, whenever the number of repetitions is deterministic rather than contingent; that is, whenever you can decide how many repetitions you require before the program executes.

## WHILE...DO: REPETITION WHILE A CONDITION REMAINS TRUE

The **while** loop is probably the most frequently used structure for controlling repetition. The general form of the while statement is

    **while** <condition> **do**
      <statement>

where <condition> is a Boolean expression yielding the value false or true and <statement> is either simple or compound. The following suggests the sequence of actions in a while statement that controls a compound statement.

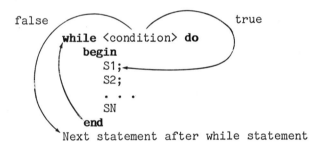

```
false                                    true
        while <condition> do
           begin
              S1;
              S2;
              . . .
              SN
           end
        Next statement after while statement
```

When first encountering the while statement, the processor evaluates its condition. If the condition is false, the processor jumps to the statement following the while statement, bypassing the while statement's body. (We find it convenient to use the term "body" for the <statement> whose execution the while statement controls.) If condition is true, the processor executes the sequence of statements contained in the while statement's body. The processor does <u>not</u> recheck <condition> until it has executed every statement in the body of the while statement. After the processor finishes executing the while statement's body, the processor rechecks condition. If the condition is false, the processor jumps to the statement following the while statement, bypassing the while statement's body. If the condition is true, the processor executes the sequence of statements contained in the while statement's body. And so on.

The while statement is useful in performing an <u>a priori</u> undeterminable number of repetitions. The while statement is most apt when our uncertainty extends to our not knowing whether we should execute <statement> even once. Suppose, for example, that a programmer wants to provide a "software" routine for the integer division of two natural numbers. The straightforward way to do this is repeated subtractions of the divisor from the dividend. How many subtractions? One does not know a priori. (If one did, one would already know the quotient.) Here's some appropriate code using a while statement.

```
Quotient := 0;
Remainder := Dividend;
while Remainder >= Divisor do
   begin
      Remainder := Remainder - Divisor;
      Quotient := Quotient + 1
   end
```

This example illustrates an important feature of the while-do loop which distinguishes it from the repeat-until loop (which we will discuss in the next section). In implementing the while loop, the processor evaluates the while condition before it performs the first execution of the while statement's body; therefore, if the condition is false, the processor completely skips the body. This ability to skip the body completely is essential for some problems. For example, suppose that the Dividend is 7 and the Divisor is 8. Then the processor sets the Quotient equal to 0 and the Remainder equal to 7, and skips the body because the while loop's condition is not satisfied. Thus the process leaves the right answers in Quotient and Remainder; but if the processor made one pass through the while loop's body, it would deposit the wrong values in Quotient and Remainder.

The next example exemplifies the second common use of the while statement (performing an a priori undeterminable number of input operations). This program adds line numbers to the text on the input file while copying this text to the output file. (The program text exhibited below is an example of the program's actions, this text having been run through the program.) One knows a priori neither how many lines there are nor how many characters there are on each line.

```
1    program AddLineNumbering(input, output);
2
3    var
4       Ch : char;
5       LineNumber : integer;
6    begin
7       LineNumber := 0;
8       while not eof do
9          begin
10            LineNumber := LineNumber + 1;
11            write(LineNumber:5, ' ':3);
12            while not eoln do
13               begin
```

```
14                      read(Ch);
15                      write(Ch)
16              end;
17          readln;
18          writeln
19      end
20  end.
```

Another example is code that reads an unbroken sequence of digits (characters) and converts them to an integer value. One does not know a priori how many digits are in a sequence.

```
read(Ch);
if ('0' <= Ch) and (Ch <= '9') then
    begin
        Number := 0;
        while ('0' <= Ch) and (Ch <= '9') do
            begin
                Number := 10*Number + (ord(Ch) - ord('0'));
                read(Ch)
            end
    end
```

The while statement is flexible. It's possible for you to write all of your programs using while repetitions only. Avoid this kind of "whilephilia." If you're implementing a repetitive structure and know the processor will execute the loop body at least once, then you ought to consider using a repeat loop, discussed in the next section. (For example, the preceding code could be more cleanly written as a repeat loop.) If you're implementing a deterministic loop--that is, if you can determine in advance how many iterations the process requires--you ought to consider using a for loop. The while statement is certainly useful; but Pascal includes two other repetitive statements for good reasons. To illustrate this point, consider these control structures:

```
1. for J := First to Last do
       Body
```

```
2. if First <= Last then
       begin
           J := First;
           Body;
           while J < Last do
               begin
                   J := succ(J);
                   Body
               end
       end
```

These two structures are equivalent. Which one is clearer to the reader? (Of course, 2 can be simplified if we know that First < Last.)

**REPEAT...UNTIL:** REPETITION UNTIL A CONDITION BECOMES TRUE

The general form of the **repeat** statement is

**repeat**
    ⟨statement sequence⟩
**until** ⟨condition⟩

where ⟨condition⟩ is a Boolean expression yielding the value false or true. The processor repeatedly executes the statement sequence between the tokens **repeat** and **until,** until it finds ⟨condition⟩ true on completion of the statement sequence. Note that the processor will execute the statement sequence at least once, because the processor evaluates ⟨condition⟩ <u>after</u> it executes the statement sequence. Note also that the programmer does not have to delimit a compound statement with **begin** and **end,** because the **repeat** and **until** tokens serve the delimiting function.

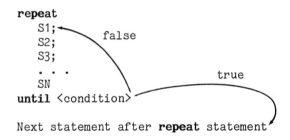

```
repeat
   S1;              false
   S2;
   S3;
   . . .                           true
   SN
until <condition>
```
Next statement after **repeat** statement

When should you use a repeat loop and when should you use a while loop? It's hard to give a specific answer. A general answer is, use whichever one yields the most natural, readable, and efficient code. Sometimes it doesn't make much difference. To see the difference between the two structures, consider the following problem. Suppose we want to write a procedure that skips blanks on the input file and leaves the first nonblank character in Ch. Here are two approaches:

```
procedure SkipBlanks1;
   begin
      read(Ch);
      while Ch = ' ' do
         read(Ch)
   end

procedure SkipBlanks2;
   begin
      repeat
         read(Ch)
      until Ch <> ' '
   end
```

For the SkipBlanks procedure, the repeat statement looks somewhat more straightforward and readable than the while statement. Note that we have to insert a read statement before the while loop to make it work; but the repeat loop requires no setting up. This is because the while loop checks the Boolean expression Ch = ' ' before it reads a value for Ch; i.e., the while loop checks its condition before it's defined it. So we have to add a statement before the while statement to make it executable. The repeat statement, on the other hand, executes its statement before it checks its termination condition; and that initial execution naturally defines its termination condition.

Now let's consider another problem. Suppose we want to read and sum a list of positive numbers, stopping when we come to the first negative number. (The negative number should not be added to the sum.) Here are two approaches:

```
program ReadAndSum1(input, output);

var
    Number, Sum : integer;
begin
    Sum := 0;
    read(Number);
    while Number >= 0 do
        begin
            Sum := Sum + Number;
            read(Number)
        end;
    writeln(Sum)
end.
```

Note the order of the statements in the body of the while loop. We placed the read statement last so that the processor checks the value of Number before it adds Number to Sum. The initialization for the while loop is fairly straightforward and the first iteration of the Sum assignment statement is meaningful. We must do something similar for the repeat version; but the initialization is not so straightforward.

```
program ReadAndSum2(input, output);

var
    Number, Sum : integer;
begin
    Sum := 0;
    Number := 0;
    repeat
            Sum := Sum + Number;
            read(Number)
    until Number < 0;
    writeln(Sum)
end.
```

The big difference between the two approaches is the initialization. The second initialization is less natural, which is to say it's less productive. Why did we replace read(Number) with Number := 0 in the second version? To make the loop work acceptably in the first iteration even if the input is negative. The Sum will be zero (correct!) even if the first Number we read is less than zero. If you find this concern for an "extreme case" obsessional or finicky, please realize that it's the "extreme" (a synonym, unfortunately, for unexpected) cases that often clobber programs most catastrophically. But our main point here is that the while loop looks more natural than the repeat loop for the second problem. The issue, of course, is that the repeat loop iterates its statements before it examines its condition. Incidentally, the same kind of issue arises when the stopping condition is the eof condition.


## IF...THEN...ELSE: CHOOSING BETWEEN TWO ALTERNATIVES


Choosing correctly between alternatives lies at the heart of intelligent action. Therefore, intelligent programs are written to leave certain decisions open, to be made by the computer processor during its execution of the program. The processor bases its course of action on current circumstances: the value of a piece of input data or the result of some calculation. There's nothing more fundamental to the power of digital computers than the principle that actions affect data and data affect actions.

Every high-level-language has some form of if-statement for selecting an alternative. Pascal's basic structure for choosing between two alternatives is

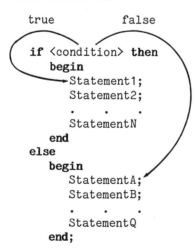

```
      true            false

  if <condition> then
     begin
        Statement1;
        Statement2;
            .   .   .
        StatementN
     end
  else
     begin
        StatementA;
        StatementB;
            .   .   .
        StatementQ
     end;
```

next statement {Not part of the if statement}

The BNF definition of the if statement is

```
if <condition> then
    <then-statement>
else
    <else-statement>;
next statement {Not part of the if statement}
```

Your intuition of what this means is probably right. First the processor
evaluates the condition, a Boolean expression. If the condition is true
the processor executes the then-statement and skips the else-statement;
if the condition is false the processor skips the then-statement and
executes the else-statement.
Note carefully where we have placed (and haven't placed!) the semicolons
in this statement. Here's an example of the if structure.

```
if X >= 0 then
    Y := sqrt(X)
else {X < 0, so}
    InvalidArg := true
```

But don't write if statements like this one!

```
if (63 < Temp) and (Temp < 78) then
    TempOK := true
else
    TempOK := false
```

because you can achieve the same effect by the simpler statement

```
TempOK :=  (63 < Temp) and (Temp < 78)
```

When we discuss the **case** statement you'll see another way to choose
one of two alternatives. Some programmers prefer

```
case sex of
    female:
        writeln('Offer fencing class.');
    male:
        writeln('Offer boxing class.')
end
```

to the if statement version

```
if sex = female then
    writeln('Offer fencing class.')
else
    writeln('Offer boxing class.')
```

We believe the **case** version is better looking and more readable.

Sometimes the decision to be taken is not to select one of two alternative actions but rather to decide whether to execute or not to execute some single action. In this case either the then-statement or the else-statement is the null statement. For example we could write

```
if Temp > 62 then
   {Do nothing}
else {Temp <= 62, so}
   StartFurnace
```

However, the empty then-statement is rather roundabout (unless you want to emphasize <u>doing nothing</u>) and we generally prefer the following **if-then** form for choosing between doing something and doing nothing:

```
if Temp <= 62 then
   StartFurnace
```

This is a very frequent form of the **if** statement.

```
if <condition> then
   <statement>
<next statement> {not part of if statement}
```

If <condition> is false, then the processor skips <statement> and continues at <next statement>.
   If statements can be nested. For example,

```
if <condition1> then
   if <condition2> then
      if <condition3> then
         <Statement>
```

However, this should usually be written as

```
if <condition1> and <condition2> and <condition3> then
   <statement>
```

which is <u>logically</u> equivalent to the first structure but more compact and readable. The nested if structure would be necessary, however, if a programmer wanted to guarantee "short-circuiting" (bypassing) the evaluation of condition2 and condition3 if condition1 is false or short-circuiting the evaluation of condition3 if condition2 is false. A programmer might want to short-circuit the evaluation of a complicated Boolean expression in order to save processing time or he may have to short-circuit an evaluation because the expression is undefined. Consider, for example, the following code.

```
if A > 0 then
   if B div A > 2 then
      A := 2*A
```

Chaining these two if statements prevents an attempt to divide B by zero in the second if condition, whereas the following form does not guarantee what the processor will do after it determines that the first expression is false.

```
if (A > 0) and (B div A > 2) then
    A := 2*A
```

Clearly, the complete condition is false if A = 0; logically, the processor does not have to evaluate B div A > 2 in this case. But the Pascal language definition leaves open the question of whether or not the processor will completely evaluate a Boolean expression when it can determine the expression's value by a partial evaluation. For this reason the second code for computing A is unsafe.

A syntactic ambiguity can arise in compound if statements: "the dangling else clause." Here's an example of a treacherous form of the ambiguity--all the more perfidious because its intent is clear from the indention.

```
if B1 then
    if B2 then
        StatementX
else {CAUTION: MISLEADING INDENTION}
    StatementY
```

Remember that the compiler pays no attention to our indention of the Pascal source code. Obviously, the writer of these lines _intended_ that the processor execute StatementY if B1 is false (independently of the value of B2). But these lines will be so compiled that the processor will execute StatementY when B1 is true and B2 is false! The misunderstanding arises from the dangling position of the else clause: does this else clause belong to the first if or to the second if? The compiler resolves the ambiguity by associating the else clause with the closest, preceding else-less if. To get the results desired by the writer of these lines, we would have to rewrite the fragment this way:

```
if B1 then
    begin
        if B2 then
            StatementX
    end
else
    StatementY
```

Now the syntax and the indention agree.

The compiler would compile the _original_ lines as if they were written as follows. (That is, the processor will associate the **else** with the closest **if**.) The lesson here should be familiar: make your semantic intention syntactically clear.

```
if B1 then
   begin
      if B2 then
         StatementX
      else
         StatementY
   end
```

## IF-ELSE IF-ELSE IF-ELSE IF: CHOOSING AMONG MANY ALTERNATIVES

The following structure:

```
if condition1 then
   statement1
else if condition2 then
   statement2
else if condition3 then
........................
else
   statementN
```

selects one alternative from N alternatives, where N can be as large as you like. The **case** statement also selects one alternative from among many; but the **else if** chain is more general. (The else-if chain is also less efficient and less compact than the case statement for those selections where the case statement works.)

The processor evaluates each condition in order; if the processor finds a true condition, it executes the associated statement and then transfers control to the statement following the else-if construction. Notice the last else clause; it deals with "none of the above" conditions. (The case statement does not have an "otherwise" or else clause for the default situation.) The programmer may omit the else part if he has no explicit action for the default situation. If the programmer has so structured his problem that one of the enumerated conditions <u>must</u> be true, then he can use the else part to report an error.

```
........................
else
   ReportError(6) {6 indicates "impossible" condition occurred}
```

Here's a simple program fragment from a program that counts positive, negative, and zero values of N.

```
if N > 0 then
   PosCount := PosCount + 1
else if N < 0 then
```

```
      NegCount := NegCount + 1
   else {N = 0}
      ZeroCount := ZeroCount + 1
```

Notice that there are no semicolons in this structure: it's one statement.


**CASE...END**: SELECTION OF ONE FROM MANY


Consider the following if structure for printing out an error message.

```
if      ErrorCode = 1 then
   writeln('**** Square root of negative number ****')
else if ErrorCode = 2 then
   writeln('**** Log of negative number ****')
else if ErrorCode = 3 then
   writeln('**** Divide by zero ****')
else if ErrorCode = 4 then
   writeln('**** Subrange variable out of range ****')
else if ErrorCode = 5 then
   writeln('**** Type incompatibility on read ****')
```

Pascal's **case** statement offers a less cluttered and more efficient way of decoding these error codes:

```
case ErrorCode of
   1 : writeln('**** Square root of negative number ****');
   2 : writeln('**** Log of negative number ****');
   3 : writeln('**** Divide by zero ****');
   4 : writeln('**** Subrange variable out of range ****');
   5 : writeln('**** Type incompatibility on read ****')
end
```

The general form of the case statement is

```
case <expression> of
   <1st case label list> : <statement1>;
   <2nd case label list> : <statement2>;
                    . . .
   <Nth case label list> : <statementN>
end
```

The case statement consists of an expression for the case "selector" (case index) followed by a list of labelled statements. The expression for the case selector (index) must be an enumerated data type or an integer subrange type, and the statement labels must be of the same data

type as the case selector. All the statement labels must be distinct.
The action of the **case** statement is to specify execution of the
statement whose label is equal to the current value of the case
selector. The target statements may be simple or compound.

Take note of the following:

**1.** Pascal considers it an error for the selector expression to yield
a value that is not equal to one of the statement labels.

**2.** The programmer does not have to declare the statement labels (in
contrast to **goto** labels). Statement labels in case statements are
defined only for the case statement in which they occur. Goto statements
may not use case statement labels as targets.

**3.** A statement may have more than one label; but a given label may
appear only <u>one</u> time in a case statement.

**4.** Statement labels do not have to appear in any order; but remember
that a statement label may appear only once in a case statement.

**5.** If a program requires no action for a particular case selector
value, a null or empty statement may be associated with the
corresponding label.

The following procedure classifies a chemical element (identified by
its atomic number, Z) into one of the groups of the periodic table. The
if statement preceding the case statement guarantees that Z has a value
equal to one of the case statement labels (see point 1 above). (In the
chapter on the **set** data type we'll show you a much more convenient and
compact way of writing the long condition of this if statement.)

```
procedure FindGroup(Z : AtomicNumber); {type AtomicNumber = 1..105}

begin
    if ((21 <= Z) and (Z <= 30)) or ((39 <= Z) and (Z <= 48)) or
       ((57 <= Z) and (Z <= 80)) or ((89 <= Z) and (Z <= 105)) then
        writeln('Element', Z:4, ' is a transition element.')
    else {Element is not a transition element.}
        case Z of
            1 :
                writeln('Element 1 is hydrogen.');
            3, 11, 19, 37, 55, 87 :
                writeln('Element', Z:3, ' is an alkali metal.');
            4, 12, 20, 38, 56, 88 :
                writeln('Element', Z:3, ' is in Group II.');
            5, 13, 31, 49, 81:
                writeln('Element', Z:3, ' is in Group III.');
            6, 14, 32, 50, 82:
                writeln('Element', Z:3, ' is in Group IV.');
            7, 15, 33, 51, 83:
                writeln('Element', Z:3, ' is in Group V.');
            8, 16, 34, 52, 84:
                writeln('Element', Z:3, ' is in Group VI.');
            9, 17, 35, 53, 85:
                writeln('Element', Z:3, ' is in Group VII.');
```

```
        2, 10, 18, 36, 54, 86:
            writeln('Element', Z:3, ' is a noble gas.')
      end {case}
   end {FindGroup}
```

**GOTO**

"I go, I don't know where!"
                    from the epitaph of Martius of Biberach, 1498

"You will go most safely in the middle."
                    Ovid

The structured control statements we have already introduced in this chapter are sufficient for you to write Pascal programs. In fact, these statements are more than a minimum set and even afford you the opportunity to exhibit programming discretion and style. So why does Pascal introduce another control construct? Sometimes we can't solve a problem neatly or clearly with one of the structured control statements. These situations are rare, however, and you should be sure that you have a genuine instance of one before you try a solution with a goto statement. There are two kinds of situations that sometimes justify the use of a goto statement:

**1.** An error or other exceptional situation arises during a process (e.g., a loop) that requires suspension of the process and perhaps the main program as well. The goto statement can transfer control to a chosen point in the program where a recovery action is taken or graceful termination is completed.
**2.** The most convenient point to exit from a particular loop is not from the top (like the while statement) or from the bottom (like the repeat statement) but from some intermediate point.

There's an example in Chapter 2 (AddAndCheckElectors) of the first kind of situation. Now's a good time to reexamine that program; it provides a goto transfer out of a for loop when the processor finds an invalid input datum. (We'll discuss the second kind of situation later in this section.) Note the following:

**1.** The label declaration for the goto must precede all other declarations (let's construct the very perfect function).
**2.** Labels are unsigned integers. (But labels have no numerical significance; they are merely statement markers or tags.) Some implementations restrict labels to four or fewer digits.
**3.** The "scope" (see the Chapter on subprograms) of a label is the entire text of the block in which you declare it; but you should prefix

a label to a statement in the statement part of the block where you
declare the label.

4. It's an error in some compilers and it's generally bad practice to
use a goto statement to jump from a higher level in a program to a lower
level. Don't, for example, use a goto statement to jump into a compound
statement or into the statement sequence enclosed by **repeat** and **until**.
It would be otiose to try to jump into a procedure or function. It's
legal (and sometimes even sensible) to jump out of subprogram in order
to return to the main program or out of a compound statement into an
enclosing compound statement.

5. Attach a label to a statement by prefixing the statement with (for
example) 9001:. Of course, you can attach a given label to only one
statement within a block. It's permissible to attach a label to an empty
statement (for example, the empty statement before the final **end** in
AddAndCheckElectors).

6. Since the goto statement occurs rarely in structured programming,
you should provide sufficient comments in the program text to explain
the goto's purpose.

To conclude this section, let's consider the pros and cons of using a
goto statement to exit from a loop. We mentioned earlier that sometimes
the most convenient point to exit from a loop is not from the top (like
the while statement) or from the bottom (like the repeat statement) but
from some intermediate point. Pascal provides two contingent loop
control statements; but neither one provides a mechanism for exiting
from a loop after any of the loop's statements. In contrast, the ADA
programming language provides this kind of generality of loop control by
permitting conditional or unconditional exit statements to appear
anywhere within the body of the loop:

```
loop
    read(Ch);
    exit when Ch = '*';
    write(Ch)
end loop;
<next statement>

loop
    read(Number);
    exit when eof;
    Sum := Sum + Number
    exit when Sum >= Limit
end loop;
<next statement>
```

When the exit statement detects that its condition is true, it transfers
control out of the loop to <next statement>. This is a general form of
loop (but still "structured" because there's only one entry point and
one exit point). It allows exit from the loop at the top, at the bottom,
or at an intermediate point. We can construct a similar loop in Pascal:

```
const
      Done = false;
      .    .    .
   begin {loop}
      repeat
         read(Ch);
         if Ch = '*' then {exit loop}
            goto 9001;
         write(Ch)
      until Done;
   9001:
   end {loop}
```

By enclosing the loop between **"begin** {loop}**"** and **"end** {loop}**"**, we have created a loop control module: the module has a single entry point and a single exit point. We have also deliberately restricted the use of the goto statement: it does not transfer control <u>outside</u> the module, but rather to the exit point of the module. When you use the goto statement--if you use it at all--use it in this kind of structured and disciplined (even stereotyped) way.

Why take all these precautions with the goto statement? Because the goto statement is intrinsically unstructured and unconstrained; it can transfer control to any label whose scope is the block in which the goto occurs. If you exercise this unconstrained freedom, your program will be hard to read, hard to test, and hard to modify.

The goto statement provides another way to attack the problem of detecting end-of-file while reading numbers.

```
   Sum := 0;
   begin {loop}
      repeat
         read(Number);
         if eof then {exit loop}
            goto 9002;
         Sum := Sum + Number
      until Done;
   9002:
   end {loop};
   <next statement>
```

or, somewhat more compactly

```
   Sum := 0;
   repeat {loop}
      read(Number);
      if eof then {exit loop}
         goto 9002;
      Sum := Sum + Number
   until Done; 9002: {end loop};
   <next statement>
```

EXERCISES

1. The following code contains nested for loops. Study the loops carefully and state what values the code leaves in SUM1 and SUM2 when:
a. M = 5 and N = 4;
b. M and N are any values >= 1 (express answer in terms of M and N).

```
Sum1 := 0;
Sum2 := 0;
for I := 1 to M do
    begin {outer loop}
        Sum1 := Sum1 + 1;
        for J := 1 to N do
            Sum2 := Sum2 + 1
    end {outer loop}
```

2. Study the following program carefully.

```
read(L);
for I := 1 to L
    begin {for loop}
        read(N);
        if odd(N) then
            Sum := Sum + 1
        else
            Sum := Sum + N div 2;
    end; {for loop}
writeln(Sum)
```

What does the program print out for an input file composed of:
a.   0  37  39  48  67
b.   1  24  37  83  63
c.   3  23  28  47  41
d.   5  49  39  83  24

3. Using one if-then, rewrite the following:

```
if Flag = Up then
    if X > -5 then
        if X < 25 then
            X := X + Increment
```

4. The following code does exactly what the programmer wants. Rewrite the code so that its function is unambiguous to anyone who reads it. Do not rely upon indention alone.

**if** Flag = Down **then if** X > 0 **then** Y := X **else** Y := 0

5. Assume a textfile F has numbered lines. Each number is immediately

followed by a colon. Write a program that reads F and writes each line of F on an empty textfile G, omitting the line numbers. Do not write the line number or the colon. (Is this specification complete?)

**6.** Write a program that reads the characters on a textfile and writes out the smallest character and the largest character
   **a.** when the number of characters is given as the first datum;
   **b.** when the sequence is terminated by a "~" symbol;
   **c.** when input provides neither number of characters nor sentinel.
("Smallest, largest" refer to lexicographic ordering of characters.)

**7.** Write a program that reads a list of integers and writes out the smallest integer and the largest integer
   **a.** when the number of integers is given as the first datum;
   **b.** when the sequence is terminated by -maxint;
   **c.** when input provides neither number of integers nor sentinel.

**8.** Write a program that reads a textfile and prints out a count of each vowel in the file.

**9.** Write a program that could print out all the consonant trigrams in the Roman alphabet. Examples of consonant trigrams are BBB, BBC, BBD,..., ZZX, ZZY, ZZZ. How many consonant trigrams are there? Estimate how many pages of printout it would take to print all the trigrams.

# 6. Structured Data Type 1:
# The Array

Most applications complex enough to merit the use of digital computers involve large masses of data; consequently, the processing of data on even the largest and fastest computers may take considerable time. Furthermore, writing complex programs that process large amounts of data with only primitive and simple data types is tedious and time-consuming. To attack these problems, computer scientists have invented data structures that help the programmer minimize both his program writing time and the computer processing time.

One of the most important ways of aiding the programmer and improving the processing time is to organize the data in memory to reflect any inherent relationship among the data and to reflect any order in the way the processor accesses the data. The array data type is the most widely used example of such efficient organization. An array variable in standard Pascal consists of a _fixed_ number of components, each a variable in its own right and all belonging to exactly the same data type. An important feature of the array is how we refer to and access the components. We explicitly refer to a component, and the processor directly accesses a component, by the array identifier followed by the component's _index_. This index, or component selector, can be a computable expression, a variable, or a constant. The time it takes for the processor to access a component does not depend on the value of the index (which is equivalent to the position of the component in the array); hence, the processor can access all components equally quickly. The array is a truly random-access data structure: it takes full advantage of the computer's high-speed primary memory.

INTRODUCTION TO INDEXED VARIABLES

Suppose it's necessary to work with a large number of variables in the same program. For example, we might want to count how many times each of the printable characters appears in this book. This kind of information would be useful to an engineer who wants to optimize the

116

placement of the characters on the print head of a character printer. There are 94 printable characters (excluding the blank character) in the America Standard Code for Information Interchange (ASCII), and all but one or two of these characters appear in this book. This means that we require 94 integer variables in which to store the number of occurrences of each of the printable characters. Therefore, it appears that we have to make up and declare 94 identifiers for these variables.

```
var
    NmbrOfExclamations    :   integer;
    NmbrOfQuotes          :   integer;
    NmbrOfNmbrSigns       :   integer;
    NmbrOfDollarSigns     :   integer;
    NmbrOfPercentSigns    :   integer;
    NmbrOfAmpersands      :   integer;
    NmbrOfApostrophes     :   integer;
    NmbrOfLeftParens      :   integer;
    et cetera                 et cetera
    et cetera                 et cetera
    NmbrOfTildes          :   integer;
```

Our burden does not end with thinking up and declaring these 94 variables. We must initialize all 94 variables with zero values, and we must write a very, very long case statement in order to increment the counts stored in the 94 variables.

```
    NmbrOfExclamations    := 0;
    NmbrOfQuotes          := 0;
    NmbrOfNmbrSigns       := 0;
    et cetera                 et cetera
    et cetera                 et cetera
    NmbrOfTildes          := 0;

read(Ch);
case Ch of
    ' ':  {empty statement};
    '!':  NmbrOfExclamations := NmbrOfExclamations + 1;
    '"':  NmbrOfQuotes := NmbrOfQuotes + 1;
    '#':  NmbrOfNmbrSigns := NmbrOfNmbrSigns + 1;
    '$':  NmbrOfDollarSigns := NmbrOfDollarSigns + 1;
    et cetera                 et cetera
    et cetera                 et cetera
    '~':  NmbrOfTildes := NmbrOfTildes + 1
end
```

Obviously, this process is tedious, wasteful, and subject to errors (spelling errors, typing errors, interpretation errors).

In order to handle this situation, most high-order languages (including Pascal) provide an extremely useful data structure: the **array.** The array is a set of variables (called <u>components</u> of the array),

all of the same data type, and bearing the same surname or family name.
We distinguish family members from one another by using their
"Christian" names or "forenames." As is often the case when
communicating with computers, we write the last name first. What is
unusual is that we call the forename the "index" or "subscript," and we
write it enclosed in square brackets. Thus we have the following 94
variables instead of the earlier ones. On the right we have indicated
(purely fictitious) possible values of these variables.

| Index Value (Subscripts) | Components (Variable Identifiers) | Some Possible Values |
|---|---|---|
| '!' | Count['!'] | 38 |
| '"' | Count['"'] | 79 |
| '#' | Count['#'] | 25 |
| '$' | Count['$'] | 102 |
| . . . | | |
| '~' | Count['~'] | 10 |

We haven't gained a great deal, however, if we still have to declare 94
variables by writing out the above 94 identifiers. Fortunately, we can
declare all 94 variables with the following compact statement.

```
var
    Count : array['!'..'~'] of integer; {ASCII only!}
```

and thereby declare our 94 variables in one swoop. The bracketed
subrange expression, '!'..'~', declares the array's index type; it
specifies the length of the array and enumerates the values which the
processor can assign to the index variable. (The printable characters
all lie between '!' and '~' in ASCII.)
    It's important to stress, before proceeding with our
character-counting problem, that the data type of the index must be an
ordered type of fixed length. Thus, the Boolean, char, user-defined
scalar type, and integer subrange types can be used to declare index
variables; but the integer and real data types cannot. The length of the
array (the number of its components) can always be determined from

Length of array = ord(index upper limit) - ord(index lower limit) + 1

In the case of our example

94 = ord('~') - ord('!') + 1

Now we can initialize all 94 variables in one compact for statement:

```
for Ch := '!' to '~' do
    Count[Ch] := 0
```

We can replace the tediously long case statement with the following computationally equivalent statement.

```
read(Ch);
if Ch <> ' ' then
   Count[Ch] := Count[Ch] + 1
```

This elegantly simple statement accomplishes the same objective as the extremely long case statement.

Be sure that you understand the meaning of Count[Ch]. Count[Ch] is a __component variable__; it refers to a single variable, a single component of the multi-variable array Count. Which component? That depends on the current value of the index variable Ch. If Ch = 'E', then Count[Ch] refers to the variable named Count['E'].

Here is the complete program for "reading" the book, counting the characters, and printing out the results.

```
program CountASCIIcharacters(input, output);

var
   Ch    : char;
   Count : array['!'..'~'] of integer;

begin
   for Ch := '!' to '~' do
      Count[Ch] := 0; {Initialize Count array}
   while not eof do
      begin
         read(Ch);
         if Ch <> ' ' then
            Count[Ch] := Count[Ch] + 1
      end;
   for Ch := '!' to '~' do
      writeln(Ch, ' occurs', Count[Ch], ' times.')
end.
```

Before proceeding to a formal discussion of arrays, let's look at one more example. Suppose that we want to maintain records and compute statistics for the monthly rainfall during a year. Before we learned about arrays, we would have declared 12 independent and unrelated variables.

```
var
   JanRainfall, FebRainfall, MarRainfall, AprRainfall : real;
   MayRainfall, JunRainfall, JulRainfall, AugRainfall : real;
   SepRainfall, OctRainfall, NovRainfall, DecRainfall : real;
```

Do these variables have any relationship to each other? Of course they do: they're all components of the annual rainfall. But as we've declared them here, they've no structure; they're not related in any

useful way. The compiler won't store them in any particular order, and
there will be no systematic way to access them. Consequently, when we
want to read values for these variables, we have to write a read
statement for twelve unrelated parameters.

```
read(JanRainfall, FebRainfall, MarRainfall, AprRainfall,
    MayRainfall, JunRainfall, JulRainfall, AugRainfall,
    SepRainfall, OctRainfall, NovRainfall, DecRainfall)
```

And if we want to add them in order to compute the average monthly
rainfall or the annual rainfall, we have to add them as twelve unrelated
variables, writing out each one of the twelve identifiers.

This is obviously inconvenient. Consider how much more inconvenient
it would be if we were dealing with <u>daily</u> rainfall for a year. If we
pursued this unstructured approach we would have to declare 365
variables, write 365 read parameters, and so on.

Whenever you have a problem which requires similar operations on a
fixed number of variables of the same data type, consider using the
array data structure. If the number of variables is large and if the
computations refer to the variables more than once, the use of an array
will probably be essential. However, in some problems, it may be
possible to process each value completely before considering the
following value. In these cases, each time the processor reads a new
value, it may destroy the previous value. Frequently, however, the
computations require all the previous values at a later stage; in these
cases it is more efficient to retain the whole set of values throughout
the process rather than reread them. The array is an efficient method
for reading and retaining a whole set of related values.

To illustrate the previous paragraph, let's consider some rainfall
problems. The first problem is to compute the annual rainfall and the
average monthly rainfall. In this elementary case an array is
unnecessary:

```
program SumAndAverageRainfall(input, output);
var
    Rainfall, Sum, Average : real;
begin
    Sum := 0.0;
    for J := 1 to 12 do
        begin
            read(Rainfall);
            Sum := Sum + Rainfall
        end;
    Average := Sum/12;
    writeln('The annual rainfall is', Sum);
    writeln('The average monthly rainfall is', Average)
end.
```

Now let's assume a more complicated problem: find the annual
rainfall, the average monthly rainfall, the deviation of the rainfall in

each month from the monthly average, and the rank order of the months by their rainfall. In the following program we do not explicitly solve the last problem because we take up sorting arrays in a later section.

```
program RainfallStatistics(input, output);
type
   RainfallType  = array[1..12] of real;
var
   Month         :  1..12;
   Rainfall      :  RainfallType;
   Sum, Average  :  real;

procedure SortRainfall;
   begin
      writeln('SortRainfall') {For development purposes only.)
   end;

begin
   Sum := 0;
   for Month := 1 to 12 do
      begin
         read(Rainfall[Month]);
         Sum := Sum + Rainfall[Month]
      end;
   Average := Sum/12;
   writeln('The monthly average is', Average);
   for Month := 1 to 12 do
      writeln('The deviation from the average for month',
              Month: 3, ' is', Rainfall[Month] - Average);
   SortRainfall
end.
```

Note that this program refers to the values of the twelve array variables two times after it computes the sum and average: it computes the monthly deviation from the average and then passes the array to the subprogram SortRainfall. Notice also that the program performs the same computations and operations on each component of the array. This is the kind of problem for which the array data structure is particularly beneficial.

## SYNTAX OF THE ARRAY

The array type definition must specify the data type of both the index variable and the component variable.

```
type
   <type identifier> = array[<index type>] of <component type>
```

where ⟨index type⟩ is an ordinal type and ⟨component type⟩ is any type, simple or structured. Here are some examples:

```
    type
       Francais   = packed array[1..4] of char;
       BoolezType = array[false..true] of Francais;
                          -or-
       BoolezType = array[Boolean] of Francais;
    var
       Boolez : BoolezType;
    begin
       Boolez[false] := 'FAUX';
       Boolez[true]  := 'VRAI'
```

Boolez translates the English false and true into the French "faux" and "vrai" respectively. Thus

```
    writeln(Boolez[0 < 1])
```

writes VRAI on the output device, whereas

```
    writeln(0 < 1)
```

writes TRUE on the output device.
    Arrays are quite useful for these mapping, translation, and transfer functions.


Scalar index-type:

```
    {Refer to EstimateTemper program in Chapter 3.}
    type
       AdjectiveType    = packed array[1..12] of char;
       ScalarToAdjective = array[TemperType] of AdjectiveType;
    var
       ScToAd : ScalarToAdjective;
    begin
       ScToAd[Cringing]    := 'Cringing    ';
       ScToAd[Placating]   := 'Placating   ';
       et cetera
       ScToAd[Murderous]   := 'Murderous   ';
```

Note: AdjectiveType is a string data type. A string is merely a sequence of characters (in this case a sequence of twelve characters long enough to hold "Eventempered"). The Pascal reserved word packed is a request to the compiler to store the twelve characters in as few memory cells as possible.... The above code provides a way to print the scalar value of

Temper as an English word: Cringing, Placating, and so on. Thus

write(SctoAd[Temper])

will print the current value of Temper as the appropriate English adjective.


Char index-type:

```
var
    Units : 3..9; {IBM 9-unit system for measuring character width}
    Width : array['!'..'~'] of Units;
    ...................................

    Width['a'] := 5;
    Width['b'] := 6;
    Width['c'] := 5;
    Width['e'] := 5;
    Width['f'] := 4;
      .         .         .
    Width['u'] := 6;
    Width['v'] := 5;
    Width['w'] := 8;
    Width['x'] := 6;
    Width['z'] := 5;
```

Note: These sample assignments are based on the IBM 9-unit system for measuring and counting character widths. (See the table in Appendix D.) The computer in an automated typesetting system requires information like that in the width array to make end-of-line decisions such as hyphenation and justification and to allocate to each character its proportional space. This example illustrates how a table of data can be incorporated in an array data structure. The array is a very fast way of "looking up" a value in a table.


Integer subrange index-type:

The integer data type is not an allowable index-type. The integer data type would typically define more components than the computer has memory cells. The real data type is also not an allowable index-type. The integer subrange, however, is a frequently used index type.

Example (component type = integer):
```
const
    ClassSize = 37;
var
    Grades : array[1..ClassSize] of integer;
    StudentNum : 1..ClassSize
```

Example (component type = array of string):
```
    const
        DeckSize = 1000;
    type
        CardImage = packed array[1..80] of char;
        CardNmbr  = 1..DeckSize;
    var
        CardDeck : array[CardNmbr] of CardImage;
```

CardImage represents one punched card; CardDeck represents a deck of 1000 punched cards.

Example (component type = real)
```
    var
        PopOfUSA : array[1776..1986] of real;
                        -or-
        Year       : 1776..1986
        PopOfUSA : array[year] of real;
```

Although population is an integer, some computers could not represent this large an integer.


SEARCHING ARRAYS


The idea of searching a list for a specified item is fundamental in data processing. Here are just a few examples.

automated composition: find a particular word in a hyphenation dictionary

police work: find the name and address of the registered owner of a license plate

telephone system: find the telephone number of a given subscriber or find the owner of a given telephone number

library system: find the borrower of a particular book

statistics: find the major city with the largest number of homocides per capita

The programmer's choice of data structure and search technique depends on several factors.

Is the list in primary or secondary storage?

Will the list fit in primary storage?

Will the job require the list of values for anything else?

Is the list ordered or random?

We are dealing with arrays in this chapter. Arrays are internally stored data, i.e., data in primary memory. In a later chapter on files we will deal with externally stored data, i.e., data in secondary memory. If the list of data will fit in primary memory, we can arrange to read the data into a array. Reading the data into internal memory--into an array--usually makes sense if we require the data for more than one operation. This is because reading data--especially reading data from input cards--is a slow and hence expensive process. By reading the data into an array we avoid reading the data a second time for subsequent operations.

For our first example, we assume that the list's items are in random order. Consequently, we must use the unsophisticated search technique of simply comparing each item in the list with the value we're seeking. We call this straightforward, serial search a _linear search_. The term "linear" comes from the fact that the time required to conduct such searches increases linearly with the number of items in the list. Later we'll see that when items in the list are sorted--like words in a dictionary or names in a telephone directory--we can conduct a _binary search_, which is more efficient than a linear search. Indeed, the reason lexicographers and directory publishers put items in alphabetic or numerical order is to make it possible for their readers to perform binary searches.

The value sought in searching is often called the "Key." We adopt this terminology and consider searching an array of integers for a particular integer equal to Key. This is a common search problem. The following code is one solution to the problem. The code is a Pascal refinement of "repeat the examination of each consecutive component of the array until you find a component equal to the Key or you come to the last component of the array. Because the stopping condition does not necessarily imply you found a component equal to the Key (you may have come to end of the array without finding the Key), check whether the last component you examined is equal to the Key; if it is not, print out an appropriate message."

Notice that this program finds the _first_ component in the array whose value is equal to Key. If there are two or more components whose values are equal to Key, this program will find only--by stopping the search at--the component which satisfies the criterion _and_ has the smallest index I. If one wants to find all the components whose values are equal to Key, one would have to modify the program. These are the kinds of questions that frequently arise in writing a program. Specifications are often vague and leave open questions like this one. The programmer must become aware of the unselected options and discuss the specification with the clients for whom he's writing the program.

```
const
    N = 1000;
```

```
var
    Key : integer;
    A   : array[1..N] of integer;
    I   : 0..N;
    begin {Assume Key and the array have already been read in.}
        I := 0;
        repeat
            I := I + 1
        until (A[I] = Key) or (I = N);
        if A[I] <> Key then
            writeln('There is no component whose value = Key.')
```

Is there any way to improve the efficiency of this program? Yes, by improving the efficiency of the termination condition. During every repetition of the repeat-until statement, the processor tests whether it's reached the end of the array: **"or** (I = N)." In an array with 1,000 components, this amounts to 1,000 tests. To eliminate these tests, we simply add a "sentinel" to the end of the array and assign the value of Key to the sentinel.

```
const
    N = 1001; {extended by one to accomodate a sentinel}
var
    Key : integer;
    A   : array[1..N] of integer;
    I   : 0..N;
    begin {Assume Key and the array have already been read in.}
        A[N] := Key; {sentinel}
        I := 0;
        repeat
            I := I + 1
        until (A[I] = Key);
        if I = N then
            writeln('There is no component whose value = Key.')
```

Suppose that when we write our program we don't know how long the list of numbers will be. Can we do the following?

```
var
    N : integer; {VARIABLE ARRAY BOUND NOT LEGAL IN PASCAL!}
    A : array[1..N] of integer;
    I : 0..N;
begin
    readln(NumberOfComponents, Key);
    N := NumberOfComponents + 1;
    for I := 1 to NumberOfComponents do
        read(A[I]);
    A[N] := Key; {sentinel}
    I := 0;
    repeat
```

```
    I := I + 1
et cetera
```

That is, can we declare N a variable and defer the assignment of a value
to N until runtime when the user provides the size of his list? Some
programming languages permit the runtime determination of array size;
but standard Pascal does not. Standard Pascal reserves the storage for
arrays at compile time, permitting more efficient and secure compilation
of the program. ("Security" relates to the index range checking possible
if the compiler knows the array size.) Some extended Pascal compilers
permit so-called "dynamic" arrays, i.e., arrays whose size can change.
In case your compiler does not permit dynamic arrays, you can deal with
the problem under discussion by providing as large an array as you
anticipate your user requiring and then checking, at runtime, his actual
requirement against your provision. Here's the relevant code.

```
const
    MaxSize = 1000;
var
    N : integer;
    A : array[1..MaxSize] of integer;
    I : 1..MaxSize;
begin
    readln(N); {The actual number of components required}
    if (N + 1)>MaxSize then
        begin
            write('Your list exceeds this program's storage.');
            write('It will process', MaxSize - 1, ' items.');
            writeln('If you want assistance call extension 000.');
            N := MaxSize - 1;
        end;
    readln(Key);
    for I := 1 to N do
        read(A[I]);
    A[N+1] := Key;
    I := 0;
    repeat
        I := I + 1
    et cetera
```

If the user wants to run the program for his longer list, we would have
to make a single change (the value of MaxSize) and recompile the altered
program.
    The linear search techniques we've been using are inefficient for
long lists. If a list is short and searches are infrequent, a linear
search may be acceptable; but in many applications the list is long and
searches are frequent and time-critical. In such situations an effective
strategy is to maintain the list sorted in either ascending or
descending order. When the list is sorted, we can employ the binary
search technique. The advantage of this technique is that each

comparison halves the number of items in which the target might be found. If you search a list of 1024 items with a linear search, you will make, on the average, 512 comparisons; but if the same list of 1024 items is sorted and you make a binary search, you will make, in the worst case, only 11 comparisons!

The processor starts a binary search by comparing the Key with the middle component of the sorted list. If this comparison yields a match, then the processor terminates the search; otherwise the processor continues the search in the appropriate half of the list. If the Key is less than the middle component, then the processor continues the search in the first half of the list. If the Key is greater than the middle component, then the processor continues the search in the second half of the list. In either case, the processor applies the same strategy to the remaining half of the list; i.e., the processor continues the binary search by comparing the Key with the middle component of the remaining portion of the sorted list. The processor continues this strategy until it finds the Key or the length of the remaining list is zero. In the latter case, of course, the Key is not in the list.

Since the range of the list undergoing search is dynamic (it changes after each unsuccessful comparison); we shall need two variables to keep track of the first and last items of the list under examination. Let's call these variables FirstItem and LastItem. These variables belong to index type. We must initialize them to the subscripts of the first and last components of the original list.

```
    var
        FirstItem, LastItem : 1..N;
........................................
    begin
        FirstItem := 1; {index of first component of original list}
        LastItem  := N; {index of last component of original list}
```

We must also declare a variable to store the index of middle item; and we must devise a way to compute its value for each iteration of the search procedure. The following will do.

```
    var
        MidItem : 1..N;
..........................................
    begin
        MidItem := (FirstItem + LastItem) div 2;
```

If a list has an even number of components, there are actually two "middle" items. The above expression for MidItem picks one of them (the earlier one) because of the truncating effect of div. This is perfectly acceptable and does not affect the efficiency of the search algorithm.

We now have the variables and the algorithm necessary for picking the middle item and defining the remaining list. Is there anything else we have to think about? We must provide a termination condition for the repetition. The processor must repeat the search until it finds a component whose value is equal to Key or until it reduces the remaining list to zero items. There is at least one item in the list if FirstItem <= LastItem. (If FirstItem = LastItem, then FirstItem, LastItem, and MidItem all refer to the same component, and there's one item remaining in the list.) Therefore, the second stopping condition is: FirstItem > LastItem. Here's the complete code for the binary search.

```
      const
         N = 1000;
      var
         A   : array[1..N] of integer;
         Key : integer;
         FirstItem, MidItem, LastItem, I : 1..N;
      begin
         {Assume that Key and the array have already been read in.}
         FirstItem := 1;
         LastItem   := N;
         repeat
            MidItem := (FirstItem + LastItem) div 2;
            if Key < A[MidItem] then {search in first half}
               LastItem := pred(MidItem)
            else {search in second half}
               FirstItem := succ(MidItem)
         until (A[MidItem] = Key) or (FirstItem > LastItem);
         if A[MidItem] <> Key then
            writeln('There is no component whose value =', Key)
         else
            writeln('The index of the target component is', MidItem)
```

## SORTING ARRAYS

As the previous section clearly illustrated, an excellent reason for sorting an array of objects is to facilitate later searches for particular components of the sorted array. Facilitating the search for a particular entry is precisely the reason why the entries in dictionaries, glossaries, directories, and subject indexes are sorted. Another reason for sorting an array is to provide a rank order of its values: to identify the students with the highest scores on an examination or to find the athletes with the greatest achievements. Computer scientists have labored hard to develop sorting algorithms with differential advantages. Consequently, there are about a dozen sorting algorithms to choose from. We'll illustrate one of the simpler ones here and a more sophisticated one in the chapter on subprograms.

For any sorting algorithm to be taken seriously, the algorithm should sort the array in situ; i.e., it should rearrange the components within the source array and not require a second array to do its processing. A strategy that requires a second array is too profligate of storage.

A straightforward solution to the sorting problem could proceed as follows: Scan the array from A[1] to A[N] to select the least component, denoting the index of the least component by L; swap A[1] and A[L]. Next, scan the array from A[2] to A[N] to select the least component in this subarray, denoting the index of the least component by L; swap A[2] and A[L]. Obviously, continuing this process will transform the original sequence into a sorted sequence of ascending order. We can state this algorithm as a **for** statement:

```
for I := 1 to N - 1 do
    begin
        "Scan A from A[I] to A[N] to select the least component, A[L];"
        "Swap A[I] and A[L]"
    end
```

How shall we translate the English between the **begin** and **end** into Pascal? The first statement suggests another **for** loop.

```
for J := I to N do
    if A[J] < A[L] then
        L := J
```

But then how do we initialize L and A[L]? One possibility would be to add a component A[N+1] = maxint to the array and initialize L to N + 1. This seems rather vamped up. A more spare solution is to assume that A[I], the first component in the inner **for** loop, is A[L] and start the inner **for** loop at I + 1 instead of I. If this first guess at L is incorrect, the algorithm will duly correct it. So our translation of

```
"Scan A from A[I] to A[N] to select the least component, A[L]"
```

is, finally,

```
L := I; {A[I] is 1st guess at least component between I and N}
for J := I + 1 to N do
    if A[J] < A[L] then
        L := J
```

The second phrase,

```
"Swap A[I] and A[L]"
```

is easily translated to

```
Temp := A[I];
A[I] := A[L];
A[L] := Temp
```

Putting together the elements we've developed we have the following program fragment:

```
const
   N = .....;
type
   IndexType = 1..N;
var
   I, J, L : IndexType;
   A       : array[IndexType] of integer;
   Temp    : integer;
begin
   for I := 1 to N - 1 do
      begin
         L := I; {A[I] is 1st guess at least value between I and N}
         for J := I + 1 to N do
            if A[J] < A[L] then
               L := J;
         Temp := A[I];
         A[I] := A[L];
         A[L] := Temp
      end
end
```

This program fragment has an interesting property: by changing the
component type in the declaration of A and Temp, we could use the same
lines of code to sort an array of real numbers, an array of characters,
or even an array of strings. (Strings are arrays of characters.) We
shall return to this point when we discuss strings later in this
chapter.


MULTIDIMENSIONAL ARRAYS


As we stated earlier, the array type definition is:

**type**
   <type identifier> = **array**[<index type>] **of** <component type>

where <index type> is a simple, ordinal type, and <component type> is
any type, simple or structured. In our extended examples we have limited
ourselves to simple component types: Boolean, char, integer, and real.
But the definition does not so limit us, and arrays of structured types
are some of the most powerful and useful structures afforded by Pascal.
In a later chapter we'll develop the extremely useful structure of **array**
[index-type] **of** component-type, where component-type is a **record**. In
this section we develop another powerful structure: arrays of arrays. By
iteration of this data structuring device we can also have arrays of
arrays of arrays (three-dimensional arrays), arrays of arrays of arrays
of arrays (four-dimensional arrays), and so on.
   As an example of a multidimensional array, suppose that our printer

engineer from the first example in this chapter wants us to provide more information on character frequencies. He notices from the count of the characters in this book that character printers spend most of their time printing lowercase letters. He decides to optimize the placement of the characters on the print head of the printer he's designing by placing close together those characters that occur most frequently in pairs. He conjectures that 'i' and 'e' should be close to each other on the print head, but 'i' and 'u' can be far apart, for example. (He wants to reduce the travel time of the print head from one character to the next.) Therefore, he asks us to create a table of the occurrences of pairs of adjacent lowercase letters in this book. (He wants to use this book as an example simply because the data are already recorded on a computer-readable medium and because he believes the book's prose is a typical sample of English writing.) We can represent the table he wants as a two-dimensional array. The table might look like this.

```
Count['a', 'a']   Count['a', 'b']   Count['a', 'c'] ... Count['a', 'z']
Count['b', 'a']   Count['b', 'b']   Count['b', 'c'] ... Count['b', 'z']
Count['c', 'a']   Count['c', 'b']   Count['c', 'c'] ... Count['c', 'z']
   ...

Count['z', 'a']   Count['z', 'b']   Count['z', 'c'] ... Count['z', 'z']
```

Each component has two subscripts. There's a mathematical convention that the first subscript refers to the table or matrix row and the second subscript refers to the table or matrix column. We have abided by this convention in the above table of components.

This two-dimensional view of the variables is a data abstraction that we impose on the computer memory, which is actually a much simpler one-dimensional sequence of memory locations. High-order languages like Pascal facilitate our making useful data abstractions like this. These data abstractions help us to organize and structure our problem solving.

For our present problem let's establish that the first subscript refers to the left letter and the second subscript refers to the right letter of a letter pair. We must be prepared to read characters that are not letters, however. Therefore we declare LeftCh and RightCh as variables of type char; but we only assign their values to the subscripts of Count when both values fall within 'a'..'z'. The heart of the PairFrequencies program looks like this.

```
read(LeftCh);
while not eof do
   begin
      read(RightCh);
      if ('a' <= RightCh) and (RightCh <= 'z') and
         ('a' <= LeftCh) and (LeftCh <= 'z') then
         Count[LeftCh, RightCh] := Count[LeftCh, RightCh] + 1;
      LeftCh := RightCh
   end
```

Assuming the following input data (and the appropriate initialization of Count)

        "This is it."

the processor would assign the following values

        Count[h, i] <-- 1
        Count[i, s] <-- 2
        Count[i, t] <-- 1

Here's the complete program.

```
program PairFrequencies(input, output);

var
   LeftCh, RightCh : char;
   Count           : array['a'..'z', 'a'..'z'] of integer;

procedure PrintResults;
   begin
      writeln('PrintResults is an exercise for the student.')
   end;

begin
   for LeftCh := 'a' to 'z' do
      for RightCh := 'a' to 'z' do
         Count[LeftCh, RightCh] := 0; {Initialize matrix}
   read(LeftCh);
   while not eof do
      begin
         read(RightCh);
         if ('a' <= RightCh) and (RightCh <= 'z') and
            ('a' <= LeftCh) and (LeftCh <= 'z') then
            Count[LeftCh, RightCh] := Count[LeftCh, RightCh] + 1;
         LeftCh := RightCh
      end;
   PrintResults
end.
```

Three dimensional arrays and even higher dimensions of arrays can be very useful in statistical analysis in the behavioral sciences. For example, suppose that we wanted to learn the effect of nutritional supplements on the academic achievement of ghetto children. The supplements could be milk, vitamins, milk and vitamins, and no supplement. The investigators might assign 50 children to each experimental treatment. The dependent variables (the outcome) could be the children's scores on standardized academic achievement tests (a set of real variables). On paper, the experiment might look like this:

| Treatment Conditions | No Vitamins | Multi Vitamins | Mega Vitamins |
|---|---|---|---|
| No Milk | 50 Children | 50 Children | 50 Children |
| Milk | 50 Children | 50 Children | 50 Children |

How would we declare an array in which to store and process the data which the experiment will generate?

```
var
    MilkLevel : (NoMilk, Milk);
    ViteLevel : (NoVite, MultiVite, MegaVite); {Vitamin dose}
    Subject   : 1..50;
    TestScore : real;
    Outcome   : array[NoMilk..Milk, NoVite..MegaVite, 1..50] of real
```

Multidimensional arrays can build up their memory requirements rapidly. To determine the number of components, and hence the number of required memory locations, form the product of the cardinalities of all the subscripts. In this case the product is 2*3*50 = 300, a component to store the outcome of the experiment for each child. Three-hundred memory locations is a modest requirement. But be careful. This array

```
var
    A : array[1..50, 1..50, 1..50] of real
```

looks fairly innocuous; but it requires 125,000 memory locations! (50*50*50 = 125,000.) This is more than the total amount of random-access memory in most microcomputers and many minicomputers.

The data structure we've created is ideal for performing a statistical analysis (e.g., analysis of variance) of the data. However, we shall not go into the statistical details here. We shall illustrate how one might arrange and read the input data and how one would compute the average scores for one of the treatment conditions. The processor should read the input data (300 test scores) by means of three nested **for** loops.

```
for MilkLevel := NoMilk to Milk do
    for ViteLevel := NoVite to MegaVite do
        for Subject := 1 to 50 do
            read(Outcome[MilkLevel, ViteLevel, Subject])
```

This structured statement reads the data in the order shown in this table.

| Treatment Conditions | No Vitamins | Multi Vitamins | Mega Vitamins |
|---|---|---|---|
| No Milk | read first | read second | read third |
| Milk | read fourth | read fifth | read last |

Therefore the first fifty data should be the test scores of the children who received neither milk nor vitamins; the next fifty data should be the test scores of the children who received no milk but did receive a multivitamin, and so on. The programmer should prepare a user's guide which explains exactly how to prepare, arrange, and submit the input data. (You should examine the structured read statement to understand why it reads the data in the order of the above table.)

Suppose that we wanted to compute the average test score for all the children who took the megavitamin--irrespective of whether they had supplementary milk. How would you find this average?

```
Total := 0;
ViteLevel := MegaVite;
for MilkLevel := NoMilk to Milk do
    for Subject := 1 to 50 do
        begin
            read(Outcome[MilkLevel, ViteLevel, Subject]);
            Total := Total + Outcome[MilkLevel, ViteLevel, Subject]
        end;
Average := Total/100
```

We have been using an abbreviated form of the multidimensional array representation. We believe the abbreviated form is better than the full form; it is both more compact and more consistent with the traditional mathematical representation of matrices. Nevertheless, you should be able to recognize and read the alternate representations (and be able to translate them into the abbreviated form). For example,

**array**[Boolean] **of array**[1..10] **of array**[size] **of** real

is an example of the full form. It's equivalent to the abbreviated form:

**array**[Boolean, 1..10, size] **of** real

which we prefer and have been using. Here's another example of the full form,

**packed array**[1..10] **of packed array**[1..8] **of** Boolean which should be equivalent to the shorter

**packed array**[1..10, 1..8] **of** Boolean

We're sorry to say there's even another representation for index specification (an ugly one with no redeeming qualities):

A[I][J][K] for A[I, J, K]

Never use it!


STRINGS AND OTHER PACKED DATA TYPES

Consider the statement

write('The product is ', X*Y)

What kind of data object is 'The product is '? Although you've seen this kind of object again and again, you might not realize that it's a constant belonging to the type

**packed array**[1..15] **of** char

'October 8, 1979' is another constant belonging to this data type. The term string type is a generic term used to refer to any type defined by

**packed array**[1..N] **of** char

We can define constant strings

**const**
    Greeting = 'Welcome to Zork'

assign constants to variable strings

**type**
    String15 = **packed array**[1..15] **of** char;
**var**
    Message, Command, Object : String15;
**begin**
    Message := Greeting;
    Command := 'Open the window';
    Object  := 'The giant''s eye';

compare strings

'ABCD' < 'ABCE'  {This expression is true}

and write strings

```
    writeln('Welcome to Zork');
    writeln(Greeting);
    writeln(Message);
    writeln(Command);
    writeln(Object)
```

These writeln statements produce the following output:

```
    Welcome to Zork
    Welcome to Zork
    Welcome to Zork
    Open the window
    The giant's eye
```

Note the assignment to Object and the resulting output: when we want to display a single quote, we must write two quotes in succession.

Strings are useful because they allow us to read, manipulate, and print natural language text. Of course, the compiler and processor do not "understand" strings. Inside the computer, they're just sequences of integers (integers from 32 to 126 in ASCII). But in Pascal they're an important abstract data type; and our interpretation of them makes all the difference between nondescript integers and meaningful variables. We can perform several useful manipulations on strings, especially comparison operations and editing and formatting manipulations.

Assuming the ASCII character set, the cardinality of a string of length N is 95 to the Nth power.

Here's an example of the string type where N equals 2.

```
    type
        Atoms : packed array[1..2] of char
```

The constants of Atoms are 'H ', 'He', Li', and so on (the symbols of the chemical elements). We can create an array of atoms:

```
    var
        Z         : 1..105; {The atomic number is generally called Z.}
        Element : array[1..105] of Atoms;
```

and then assign values to the array components that match (according to the periodic table) the values of the array subscripts:

```
    begin
        Element[1]    := 'H ';
        Element[2]    := 'He';
        Element[3]    := 'Li';

        .       .      .
        Element[104] := 'Ku'; {Kurchatovium}
        Element[105] := 'Ha'  {Hahnium}
```

By means of these assignments, we have created an array, Element[Z], that maps atomic numbers into the symbols of the corresponding chemical elements. Thus

    Element[Z] = symbol for element with atomic number Z

We can print strings; hence

    write(Element[11], Element[17])

prints

    NaCl

on the output device.

Remember our definition of data type: a variable's <u>data type</u> characterizes the set of values (constants) that a processor may assign to the variable, and the set of operations that a processor may perform on these values. The values assignable to a variable of the string data type should be clear from our examples: sequences of characters of length N. Thus we can assign the following values to the variable ElementName: ' ', 'Xe', and '??' (all useful since '??' could be used if we extended the array index range to Z = 106 and 107) and '!!' and '@~' (not so useful!).

Besides the operation of assignment, we can perform relational operations on string variables. This is quite significant because relational operations on string variables permit us to sort and search names, titles, keywords, what have you--alphabetic material of any kind. The enumerative order of the underlying character set determines the order of character strings. Strings of length one (N = 1) are constants of type char; and the order of Ch1 and Ch2 is the order of ord(Ch1) and ord(Ch2). (The function ord( ) is <u>not</u> available for strings of length greater than one, however.) Alphabetic strings of length greater than one are ordered in exactly the the same way as words in a dictionary and names in a telephone directory. Strings are first ordered on their initial character; strings which have the same initial characters are ordered on their second characters; and so on. Thus if Name is a variable of type Atom and we make this assignment

    Name := 'H '

then all the following Boolean expressions yield the value true.

    Name < 'He'          Name > ' '          Name >= 'Be'
    Name < 'Ha'          Name < 'K '          Name <> 'Ho'

Note that, for the ASCII character set,

    ' ' < ',' < '.' < 'A' < 'Z' < 'a' < 'z'  (In ASCII!)

The ASCII character sequence implies that ' ' < 'H ' and 'H ' < 'Ha'. This is the conventional lexicographic order. Unfortunately, the enumerative order of the ASCII character set has the following undesirable effects:

Zzyytron, Robert < cummings e e < cummings, e e < cummings, e. e.

We can prevent these effects by using the same rules of capitalization for all columns in a field; assigning separate fields to last, first, and middle names; and by not sorting on punctuation tokens like ',' and '.'. Applying these principles we get

Cummings E E = Cummings, E E = Cummings, E. E. < Zzyytron, Robert

Returning to the names of the chemical elements, suppose that we decide to put them in alphabetical order so that we can find them faster. (This exercise makes more sense if the names are fields in a array of records and the records contain additional information like atomic number, atomic weight, and so on. We'll take up the record data type in Chapter 8 and return then to the problem of a convenient representation of the table of chemical elements.) When we introduced code on page 131 for sorting an array of integers, we mentioned that we could use the same algorithmic actions to sort other data types, including arrays of strings. We now introduce the necessary definitions and declarations to use the statement part of the code on page 131 to sort the Element array.

```
const
   N = 105;
type
   IndexType = 1..N;
   String2   = packed array[1..2] of char;
var
   I, J, L : IndexType;
   A       : array[IndexType] of String2;
   Temp    : String2;
begin
   A := Element;
   for I := 1 to N - 1 do
      begin
         L := I; {A[I] is 1st guess at least value between I and N}
         for J := I + 1 to N do
            if A[J] < A[L] then
               L := J;
         Temp := A[I];
         A[I] := A[L];
         A[L] := Temp
      end
end
```

Note the first assignment in the statement part of the code. This is an array assignment; it's equivalent to 105 separate assignments of the components of Element to the components of A.

```
A[1] := Element[1]; {'H '}
A[2] := Element[2]; {'He'}
A[3] := Element[3]; {'Li'}
. . .
A[104] := Element[104]; {'Ku': Kurchatovium}
A[105] := Element[105]; {'Ha'}
```

Some Pascal compilers may not permit this statement. In that case one would have to write a for loop to make the 105 assignments.

If we sorted the Element array rather than copying it and then sorting the copy, we would destroy the mapping relationship of Element; namely, that Element maps the atomic number of an element into its symbol. After the sorting process, we have the following values stored in the A array:

```
A[1] <-- 'Ac'
A[2] <-- 'Ag'
A[3] <-- 'Al'
. . .
A[104] <-- 'Zn'
A[105] <-- 'Zr'
```

## APPLICATIONS: TEXT EDITING AND TEXT FORMATTING

Digital computers are particularly well suited to text editing and text formatting: creating, modifying, and printing textual information like computer programs, numerical data, books, letters, catalogs, dissertations, and so on. In this section we shall give only a few hints and examples of text editing and text formatting. Nevertheless, the first eight chapters of this book lay the groundwork for your writing a respectable editor or formatter. An editor and/or formatter would make an excellent term project or personal learning experience. An advantage of such a project is that the student requires only elementary mathematical knowledge. Yet the project is quite challenging.

We are especially interested in arrays of characters in this section. A short array can store a word or title; a medium-length array can store a phrase, character pattern, or running head; a long array can store a paragraph; and a very long array can store a textbook chapter. Here are some examples:

```
Word     : packed array[1..12] of char;
Title    : packed array[1..20] of char;
Pattern  : packed array[1..40] of char;
```

```
Paragraph  : packed array[1..2500] of char;
Chapter    : packed array[1..60000] of char;
```

The first programming example we'll discuss is relevant to text editing. Some text editors number each line of text. To refer to a line of text you want to modify, you must specify its line number. Another approach is often more convenient--and more general. In this approach you specify a pattern of characters in or near the text you want to work on. If your text has numbered lines, this method can also find a line-number pattern. (However, there are faster numerical searches: for example, the binary search. The search tactic we'll develop is linear.) Pattern finding is an important technique for many reasons. Therefore, we shall give a short function which searches for a pattern in an array of characters. We'll call this function "Find." Its heading is:

**function** Find(StartSearchAt : TextIndex) : FindType;

and it uses the following global definitions and declarations:

```
const
    MaxPattern = 40;
    MaxText    = 32000;
type
    PatternIndex = 1..MaxPattern;
    PatternType  = packed array[PatternIndex] of char;
    TextIndex    = 1..MaxText;
    TextType     = packed array[TextIndex] of char;
    FindType     = 0..MaxText
var
    Pattern : PatternType;
    Text    : TextType; {precludes using predefined identifier text}
    LastP   : PatternIndex; {Index of last character in Pattern}
    LastT   : TextIndex; {Index of last character in Text}
```

Find's job is to search through the text stored in the array named Text. Find's caller supplies the index of the position in Text where he wants the search to start. The caller expects Find to return the value of the index where the pattern actually begins. In the event that Find does not find the pattern in Text, Find returns the value zero, which does not correspond to any index value of Text. (Thus, we defined the result type of Find as "0..MaxText": see the heading for Find and the definition of the type identifier, FindType.)

Typically the length of Text is many times greater than the length of Pattern. In microcomputers configured for word-processing, the bulk of random access memory may be devoted to the array Text.

We assume that the pattern sought is stored in Pattern. We also assume that the character pattern is stored <u>left-justified</u> in the Pattern array. This means that the relevant indices of Pattern lie on the interval 1..LastP, where LastP <= MaxPattern. It's conventional to store characters left-justified in arrays of characters. Padding blanks,

if necessary, are added to the right end of the array. (This is the
convention we used when storing the symbols for the chemical elements in
Atom and Element[Z].)

The Find function conducts its search by means of a
character-by-character test for match between Pattern and successive
subsequences in Text. Find accomplishes this by two nested repeat-until
loops. The outer repeat loop picks successive starting indexes in Text.
The inner repeat loop tries to find a match between the string in
Pattern and a substring in Text, starting at the index in Text picked by
the outer loop. The inner loop repeats the comparison of individual
characters until it finds a character mismatch or until it has compared
all the characters in Pattern to the characters in the current selected
substring in Text. The outer loop repeats until the inner loop finds the
pattern in Text or until there aren't enough characters left in Text for
a match to be possible.

```
function Find(StartSearchAt : TextIndex) : FindType;

  var
     T : TextIndex;
     P : PatternIndex;
     Match : Boolean;

  begin {Find}
     T := StartSearchAt;
     repeat
        P := 1;
        repeat
           Match := (Pattern[P] = Text[P + T - 1]);
           P := P + 1
        until not Match or (P > LastP);
        T := T + 1
     until Match or ((T + LastP) > LastT);
     if Match then
        Find := T - 1
     else
        Find := 0
  end; {Find}
```

Our next program is a simple but important example of text
formatting. One reason for its importance is that an effective strategy
for tackling a complex problem is to solve a similar but simpler
problem. We can make a complex problem simpler by breaking it into
several parts and then solving one of the parts. Or we can make a
problem simpler by leaving out one or more of the complicating factors
and then solving the stripped-down problem. After we solve the reduced
problem in either approach, we often gain the insight and momentum to
solve the rest of the problem. The complex problem we'll divide to
conquer in this section is the printing of a page for a book. This
already represents some break-down of the problem because no author or

publisher is interested in printing just one page. But note that we can
print a whole book if we can properly print a single page:

```
begin
   Initialize;
   while not eof do
      PrintOnePage;
end
```

We have expressed the book-printing algorithm as two procedures which
may be very complicated indeed. But this gives a sort of high-level view
of how to proceed.

What is involved in printing one page? A great deal. We have to
control top and bottom margins, left and right margins, line length and
number of lines per page, paragraph indention, the counting and printing
of page numbers, the printing of running heads, and other values and
parameters. A particularly knotty problem is the placing of characters
on a line so that both margins are justified; that is, to so place words
and blanks on a line that the line has an exact specified length. Let's
tackle this problem in isolation from the rest of the problems.

Now that we've isolated a problem to be solved, let's consider
whether the isolated problem is simple enough. If we've solved such
problems before, we may not have to simplify this one any further before
we take it on. But assuming that this is the first time we've tried to
solve such a problem, we should try to simplify it further. Let's relax
the specification of exact justification of the line length. Instead,
we'll try to develop a program that places as many words as possible on
each line up to a certain specified line length. Typesetters call this a
"ragged right" margin because the right margin has a "ragged" look. The
ragged right style has an intrinsic interest because some typographers
prefer it to the fully justified look; and it's certainly the style of
choice in informal letters where the mechanical precision of justified
margins is out of place. This paragraph has been set ragged right to
illustrate the technique and the appearance. When we printed this
paragraph we specified that no line should contain more than 72
characters. The program then squeezed as many words as it could (without
intra-word breaks or hyphenations) onto each line. (The rest of the book
is printed with fully justified margins and an average of 72 characters
per line.) Once we solve the relaxed problem we are well on the way to
solving the original problem. For example, we could add full
justification to our simple program by increasing the spacing between
each word until the line length becomes equal to an exact specified
quantity.

Before we try to develop a solution to the simpler problem, let's
write an exact specification of what we want to accomplish. It's
important in programming to have such a specification. Without it, one
is never certain whether a program is correct because one cannot
possibly be clear about what the program should do to begin with.

The input to the program will be a textfile, a sequence of characters
whose end is signified by the eof condition. Textfiles are composed of

visible characters, blanks, and line markers. We may think of blanks and
line markers as word separators. For our purpose we define a "word" as a
sequence of characters delimited by word separators. Thus

```
let's
it's
whose
predicate.
characters,
"word"
separators.
```

are all examples of words occurring in this and the preceding paragraph.
No harm is done by treating puntuation marks as part of the word with
which they're contiguous, and this treatment eliminates the problem of
punctuation marks as a special case.

Thus we view the input file as a sequence of words delimited by word
separators (possibly multiple separators) and ending with a true eof
condition. The line markers on the input textfile will not in general
occur at the right places in the sequence of words. Our job is to
generate the desired sequence of words and line markers. Sometimes we'll
replace a line marker in the input file with a blank on the output file;
sometimes we'll replace a blank in the input file with a line marker on
the output file.

We specify that the program's output should be the same sequence of
words that appear on the input file (with the exception that an
excessively long word should cause termination of the program). The
program's output should comply with these specifications:

**1.** New lines will start only <u>between</u> words (except, of course, the
new line that starts at the beginning of the output text).

**2.** Word separator(s) on the input file will be written as a single
separator on the output file.

**3.** Each line of output will have a maximum length of MaxLength
(characters in words plus blanks).

**4.** As many words as possible will be placed on each line of output.

We have written, as a procedure, code that meets the above
specifications. The relevant declarations which exist outside the
procedure and the procedure itself follow.

```
var
    MaxLength   : 8..PrinterLimit; {163 for our printer}
    WordTooLong : Boolean;

procedure PrintLines;

var
    Word        : array[1..PrinterLimit] of char;
    J           : 1..PrinterLimit;
```

```
   Ch           : char;
   WordLength : 0..PrinterLimit;
   LineLength : 0..PrinterLimit;

begin {PrintLines' statements}
   WordTooLong := false;
   WordLength  := 0;
   LineLength  := 0;
   repeat
      read(Ch);
      if (Ch <> ' ') then {we're reading a word}
         if WordLength < MaxLength then
            begin
               WordLength := WordLength + 1;
               Word[WordLength] := Ch
            end
         else
            WordTooLong := true
      else {we're reading a word separator}
         if WordLength > 0 then {there's a word to print}
            begin {print the word}
               if (LineLength + WordLength < MaxLength)
                                 and (LineLength > 0) then
                  begin {print word at end of current line}
                     write(' ');
                     LineLength := LineLength + 1
                  end
               else
                  begin {print word at beginning of new line}
                     writeln;
                     LineLength := 0
                  end;
               for J := 1 to WordLength do {actually print word}
                  write(Word[J]);
               LineLength := LineLength + WordLength;
               WordLength := 0
            end {print the word}
   until WordTooLong or eof
end {PrintLines' statements}
```

To understand this program, try tracing it. But pick a short text and small value of MaxLength: you'll quickly weary of the monotonous repetition which is only fit for machines. To see that the program works for even "extreme" values such as a "word" whose length is MaxLength, the test case should provide such a "word." Here's a good test case to trace: (Assume that the calling program has set MaxLength to 9. MaxLength is a constant as far as Printlines as concerned.)

********* The miser is always poor. *********

PrintLines writes this input as:

```
*********
The miser
is always
poor.
*********
```


EXERCISES


1. Assume that previous processor operations have assigned the following values to these two arrays and seven simple variables: (? indicates that the variable's value is still undefined.)

| | | |
|---|---|---|
| Hours[1] <-- 32 | WageRate[1] <-- 3.50 | I <-- 1 |
| Hours[2] <--  0 | WageRate[2] <-- 6.80 | J <-- 2 |
| Hours[3] <-- 42 | WageRate[3] <-- 2.75 | K <-- 3 |
| Hours[4] <-- 38 | WageRate[4] <-- 4.00 | M <-- 4 |
| Hours[5] <-- 37 | WageRate[5] <-- 5.00 | Sum <-- ? |
| Hours[6] <-- 40 | WageRate[6] <-- 3.50 | Max <-- ? |
| Hours[7] <-- 56 | WageRate[7] <-- 2.50 | Min <-- ? |
| Hours[8] <-- 39 | WageRate[8] <-- 4.55 | Wages <-- ? |
| Hours[9] <-- 15 | WageRate[9] <-- 6.00 | |

**a.** What are the values of Hours[9], WageRate[5], Hours[I], and WageRate[J + K]?

**b.** Evaluate the following expressions;

```
Hours[2] + Hours[5] + Hours[9]
Hours[5]*WageRate[5]
Hours[3]*WageRate[3] - 3.00
1.5*(Hours[7] - 40)*WageRate[7]
```

**c.** What is the name of the component which has the smallest value in the WageRate array? What is the index of the component which has the largest value in the Hours array?

**d.** Which one(s) of the following are not defined?

```
Hours[J*K + I]    WageRate[K*M]    WageRate[K div M]    Hours[M
div K]
```

**e.** Write variable declarations for the above arrays and simple variables. Considering problem **d.**, what data type must I, J, K, and M be? Assume that Sum, Max, and Min are real.

**f.** Write a read statement to assign the values shown to the Hours array. Write assignment statements to assign the values shown to the other variables.

**g.** What would Employee 7's wages be if his wage rate were increased to the maximum value in WageRate?

2. Assume the variables and value assignments given in example **1.** What values do the following program fragments assign to Sum, Max, Min, and M? (Employee is a previously declared index variable.)

**a.** Sum := 0;
```
for Employee := 1 to 5 do
    Sum := Sum + Hours[Employee]*WageRate[Employee]
```

**b.** Sum := 0;
```
for Employee := 1 to 5 do
    Sum := Sum + Hours[2*Employee]
```

**c.** Min := WageRate[1]
```
for Employee := 2 to 10 do
    if WageRate[Employee] > Min then
        Min := WageRate[Employee]
```

**d.** Max := 0;
```
for Employee := 1 to 10 do
    begin
        Wages := Hours[Employee]*WageRate[Employee];
        if Wages > Max then
            begin
                Max := Wages;
                M   := Employee
            end
    end
```

**e.** Make the Boolean expression in problem **c.** consistent with the identifier "Min."

3. Add code to Printlines (page 145) that allows the user to specify a "reasonable" left margin. What's a "reasonable" left margin? Add a test to PrintLines to verify that the margin is reasonable. Do not make the reasonableness test any stricter than logically necessary.

4. Add code to Printlines that justifies (i.e., makes each line's length exactly equal to MaxLength) by adding extra blanks to the blanks that PrintLines would normally write. Distribute the extra blanks as evenly as possible. Hint: you will have to buffer each line before you print it. Define a buffer array named Line that has the same dimension as the Word buffer.

**5.** Modify PrintLines to work with a printer or typesetter that uses proportional spacing. In proportional spacing, the space the printer allocates to each character depends on the character's type width. Thus the printer should allocate less space to "i" and "!" than "m" or "w." (Proportional spacing looks more professional and saves paper.) Assume that the printer allocates space according to the IBM 9-unit system for measuring character width. See page 123 and Appendix D. You must redefine LineLength and WordLength in these units. For example, PrinterLimit will be about 1,000 and

    WordLength := WordLength + 1

will become

    WordLength := WordLength + Width[Ch]

# 7. Subprograms:
# Functions and Procedures

## THE NECESSITY AND BENEFITS OF HIERARCHICAL ORGANIZATION

Human cognitive limits are a basic obstacle to writing correct computer programs. The fact is that human beings can keep only a handful of items in awareness simultaneously. For this reason we like (and require) simplifying diagrams, mnemonic devices, and short lists (preferably fewer than seven items) summing up all that is known on a subject. It's reassurring, for example, to realize that a Pascal program has only seven main syntactic parts: program heading, label declaration, constant definition, type definition, variable declaration, procedure and function declaration, and statement. It's also reassuring to remember that Pascal has only five simple data types, four structured data types, and six or seven (depending on how you count) structured control statements. It's not so reassuring that Pascal has 35 reserved words! But we have a strategy to cope with proliferating complexity. We divide and conquer. We can divide Pascal's reserved words into a small number of categories. For example, we assign **begin, end, case, of, for, downto, to, do, if, then, else, repeat, until,** and **while** to the structured control category; **goto** and **label** to the unstructured control category (or the somewhat disreputable category); **label, const, type, var, procedure,** and **function** to the definition and declaration category; **array, file, record,** and **set** to the structured data category; and so on. And thus we conquer.

You might want to try the following experiment. Ask a classmate to try to recall all of Pascal's reserved words. On the first trial don't give your subject any categories. After your classmate has recalled as many words as he can, give him some categories (structured control, unstructured control, definition and declaration, structured data, or any other categories you can think of). Psychologists have performed this kind of memory experiment many times, and they always obtain the same results: Subjects recall more words when the experimenter gives them categories or directs them to think up categories themselves.

What does this have to do with overcoming our cognitive limitations when we have to write an large and complex program? The point is this: when we can keep the number of items, chunks of information, or ideas down to around a handful we feel (usually justifiably) that we can understand, comprehend, and control the situation. The chief operating officer of a large enterprise does something like this. He makes the complexity manageable by making a <u>hierarchical</u> organization. You can't divide the United States Government or the General Electric Company into seven big chunks and stop there. But you can divide either enterprise into about seven chunks, divide each chunk into about seven chunks, and keep dividing until you reach the point where you have subsub...subchunks that are elemental. This is what we do when we outline a complicated subject or topic. The idea is to divide the subject into six or seven (preferably even fewer) divisions, to subdivide each division into simpler subdivisions, and to keep subdividing until we attain subdivisions in our outline that we can implement by a simple paragraph or two in the finished paper.

I. _____
   A. _____
   B. _____
   C. _____
      1. _____
      2. _____
II. _____
   A. _____
      1. _____
      2. _____
         a. _____
         b. _____
      3. _____
   B. _____
III. _____
   A. _____
      1. _____
      2. _____
      3. _____
   B. _____
   C. _____
      1. _____
      2. _____
         a. _____
         b. _____
         c. _____
IV. _____
   A. _____
   B. _____
   C. _____
      1. _____
      2. _____
         a. _____
         b. _____
         c. _____

It's notoriously difficult to write a paper on a complex subject without such an outline: we lose our way, forget how the parts fit together, lose our confidence that we are covering the important points, and so on. We repeat: the problem is that we can keep only so many things in our awareness at the same time. The total number of elements in the above outline utterly exceeds our mental capacity--if we try to consider all the elements at the same time. The strategy we use to defeat the complexity is to focus our attention on only one level of abstraction at a time, forgetting for the time-being the other levels, which must wait their turn for our consideration. We might choose to focus our attention on the highest or most abstract level, the level of I, II, III, and IV. This outermost level gives us the "big picture" of the subject. The top level's suppression of details is beneficial because our consciousness cannot hold the big picture <u>and</u> the details all at once.

Suppressing the details while we're reasoning at the top level is necessary; but ultimately we must grapple with the details. Therefore, we must refine the big picture and break I, II, III, and IV down. At the top level, IV is an undivided and unanalyzed entity; but at the next level of refinement (of detail) we allow ourselves to consider that IV is composite and we subdivide it into A, B, C,.... While we analyze IV into its logical constituents we isolate it (ignore I, II, and III). When the detail comes in, the big picture goes out (of our minds, temporarily). We do not have to think about the details of IV <u>and</u> IV's relationship to I, II, and III <u>at the same time</u>. But we can return to the top level at any time we require reassurance that our step-wise refinement of IV is harmonious with the top level. An orderly way to start this process is to try to settle the top level first. In computer programming we call this <u>top-down design</u>. An orderly way to consummate the process is to refine each element to the required level of detail. Thus we refine I into A, B, C,...; A into 1, 2, 3...; 1 into a, b, c...; and so on. At each lower level we bring in more detail, detail which is irrelevant and distracting at the higher level but essential and engaging at the lower level. We call this <u>step-wise refinement</u>. If we put these two ideas together we have the programming technique called <u>top-down design using step-wise refinement</u>.

## FUNCTIONS: SUBPROGRAMS THAT COMPUTE A SINGLE VALUE

What does the previous section have to do with subprograms? Subprograms permit us to design our programs as hierarchical structures. They facilitate top-down design using step-wise refinement. They permit a constructive suppression of details ("information hiding," and so on).

The first stage of abstraction is to associate a name with a program segment that computes a single value. In Pascal and most programming languages we call this method of abstraction a function. The program segment may be very short; then the main advantage of the function is to substitute a meaningful name for a less meaningful expression. Here's a short <u>function</u> <u>declaration</u>:

```
function LogBase2(X : real) : real; {Compute Log to the base 2 of N}
begin
   LogBase2 := 1.442695*ln(X) {1.442695 = LogBase2(e)}
end;
   . . .
```

The first line of the function declaration is the function heading, which is analogous to a program heading. Let's examine the parts of the function heading.

**"function"** is a reserved word indicating that this is a function declaration.

"LogBase2" is the name (identifier) of the function.

"(X : real)" is a list of the function's <u>formal parameters</u> and their data types. In this case there is only one formal parameter, X; its type is real.

": real" identifies the data type of the function's result. (A function must return a <u>simple variable</u>.)

The program activates the function LogBase2 with a <u>function designator</u>, which consists of the function identifier and a list of actual input values (called <u>actual parameters</u>) on which the function will operate. In the case of LogBase2 the list has only one value. The actual parameters can be in the form of expressions. The function designator itself can appear in an expression. Thus the program could activate LogBase2 in the following assignment statement:

```
   Bits := LogBase2(32*1024) + 1
```

This statement calculates the number of bits required to represent the integers from -maxint to maxint, maxint = 32,767. The "+ 1" provides a bit for the sign. The result is Bits = 16. (This logarithm is also useful in information theory.)

It is clearer to use the function identifier LogBase2( ) than the rather obscure expression 1.442695*ln( ). Furthermore, if the programmer wants to change the computation for LogBase2 to a more accurate or efficient expression, he can make his change in <u>one</u> place without concern for the number and locations of the function invocations.

Let's consider what happens when the processor executes the above statement. First, the processor evaluates the value of the actual parameter (32768 := 32*1024); then, the processor assigns this value to X, the function's formal parameter. The actual parameter's data type must be compatible with the declared data type of the function's formal parameter, which in this case is real. (Remember that you can usually assign an integer value to a real variable in Pascal.) After the processor assigns the values of the actual arguments (or parameters) to the formal parameters, it executes the statement part of the function declaration. In the case of LogBase2 there is only one statement, the statement which assigns an appropriate value to the function identifier.

    LogBase2 := 1.442695*ln(X) {1.442695 = LogBase2(e)}

Every function declaration must have such an assignment statement; it is the agreed upon way for the function to return its result to the calling statement. After the processor has assigned a value to the function identifier, it transfers control back to the statement that invoked the function and finishes evaluating the expression of which the function designator is a part. Note that the function returns a value; the processor simply substitutes this value for the function designator. Note also that the data type of this value must be compatible with the expression in which the function designator appears. In this case that data type is real.

When there's more than one parameter, the type and number of the lists of actual parameters and formal parameters must match. Assignment is by positional correspondence, in much the same way that a read statement assigns external data to the read procedure's parameters. Although the result type of a function must be a single value, its parameters may be a list of simple and structured variables. Names do not play a role in communicating data _between_ the actual parameter list and the formal parameter list: positional correspondence rules.

The formal parameter is _local_ to the function declaration: we say that the function declaration is the _scope_ of the formal parameter. In fact, the scope of _any_ identifiers which we define or declare in the function declaration is the function itself. If the function declaration defines or declares any labels, constants, data types, variables, procedures, or functions, these objects, like the formal parameters, are local to the the function and exist only during the activation of the function. Therefore, assuming that the function has no side effects (i.e., does not affect any variables except its local variables and the function identifier), after the function returns its result value and terminates, there is no memory of its having run except for its assignment to the function designator and, of course, the processor time it required.

Let's look at a function that has simple _and_ structured formal parameters. This function computes the "entropy" or average information available from observing a set of possible events. We assume that there are N of these events, that one and only one of the events will occur on any occasion, and that the probability that the Ith event will be the one that occurs is P[I]. (We usually use the term "outcome" to refer to the event that actually occurs.) Then the information available, on the average, from many observations of the outcomes is

    Entropy = -P[1]Log(P[1]) -P[2]Log(P[2]) - ... -P[N]Log(P[N])

where each term is actually positive because Log(P[I]) is negative (or zero) for all valid P[I]s. If the logarithm uses base 2, then the answer is in bits. Using base two logarithms leads to the interesting notion that entropy is the number of bits required to learn about or keep track of the system's outcome. For example, if the set of events has just two equally likely outcomes, then the probability of each outcome is 0.5 and the number of bits required to keep track of the outcome is

Entropy = -0.5*LogBase2(0.5) -0.5*LogBase2(0.5)

which evaluates to exactly one bit. If you flip a fair coin and tell someone the outcome of the flip, you are sharing exactly one bit of information.

Now let's write a program that reads a list of probabilities corresponding to a set of events, calcuates the average information (using a function) available from the set, and prints the results. Although it is not strictly necessary, we will use an array to store the set of probabilities. The program, proceeding in a top-down manner, might look like this:

```
program Information(input, output);

const
   MaxSize = 20;
type
   Index = 1..MaxSize;
   Probabilities = array[Index] of real;
var
   I : Index;
   P : Probabilities;
   N : Index; {Actual number of probabilities: <= MaxSize}

function Entropy(N : Index; P : Probabilities);
   begin
      {define later}
   end;

begin {Information}
   ReadProbabilities;
   CheckProbabilities;
   AverageInformation := Entropy(N, P);
   PrintResult
end. {Information}
```

We'll defer the refinement of the function Entropy until last, illustrating that we can often put off thinking about some computational detail. All we need to know now is that we will pass the function two parameters: the first will be an integer representing how many probabilities there are; the second will be the array of probabilities. We expect the function to return the number of bits of information, stored in the function designator, Entropy( ).

Let's consider the refinement of ReadProbabilities and CheckProbabilities first. We should probably check the input data as we read it in order to reduce handling of the data. What checks should we make on the input data? Theoretically, the value of each individual probability should lie on the __closed__ interval [0.0 to 1.0]; but the value of P[I]*LogBase2(P[I]) is undefined when P[I] = 0. (In particular, the log function "blows up (down!)" for zero arguments.) Furthermore, it makes little sense for the user to specify that there's an event in his system that occurs with zero probability. Such events are better ignored. Therefore, we'll assume that any zero inputs are invalid. (We could also simply ignore zero inputs; but we'll take the tack of calling a zero value invalid.) Let's consider the other end of the interval (0.0 to 1.0): should we accept an input of 1.0? If a system has an event whose probability of occurrence is 1.0 (such a system can have only one outcome!), then its entropy is just zero. After all, there's no uncertainty about the outcome in such a system; and no information is imparted to us when an observer announces its predictable monotonous outcome. Therefore, we should not expect a reasonable or knowledgeable user of our program to submit a system of probabilities with one probability identically equal to 1.0. What all this comes down to is that we should reasonably expect valid inputs to lie on the __open__ interval (0.0 to 1.0). What other tests should we make on the input data? Certainly, all the probabilities in the system should add up to a sum very close to 1.0 since the system must always have __some__ outcome. However, we should not be too rigorous about checking the sum of the probabilities: the user's values may be empirical and approximate; and besides, our real arithmetic is not perfectly precise. Let's just add up all the probabilities and display the result. We'll let the user decide whether the sum is close enough to 1.0.

   The philosophy we're using here is reasonable: when an input doesn't make much sense and that input also gives us a great deal of trouble, we tend to reject the input; but if the input is somewhat questionable but also somewhat sensible, we accept the input with an appropriate message to the user to make sure that he's aware of the questions one could raise. Do not be trigger happy to shoot down a user's inputs; write "friendly" programs!

   Here's the refinement of Read Probabilities and Check Probabilities. (We should also check that N is on the interval (1..MaxSize); we leave that detail to the reader).

```
Sum := 0;
readln(N); {assuming N is reasonable; not a safe assumption}
for I := 1 to N do
   begin
      read(P[I]);
      if (P[I] <= 0.0) or (P[I] >= 1.0) then
         begin
            writeln('The ', I:2, 'th probability is invalid);
            goto 9001 {for termination}
         end;
      Sum := Sum + P[I]
   end; {for loop}
```

```
      writeln('The', N : ?, ' probabilities sum to', Sum : 11:7, '.');
      writeln('They should sum to 1.000000.');
      writeln;
      writeln('The probabilities are:');
      for I := 1 to N do
         writeln(P[I] 11:7)
```

Now let's refine the next two statements in our top-level cut at the program:

```
      AverageInformation := Entropy(N, P);
      PrintResult
```

Actually, we don't have to assign the value of Entropy to another variable. All we want to do is print the value of Entropy: we can use the function designator exactly like any other operand or factor. Consequently, we can use Entropy( ) as the parameter in a writeln statement:

```
      write('The information in this system is');
      writeln(Entropy(N, P) : 8:3, ' bits.')
```

We're now ready to write the Entropy function and complete the program. Here's the completed program:

```
program Information(input, output);

label
   9001; {for termination on invalid input}
const
   MaxSize = 20;
type
   Index = 1..MaxSize;
   Probabilities = array[Index] of real;
var
   I   : Index;
   P   : Probabilities;
   N   : Index; {Actual number of probabilities: <= MaxSize}
   Sum : real; {To check the sum of the probabilities};

function Entropy(N : Index; P : Probabilities) : real;
   var
      J   : Index;
      Sum : real;

   function LogBase2(X : real) : real; {Compute Log to the base 2 of N}
      begin{Logbase2}
         LogBase2 := 1.442695*ln(X) {1.442695 = LogBase2(e)}
      end; {LogBase2}
```

```
      begin {Entropy}
         Sum := 0;
         for J := 1 to N do
            Sum := Sum - P[J]*LogBase2(P[J]);
         Entropy := Sum
      end; {Entropy}
begin {Information}
   Sum := 0;
   readln(N); {assuming N is reasonable; not a safe assumption!}
   for I := 1 to N do
      begin {for loop}
         read(P[I]);
         if (P[I] <= 0.0) or (P[I] >= 1.0) then
            begin
               writeln('The ', I:2, 'th probability is invalid);
               goto 9001 {for termination}
            end;
         Sum := Sum + P[I]
      end; {for loop}
   write('The', N : 2, ' probabilities sum to', Sum : 11:7, '.');
   writeln('They should sum to 1.000000.');
   writeln;
   writeln('The probabilities are:');
   for I := 1 to N do
      begin
         write(P[I] : 11:7);
         if I mod 4 = 0 then
            writeln
      end;
   writeln;
   write('The information in this system is');
   writeln(Entropy(N, P) : 8:3, ' bits.');
   9001:
end. {Information}
```

Input:
```
   8 probabilities follow:
      0.0078125      0.0546875      0.1640625      0.2734375
      0.2734375      0.1640625      0.0546875      0.0078125
```

Output:
```
   The 8 probabilities sum to 1.0000000. They should sum to 1.00000.

   The probabilities are:

      0.0078125      0.0546875      0.1640625      0.2734375
      0.2734375      0.1640625      0.0546875      0.0078125

   The information in this system is 2.447 bits.
```

This program illustrates many important points about function declarations and invocations:

**1.** Formal Parameters: A function can have many formal parameters, including parameters that stand for structured variables such as arrays.

**2.** Result Value: A function can return only one simple value; therefore the data type of the result must be Boolean, user-defined scalar, char, integer, scalar subrange, or real. In our example the result data types are real.

**3.** Global Variables: Variables I, P, N, and Sum are global variables. Their declarations occur before any function, procedure, or, of course, the statement part of the program itself. We call these variables <u>global</u> because their scope is program-wide. Any function, procedure, or, of course, the program statement itself can refer to and assign values to these variables.

**4.** Global Versus Local Variables: Note that Sum is a global variable because we declared Sum in the variable declaration part of Information. But then we declared <u>another</u> variable with the <u>same</u> name in the variable declaration part of Entropy. What is the consequence of these two declarations? The consequence is that the compiler creates <u>two</u> completely independent and different variables. The scope of the main program's Sum no longer includes the function Entropy: by declaring a variable identified as Sum, Entropy can no longer refer to the main program's Sum. This is the only mechanism by which a function can lose access to a global variable; to wit, by using the global variable's identifier in a local definition or declaration.

**5.** Local Variables: Both variables named Sum--the program's global Sum and Entropy's local Sum--are real variables. Why did we declare a local variable named Sum in Entropy and thereby create another variable? Why didn't we simply use the global variable Sum in Entropy? The reasons are independence and security. By declaring its own variables, Entropy does not have to depend on its environment to create its variables. The author of Entropy does not even have to know what identifiers have already been used in other parts of the program: he can pick his identifiers to describe his variables rather than worrying about duplication or coordination.

**6.** Side Effects: The most important reason for using local variables in a function is to avoid "side effects." A side-effect occurs whenever a function alters any nonlocal variable (other than the function designator, which is a kind of nonlocal variable). In the case of the present program, no harm would have been done by Entropy's using the nonlocal variable Sum. But consider the harm that would ensue if we rewrote Information in a certain way. Suppose that we decide to rearrange the output statements so that we print the Sum of the input probabilities <u>after</u> we print the Entropy of the probabilities. In that case, Entropy would have a serious side effect: it would destroy the value of the sum of the input probabilities before the program printed this quantity. In general, functions should not produce side effects. One way to avoid side effects (the most secure way) is to declare all the variables used by a function (except, of course, the parameters).

This is the reason that we declared the index variable J in Entropy rather than using the global index variable I. Again, in this particular program, we could have safely used the global variable I as the index variable in Entropy. But consider what would happen if someone rewrote Information so that the program called Entropy from a loop indexed by I.

**7.** Initialization of Formal Parameters: The formal parameters of a function are a kind of local variable. They are special local variables, however, because the processor initializes them to the values of the function designator's corresponding actual parameters. For example, consider the function LogBase2 whose formal parameter is X : real. Each time Entropy invokes LogBase2, the following assignment takes place:

```
X := P[J];
```

**8.** Value Parameters: The initialization or copying process mentioned in **7.** takes place even when a formal parameter happens to have the same identifier as the corresponding actual parameter. Consequently, when Information invokes Entropy, the value of N and the values of P are assigned to Entropy's **local** N and P. Indeed, if Entropy assigned a value to its formal parameter N, this assignment would have absolutely no effect on the the actual parameter N. Thus, a function cannot create a side effect by modifying the value of its formal parameters. Parameters of this kind are called **value parameters**. They're called value parameters because they communicate or transmit a **value** from the actual parameter to the formal parameter; but they don't allow the function's statements to have access to the **variable** that corresponds to the actual parameter.

**9.** Inaccessibility of Local Labels and Identifiers: Any labels, constants, types, variables, functions, or procedures defined and declared in a function are local to that function. In effect, they don't exist outside the function. For example, LogBase2 is unknown outside the function Entropy: the main program cannot invoke LogBase2 (except indirectly by invoking Entropy). This is as it should be: from our hierarchical viewpoint, certain details are beneficially hidden from higher levels. On the other hand, if the main program or some other subprogram required the function LogBase2, this function could be taken out of Entropy and declared as a global function so that other subprograms could invoke it.

**10.** Transience of Local Labels and Identifiers: Similarly, any labels, constants, types, variables, functions, or procedures defined and declared in a function exist only during the time the processor is actually executing the function. The formal parameters share in this transience.

Many of the above rules and points are consequences of Pascal's block structure and scope rules. We shall sum up Pascal's scope rules later in this chapter.

## RECURSIVE FUNCTIONS

Before we leave Information, let's discuss one more point concerning that program. The body of the function Entropy is

```
begin {Entropy}
   Sum := 0;
   for J := 1 to N do
      Sum := Sum - P[J]*LogBase2(P[J]);
   Entropy := Sum
end; {Entropy}
```

Why not rewrite the body this way:

```
begin {Entropy}
   Entropy := 0;
   for J := 1 to N do
      Entropy := Entropy - P[J]*LogBase2(P[J])
end; {Entropy}
```

replacing the identifier Sum with the identifier Entropy. This is completely wrong! Entropy is a __function__ identifier--not a variable identifier. It's a syntactic peculiarity of Pascal that we assign a value to a function identifier as though it were a variable identifier. When the function identifier appears on the right-hand side of a statement in the function declaration, it isn't playing the role of a simple variable. It's a function designator: it invokes the function. Invokes the function from inside the function? Yes, it's called a recursive invocation. Functions which invoke themselves are called __recursive functions__. Pascal permits and encourages recursive functions and procedures.

But what good are recursive functions? What can a function accomplish by invoking itself? It turns out that the solutions to many problems are naturally stated in the form of recursive algorithms. For example, on page 26 we showed an iterative solution to the problem of finding the greatest common factor (GCF) of two integers. Here's that program, rewritten as a function.

```
function GCF(M, N : integer) : integer;
   begin
      while M <> N do
         if M > N then
            M := M - N
         else
            N := N - M;
      GCF := M
   end
```

Let's look at Euclid's algorithm again. Here it is, slightly rephrased:

**1.** If M = N then the GCF = M.
**2.** If M > N then find the GCF of the integers M - N and N.
**3.** If N > M then find the GCF of the integers M and N - M.

This definition may appear to be circular and therefore ineffective: the algorithm tells us (in **2** and **3**) to find the GCF of two integers by finding the GCF of two other integers. Where does this process end? Does it end? The process ends at line **1** when the algorithm finally invokes itself with M = N. The process does eventually end because the algorithm continues subtracting the smaller integer from the larger until the remainder is equal to the smaller integer. The straightforward way to code this algorithm is to write it as a recursive function:

```
function GCF(M, N : integer) : integer;
    begin
       if M = N then
          GCF := M
       else if M > N then
          GCF := GCF(M - N, N)
       else {N > M}
          GCF := GCF(M, N - M)
    end
```

Let's compare the two GCF functions. Both achieve their results by repetition. The repetition in the iterative function is explicit: a while statement. But the recursive function is also repetitive: it repeatedly invokes itself (until M = N). There's one big difference between the two functions: the recursive function requires additional storage for its method of repetition. <u>Every</u> time the recursive function invokes itself, the processor must create a whole set of local variables for the function. The processor must also save the location of the function designator so that it can return to the point of invocation after it's executed the function's statements. The runtime overhead associated with many invocations (the allocations of the local variables, the initializations of the formal parameters, and then the deallocations of the local variables) can make the recursive function run more slowly than the equivalent iterative function. Even more seriously, a long sequence of recursive invocations could exhaust all the memory available for local variables.

These caveats have not been written to convince you that recursive functions are impractical; recursive solutions are often very attractive: easy to formulate, easy to write, and easy to read. And that's what a high-level language should be all about. We want you to know, however, that the elegance and simplicity of a recursive function can be somewhat beguiling. At some point you should trace a recursive function in order to get a sense of the large amount of bookkeeping that even a simple problem can generate. (The Appendix on tracing programs shows you a neat and orderly way to trace recursive subprograms.) Fortunately, the execution of recursive solutions is a low-level task properly delegated to a machine. We don't recommend tracing a recursive subprogram as a method of understanding it or proving it correct. A more fruitful way to create, understand, and prove recursive functions is a form of mathematical induction. We'll return to this point later.

When we wrote the first solution to the problem of finding the GCF of two integers, we didn't know about the **mod** operator. Let's use the mod operation now in a recursive GCF function. Because the mod operation substitutes the speed and efficiency of division and remainder for repeated subtractions, we can write an elegant <u>and</u> efficient recursive GCF function. Because the division process invokes fewer recursive calls, this function is quite practical.

```
function GCF(M, N : integer) : integer;
   begin
      if N = 0 then
         GCF := M
      else
         GCF := GCF(N, M mod N)
   end;
```

How does this function find the GCF of two integers? It's obviously correct if one of the integers, N, is zero, because the GCF of 0 and any integer M is M. (Zero has M as a factor and M has itself as its greatest factor.) Now consider the else part: N is not zero and the function invokes itself so that

GCF(M, N) = GCF(N, M **mod** N)

and this is also correct. That is, the GCF of the integers M and N <u>is</u> <u>the same as</u> the GCF of the integers N and M **mod** N. To see this, reread the description of the GCF algorithm on page 24 and especially the worked-out example on page 25. This function finally terminates and gives the GCF as a single integer (by executing the then part of the if statement): that is, the repeated division of M by N and the replacement of M with the remainder from this division is certain to reduce one of the integers to zero (and then the other integer is the GCF).

It's possible to define many operations and functions recursively:

```
Multiplication of two integers, Mult(M, N):
   Mult(M, 1) = M
   Mult(M, N) = M + Mult(M, N - 1) for N > 1

The factorial function, N! or Factorial(N):
   Factorial(0) = 1
   Factorial(N) = N*Factorial(N - 1) for N > 0

X raised to the power N, Power(X, N):
   Power(X, 0) = 1
   Power(X, N) = X*Power(X, N - 1) for N > 0
```

We can translate any one of these definitions directly into a recursive

Pascal function. For example:

```
function Power(X : real; N : integer) : real; {N >= 0}
   begin
      if N = 0 then
         Power := 1
      else
         Power := X*Power(X, N - 1)
   end
```

However, as we shall show in the next section, we can easily devise a more efficient nonrecursive function.


EXTENDING PASCAL WITH NEW SUBPROGRAMS


There are many operations and functions that you can find in this or that high-level language that you won't find in standard Pascal. A language designer cannot anticipate and satisfy every programmer's needs; those who try sometimes create bloated monsters. Instead, Pascal provides rich data structures, versatile control features, and convenient subprogram facilities. In short, Pascal encourages the user to provide his own "extensions" to the language through the development of customized data structures, functions, and procedures.

For example, some programmers are surprised to learn that Pascal does not provide an exponentiation operator. BASIC allows the programmer to write

4 ^ 5

and FORTRAN and other languages allow

4**5

to represent 4 to the 5th power. But for many applications the exponentiation operator is very rarely needed. When an application does require raising numbers to an integral power, it's easy enough to construct a function to supply this facility. For example, here's an efficient function, Power(X, N), that can be used to raise X to the Nth power. (The recursive function we gave in the last chapter is not as efficient.) This function exploits the fact that Power(X, N) can be expressed as shown:

```
Power(X, 1) = 1*X
Power(X, 2) = 1*Sqr(X)
Power(X, 3) = 1*X*Sqr(X)
Power(X, 4) = 1*Sqr(Sqr(X))
Power(X, 5) = 1*X*Sqr(Sqr(X))
```

```
Power(X, 6) - 1*Sqr(X)*Sqr(Sqr(X))
Power(X, 7) = 1*X*Sqr(X)*Sqr(Sqr(X))
Power(X, 8) = 1*Sqr(Sqr(Sqr(X)))

function Power(X : real; N : integer) : real; {N >= 0}
   var
      Y, Z : real;
      I    : integer;
   begin
      Y := X;
      Z := 1;
      I := N;
      while I > 0 do
         begin
            if odd(I) then
               Z := Z*Y;
            I := I div 2;
            Y := Sqr(Y)
         end;
      Power := Z
   end
```

## PROCEDURES: PROGRAMS WITHIN PROGRAMS

In an earlier section we discussed functions; they are subprograms that accept one or more values and calculate a single value which they assign to a function designator. The function designator appears as an operand in a statement. The function designator represents a welcome piece of abstraction. The details and specifics of the function's calculations are relegated to the function declaration where they won't distract us from reading and understanding the statement in which the function designator appears.

We require a subprogram that's a more general abstraction than the function. We want to be able to associate an identifier with an arbitrarily complex set of program actions: reading and checking data, calculating and assigning many results, changing the values of many operands, formatting and printing program outputs, in short, the execution of any coherent actions we can describe and invoke with a single identifier and carry out with a self-contained program within a program. A procedure is a subprogram that gives us this general abstraction.

A procedure, then, is a self-contained program block preceded by a procedure heading. The heading contains a procedure identifier which has the power to activate the program block. Unlike the function identifier, the procedure identifier has no data type and no value. Instead, the procedure identifier (when it appears anywhere other than the procedure heading) is an executable statement; it causes the processor to create the local variables and execute the statements declared in the procedure's block. It's as though the statements in the procedure were copied at every place in the program text where the procedure identifier appears. Here are some procedure identifiers gleaned from several programs: InitializeConstants, GetSymbol, CompareFiles, FindMatch, FindMismatch, ReadACharacter, ReadSymbol, StartNewLineAndIndent, WriteSymbol, MoveChecker, GraphFunction, JustifyLine, FindGCD, and FindMinAndMax. Notice that every one of these identifiers is a verb, usually followed by the object upon which the verb acts. This grammatical form is appropriate for the procedure identifier: the identifier names, even causes, an <u>action</u>. The literary ancestor of the procedure statement is "Open, Sesame."

The following is a simple illustration of a program employing procedures. Its execution prints these four lines:

```
Bring me my Bow of burning gold:
Bring me my Arrows of desire:
Bring me my Spear: O clouds unfold!
Bring me my chariot of fire.
```

Here's the program:

```
1.    program UsingSubprograms(output);

2.    procedure PrintFirstPart;
3.       begin {PrintFirstPart}
4.          write('Bring me my ')
5.       end {PrintFirstPart};

6.    procedure PrintLine1;
7.       begin {PrintLine1}
8.          PrintFirstPart;
9.          writeln('Bow of burning gold:')
10.      end {PrintLine1};

11.   procedure PrintLine2;
12.      begin {PrintLine2}
13.         PrintFirstPart;
14.         writeln('Arrows of desire:')
15.      end {PrintLine2};

16.   procedure PrintLine3;
17.      begin {PrintLine3}
18.         PrintFirstPart;
19.         writeln('Spear: O clouds unfold!')
20.      end {PrintLine3};

21.   procedure PrintLine4;
22.      begin {PrintLine4}
23.         PrintFirstPart;
```

```
24.          writeln('Chariot of fire.')
25.       end {PrintLine4};

26.  begin
27.       PrintLine1;
28.       PrintLine2;
29.       PrintLine3;
30.       Printline4
31.  end.
```

(You must forgive our pedagogical illustration: UsingSubprograms may seem like the proverbial elephant that labors to bring forth a pea.)

UsingSubprograms produces its output by invoking (lines 27-30) four procedures, each of which invokes a fifth procedure (to write the first part of a line) and then executes a writeln statement to print the rest of the line.

Notice that the procedure identifiers appear in two roles: first, in procedure headings as ways of associating an identifier with the procedure; and, second, in procedure statements as ways of invoking (executing) the named procedure. For example, "PrintLine3" appears in the first role in line 16; it appears in the second role in line 29. When an identifier appears in the first role, we call this appearance its "defining occurrence." The procedure identifier "PrintLine4" has its defining occurrence in line 21. The defining occurrence of a procedure identifier (in fact of all identifiers save one kind you have not met yet) must precede all corresponding occurrences of that identifier. Thus, we declared PrintFirstPart before we declared PrintLine1, PrintLine2, and so on, so that PrintFirstPart's defining occurrence preceded references to it in the other four procedures. We declared PrintFirstPart in lines 2-5 and invoked this procedure in lines 8, 13, 18, and 23. This should not be a new idea to you: you are used to declaring variable identifiers before you refer to them. It's easier to violate the rule with procedures, however, because they're all declared in the same section of the program.

A well chosen procedure identifier abstracts what a procedure does; the procedure declaration explains how the procedure carries out this task. For example, "PrintLine2" tells what the procedure does; and

```
  begin
     PrintFirstPart;
     writeln('Arrows of desire:')
  end
```

tells how the procedure does it. In a complex program with nontrivial procedures, the procedure identifiers provide a welcome abstraction from the multitudinous details of the procedure declarations. In the top-down design strategy, the abstract statement comes first, the implementing details later.

Note that the processor does not execute the procedure at the point in the program text where we place its declaration: the processor executes the procedure when (and if) the program refers to the procedure by its name. Procedure declarations must occur after the program's variable declarations and before the program's statement part. Procedure declarations are very much like program declarations; they must have a heading and statement part and they may have **label, const, type, var, procedure,** and **function** parts. Thus procedures may have their own labels, constants, data types, variables, and even their own procedures and functions. These entities, if they exist at all, exist only within the scope of the subprogram in which they are defined or declared. (As you see, UsingSubprograms has rather impoverished procedures.) A procedure is really a program within a program. The main differences between a program and a procedure are their environment, their method of invocation, and their headings. The environment of the program is the computer's operating system; the operating system "invokes" (runs) the program. The environment of the procedure is the program; the program invokes the procedure. Their headings reflect these first two differences. Outside of the obvious heading differences of the reserved words **program** and **procedure,** there are differences in the way input and output parameters are indicated in their headings. We will discuss later how data is imported into and exported from procedures. The procedures in UsingSubprograms do not require data from or provide data to the main program. The only "communication" between UsingSubprograms and PrintLine3, for example, is that the main program "turns on" PrintLine3 and PrintLine3 returns control to the main program after printing "Bring me my Spear: O clouds unfold!"

A procedure statement activates a procedure by identifying the procedure and transferring control to its first executable statement. For example, the main program activates PrintLine4 by executing the procedure statement "PrintLine4" in line 30, which transfers control to line 23.

But where does the execution of the program begin? The operating system starts the execution of a Pascal program at the first statement in the main program. The first statement in the main program can be a procedure statement; in the case of UsingSubprograms the first statement that the processor executes is a procedure statement, and the second statement that the processor executes is the first statement in the activated procedure. But between these two statements the processor may carry out additional operations; for example, it might have to import certain data into the activated procedure. In the case of our simple illustration, UsingSubprograms, this is not necessary. We will discuss transferring data into and out of procedures later.

Let's look now at the details of the execution of UsingSubprograms. The operating system starts the execution of this program at line 27, where the processor finds a procedure statement. The processor executes the procedure statement, PrintLine1, by transferring control to line 8 where it finds PrintLine1's first statement: PrintFirstPart. The processor executes this statement by transferring control to line 4, executes this line, and then returns control to the statement immediately following the procedure statement that activated

PrintFirstPart; i.e, the processor returns control to line 9. After the processor executes line 9, it has finished the execution of PrintLine1; consequently, it returns control to the main program, to the line following the line which activated PrintLine1, i.e., to line 28. The processor executes line 28 by transferring control to the first executable statement in PrintLine2, which is PrintFirstPart. Thus the processor must execute PrintFirstPart again. If you trace through all fours lines of the main block, you will see that the program executes PrintFirstPart four times.

The multiple execution of the same procedure is sometimes given as the main or even sole reason for casting actions in the form of procedures. Certainly, this is one of the economies of text that procedures provide. However, programmers should break their programs into procedures even when the program invokes most of the procedures just one time. There are many advantages of breaking programs into procedures:

**1.** Procedures facilitate carrying out the top-down development strategy.

**2.** The set of procedures that compose a program can be written and tested relatively independently of each other, avoiding a monolithic task that's hard to divide and conquer.

**3.** The reader, maintainer, or modifier of the program finds much easier his cognitive task of mastering the program.

## COMPAREFILES: AN EXAMPLE OF HIERARCHICAL STRUCTURE IN A NONTRIVIAL PROGRAM

A fairly large program may contain many procedures. For the reasons we've mentioned, procedures are essential in the orderly and comprehensible development of large programs. Unfortunately, in a textbook we cannot take the space or time to develop programs large enough to illustrate realistically the role of subprograms. It may be difficult for you to "get the feel" of the necessity and power of subprograms from programming examples that are fifty lines or less long. To give you some "feel" for how procedures help modularize and organize a fairly long program, we have included Figure 7.1 to illustrate the procedure references in a program, named Compare, that's about 400 lines long. The program's author is James F. Miner, and his program bears the following copyright notice:

Copyright (C) 1977, 1978
James F. Miner
Social Science Research Facilities Center
University of Minnesota

The Pascal User's Group published this program in the June, 1978 issue of Pascal News.

Quoting (selectively) from the author's comments at the beginning of the program:

COMPARE--Compare two text files and report their differences....
Compare is used to display on "output" the differences between two
similar texts ("FileA" and "FileB")....
Compare is line-oriented. The smallest unit of comparison is the
text line (ignoring trailing blanks)....
By manipulating a program parameter, the user can affect Compare's
sensitivity to the "locality" of differences. More specifically,
this parameter, "MinLinesForMatch," specifies the number of
consecutive lines on each file which must match in order that they
be considered as terminating [any] prior mismatch.... The value
six appears to give good results on Pascal source files....
Compare employs a simple backtracking search algorithm to isolate
mismatches from their surrounding matches....

The boxes in Figure 7.1 represent the program's procedures. The lines
between the main program and the procedures and between the procedures
themselves represent invocations of procedures. An arrow head indicates
the direction of an invocation. For example, the main program, Compare,
invokes Initialize and CompareFiles. CompareFiles invokes FindMismatch
and FindMatch. FindMismatch invokes Comparelines. FindMatch also invokes
Comparelines, but indirectly: FindMatch invokes Search, Search invokes
CheckFullMatch, and CheckFullMatch invokes CompareLines. CompareLines is
a central procedure because the Compare algorithm is line oriented;
i.e., Compare's smallest unit of comparison is the text line.
  Our objective in showing you Figure 7.1 is not that you thoroughly
understand the program Compare. Our objective is that you perceive how
the author of Compare has used subprograms to organize his program into
a hierarchical structure, and how you can use that same hierarchical
structure to begin to understand the program. This hierarchical
structure helps the program's author as well as the reader to understand
and master the program.
  The highest level in the hierarchy is the main program, Compare.
Compare invokes Initialize and CompareFiles, which constitute the next
level in the program hierarchy. Here's the text of Compare's statement
part. (The main program statements start on line 381 of Compare. We have
changed slightly some of the program's typography to be consistent with
the conventions we've been using.)

```
381 begin {Compare}
382     Initialize;
383     page(output);
384     writeln('Compare. Version ', version);
385     writeln;
386     writeln('Match criterion = ', MinLinesForMatch :1, ' lines.');
387     writeln;
388     if A.EndFile then writeln('FileA is empty.');
389     if B.EndFile then writeln('FileB is empty.');
```

```
390     if not EndFile then
391        begin
392           Same := true;
393           CompareFiles;
394           if Same then
395              writeln('No differences.')
396        end
397 end. {Compare}
```

**Note.** Perhaps you are puzzled by the unusual syntax (embedded .) of the Boolean variables A.EndFile and B.EndFile in lines 388 and 389. A and B are variables of data type **record**, and EndFile is a "field" in each of the **records**. To refer to the EndFile field in variable A, you may write A.EndFile. We discuss the **record** data type in the next chapter. **End of note.**

Note particularly the invocation in Compare of its two main procedures, Initialize (in line 382) and CompareFiles (in line 393). Compare accomplishes most of its processing through CompareFiles.

CompareFiles (See Figure 7.1) is subdivided into the two main modules of the comparison algorithm: FindMismatch and FindMatch. The division of CompareFiles into two main processes is illuminating. The algorithm starts in FindMismatch which repeatedly reads and compares the two files line-by-line until it encounters the ends of the files or finds a mismatch. If FindMismatch succeeds in finding a mismatch, CompareFiles transfers control to FindMatch which searches forward (and backward) in the files until it finds a specified number of lines ("MinLinesForMatch") which match. If FindMatch can find MinLinesForMatch number of matching lines, then FindMatch has delineated the mismatched lines; thereupon, FindMatch terminates the prior mismatch, prints the mismatch, and returns control to CompareFiles, which recalls FindMismatch.

We can express the hierarchical structure of Compare in the form of an outline just as well as in the form of Figure 7.1.

                  Compare

    I. Initialize; InitStream
   II. CompareFiles
       A. FindMismatch
          1. MoveCursor; ReadLine
          2. Mark
          3. CompareLines
       B. FindMatch
          1. Search
             a. MoveCursor; ReadLine
             b. BackTrack
             c. CheckFullMatch
                (1) MoveCursor; ReadLine
                (2) CompareLines
          2. PrintMismatch

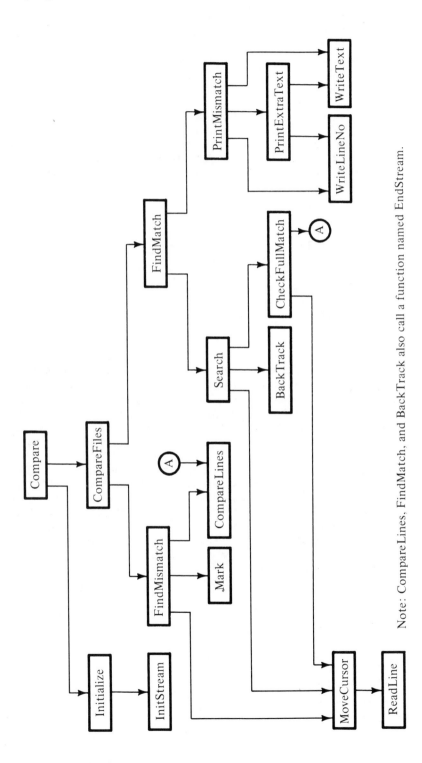

**Figure 7.1** Compare

Note: CompareLines, FindMatch, and BackTrack also call a function named EndStream.

```
?  PrintMismatch
   a. PrintExtraText
      (1) WriteLineNo
      (2) WriteText
   b. WriteLineNo
   c. WriteText
```

**Hint.** If you want to understand a complex program, try <u>starting</u> this way: 1. Read all the author's comments appearing at the beginning of the program. 2. Turn to and read the main actions of the program, noting especially the subprograms invoked by the main statements. 3. Make a subprogram diagram like the one in Figure 7.1 or an outline like the above. **End of hint.**

VALUE AND VARIABLE PARAMETERS

Consider these headings:

**procedure** A1(X : SomeType)

**procedure** A2(**var** X : SomeType)

What's the syntactical difference between the formal parameter in procedure A1 and the formal parameter in procedure A2? In procedure A1, X is a <u>value parameter</u>; in procedure A2, X is a <u>variable parameter</u>. When the formal parameter list of a subprogram heading does not prefix a parameter with the reserved word **var**, then that parameter is a value parameter. Thus, formal parameters are value parameters by default; they are variable parameters by explicit marking with the prefix **var.**
    <u>Formal Value Parameter</u>: Within the subprogram the formal value parameter exists as a local variable whose initial value is provided by the value of the corresponding actual parameter. Thus the actual value parameter can be any expression yielding a value of the same data type as the formal value parameter. The processor assigns the current value of this expression to the formal value parameter upon activation of the block in which the formal value parameter has its defining occurrence. Assuming this heading declaration:

**procedure** A1(X : real)

all the following invocations of A1 are correct.

```
A1(C/D); {C and D are numeric data types}
A1(Pi); {Pi = 3.14159}
A1(X*(Y + Z)/W);
A1(1)
```

Especially note that formal value parameters are strictly local to their blocks. Assignment to a formal value parameter has no effect on the corresponding actual parameter. Thus, a subprogram can import values by means of value parameters; but it can't export results by means of value parameters. To export results, subprograms must resort to some other means.

Formal Variable Parameters. Within the procedure the formal variable parameter exists as a local variable which has access to and can assign values to the corresponding actual parameter. You may, if you wish, think of the formal variable parameter as a synonym for the corresponding actual parameter. Thus the actual variable parameter cannot be an expression. It must be a variable of the same data type as the formal value parameter. The processor considers references to the formal variable parameter to be identical to references to the actual parameter--during the entire activation of the block. When the processor performs an operation on the formal variable parameter it immediately performs the same operation on the corresponding actual parameter.

Whenever a procedure has to effect a permanent change in the values of its formal parameters, those parameters must be variable parameters. For example, consider the subprogram Swap:

```
procedure Swap(var X, Y : SomeType);
    var
        Temp : SomeType;
    begin
        Temp := X;
        X := Y;
        Y := Temp
    end
```

If this procedure were written with value parameters (without the **var** in the parameter list) it wouldn't work. It would indeed exchange the initial values of X and Y; but this exchange would have no effect on the corresponding actual variables in the procedure call statement. Therefore, X and Y must be variable parameters. Similarly, if a procedure has the task of sorting an array, the array must be a variable parameter (or the procedure must refer to the array as a global variable). On the other hand, if a procedure has the task of finding the largest component in an array, the array could be a value parameter (or, again, simply a global variable). There are reasons, however, to declare an array as a variable parameter even for those subprograms which don't alter the array. We'll discuss those reasons in a moment.

The formal parameter list is not restricted to one mode of parameter. For example, the following procedure, which returns the maximum value of an array A, has both value and variable parameters.

```
procedure Maximum(A : List; var Max : integer);
   var
      I : Index;
   begin
      Max := A[1];
      for I := 2 to N do
         if A[I] > Max then
            Max := A[I]
   end
```

where we have assumed the following nonlocal definitions of Index and
List:

```
type
   Index = 1..N;
   List  = array[Index] of integer
```

Since this procedure does not modify the array, A can be a formal value
parameter. Because the procedure returns its result in the parameter
Max, Max must be a variable parameter.

Despite the fact that Maximum does not alter A, the programmer may
still want to make A a variable parameter. To understand why, let's look
at the processor's actions when it invokes a subprogram.

For each procedure invocation, the processor must allocate new
storage locations for the value parameters; these storage locations are
the local variables corresponding to the value parameters. The processor
must also copy the value of each actual value parameter into its
associated local variable. This is the way the processor initializes the
formal value parameters. When the processor finishes executing the
procedure it releases this local storage.

If a parameter is not used to export a value from the procedure, then
we generally prefer to use a value parameter. Value parameters help
prevent the unintended alteration of nonlocal variables. However, in the
case of array variables we must exercise caution: the copying operation
takes processor time and the amount of storage allocated to the
subprogram's local variables may be large. Therefore, it may be
desirable to define an array parameter as variable.

In general, all the parameters of a function subprogram should be
value parameters. Functions return their results by means of the
function designator (assignment to the function identifier) and hence
functions never require variable parameters. Furthermore, as we
discussed earlier, functions should not produce side effects; and the
danger of side effects is always present with variable parameters.
Despite these reasons for not using variable parameters, the argument in
the preceding paragraph for using variable array parameters holds for
functions also. Therefore, the previous procedure for finding the
maximum value in an array might be better rewritten with a variable
array parameter or as the following function.

```
function Maximum(var A : List) : integer;
   var
      I   : Index;
      Max : integer;
   begin
      Max := A[1];
      for I := 2 to N do
         if A[I] > Max then
            Max := A[I];
      Maximum := Max
   end
```

To complete our discussion of variable parameters, we must mention
two more rules. While it's often desirable to specify array parameters
as variable parameters, it's mandatory to specify file parameters as
variable parameters. Second, Components of variables of any packed data
type should not be used as actual variable parameters.


GAINING FLEXIBILITY THROUGH PARAMETERS


   Parameters are an effective way to vary the actions of a subprogram.
Without parameters a subprogram would always have to take its arguments
from the same variables. For example, the procedure Swap in the previous
section can be used to Swap any two real variables. Indeed, the
variables to be swapped are not known until the program invokes Swap.
Thus

```
Swap(W, X);
Swap(Y, Z);
Swap(U, V);
```

are all valid invocations of Swap (assuming the actual parameters are
real).
   To demonstrate how value parameters facilitate flexibility in a
procedure, we'll develop a procedure useful in text-formatting systems.
This procedure prints the folio on a page of text. (Typesetters use the
term "folio" for the page number.) There are several choices in printing
the folio:

   Flush right; i.e. justified against the right-hand margin
   Centered; i.e., centered on the text line
   Alternating; i.e., flush left on even pages and flush right on odd
   pages

In addition to the folio location, there are other variables we must
consider: the left margin, the text line length, and of course the folio
(page number) itself. By passing all the above parameters to the

procedure, the caller has extensive control of its actions. (One could expand the flexibility by passing parameters designating Roman or Arabic numerals and supplying a running head to be printed on the same line as the folio.)

We assume these global definitions and declarations:

```
type
    Location   = (FlushRight, Centered, Alternating);
    ZeroTo128  = 0..128; {Range of left margin}
    EightTo136 = 8..136; {Range of line length}
var
    Folio          : integer; {Folio >= 1}
    FolioLocation : Location;
    LeftMargin    : ZeroTo128;
    LineLength    : EightTo136;
```

To simplify reading the procedure, we'll use the same identifiers for the formal parameters as we use for the actual parameters.

Let's attack the problem with these top-level actions:

```
Determine the number of digits in the folio
Interpret the command (FolioLocation)
Compute the number of leading blanks
Print the number of leading blanks
Print the Folio
```

Here's the final refinement of this sequence of actions:

```
procedure PrintFolio(Folio : integer; FolioLocation : Location;
                LeftMargin : ZeroTo128; LineLength : EightTo136);
    var
        M : 0..5; {Number of digits in folio}
        Q : integer;
        LeadingBlanks : 0..135;
    begin
        M := 0;
        Q := Folio;
        while Q > 0 do
            begin
                Q := Q div 10;
                M := M + 1
            end;

        case FolioLocation of
            FlushRight:
                begin
                    LeadingBlanks := LeftMargin + LineLength - M;
                    writeln(' ' : LeadingBlanks, Folio : M)
                end;
```

```
        Centered :
          begin
            LeadingBlanks := LeftMargin + (LineLength - M) div 2;
            writeln(' ' : LeadingBlanks, Folio : M)
          end;
        Alternating:
          if odd(Folio) then
            begin
              LeadingBlanks := LeftMargin + LineLength - M;
              writeln(' ' : LeadingBlanks, Folio : M)
            end
          else
            writeln(' ' : LeftMargin, Folio : M)
    end {FolioLocation case}
  end {PrintFolio}
```

## Procedural and Functional Parameters

In the previous sections of this chapter we have described two kinds
of parameters in detail: value parameters and variable parameters.
Pascal offers additional flexibility to subprograms by allowing
procedural parameters and functional parameters. Procedural and
especially functional parameters can make certain kinds of subprograms
more useful and general. For example, consider a procedure that
tabulates the values of a function F or makes a graph of the function F.
By making the function F a functional parameter, the tabulating or
graphing procedure can operate on a function which the caller specifies.
Or consider a function that returns the value of the integral of a
function G; by making G a functional parameter the integral function can
operate on a function specified by the caller.

To illustrate the usefulness of a functional parameter, we have
developed a subprogram called Maximum that finds the maximum values of
integer functions. Maximum closely parallels the function in an earlier
section for finding the maximum value of an array. We assume the formal
functional parameter F receives a single integer parameter and yields an
integer result. The caller specifies, besides the actual functional
parameter, the interval A..B on which Maximum should search for the
maximum of F. Assuming the following declaration of an integer function

```
  function SecondDegree(J : integer) : integer;
    begin
      SecondDegree := -2*sqr(J) - 4*J + 6
    end
```

the following statement would write the maximum value of SecondDegree on
the interval -5..5.

```
  writeln(Maximum(SecondDegree, -5, 5))
```

```
function Maximum(function F : integer; A, B : integer) : integer;
   var
      I, ValueOfF, Max : integer;
   begin
      Max := F(A);
      for I := A + 1 to B do
         begin
            ValueOfF := F(I); {To avoid evaluating F twice}
            if ValueOfF > Max then
               Max := ValueOfF
         end;
      Maximum := Max
   end
```

The following rules and operations apply to functional parameters:

   **1.** The actual parameter must be, of course, a function identifier. (In the above writeln statement, for example, the function identifier SecondDegree is the actual parameter.)

   **2.** The formal parameter stands for the actual function during the entire activation of the block. (The formal parameter F stands for the actual function SecondDegree during the entire activation of Maximum.)

   **3.** If, upon its activation, the functional parameter accesses any nonlocal entity, this entity must be one that was accessible to the function when its functional identifier was passed as a parameter. This restriction will be more understandable when we discuss Pascal's block structure and its rules for the scope of identifiers. Many implementations of Pascal may limit actual functional parameters to functions having value parameters only. You must check your Pascal compiler to find its actual limitations. (The only entities accessed by SecondDegree meet all the above requirements: J was in the scope of SecondDegree when it was passed as a parameter; J is a local entity; J is a value parameter.)

   **4.** The actual function and the formal function must have compatible formal parameter lists and identical result types. This should be obvious but bears repeating. Some Pascal compilers may not check the compatibility of the formal parameter lists. The proposed standard we mentioned in the preface requires that the formal functional parameter contain a formal parameter list; but the previous standard did not. (The actual function, SecondDegree(J : integer) : integer, and the formal function, F(I : integer) : integer, have compatible formal parameter lists and identical result types. We wrote the heading of Maximum without F's formal parameter list. This is consistent with the earlier Pascal standard (Jensen & Wirth, 1974); but may be inconsistent with the new standard.)

   All the above rules and operations apply identically to procedural parameters (with the exception, of course, of the statement in 4 that the actual function and the formal function must have identical result types: procedures do not have result types).

RECURSIVE PROCEDURES

We already met recursive subprograms in the section on recursive functions. Pascal procedures can also be recursive; i.e., they can call themselves. Most recursive procedures can be written in the same pattern as the recursive functions we examined in the earlier section. In those functions the subprogram defines the result nonrecursively for one or two values of the argument, usually for 0 or 1. For larger values of the argument, the subprogram defines the result recursively. For example, examine the functions on page 162 as well as this recursive function for Factorial(N):

```
function Factorial(N : integer) : integer;
   begin
      if N = 0 then
         Factorial := 1
      else
         Factorial := N*Factorial(N - 1)
   end
```

This pattern is a desirable way to express recursive subprograms. We show the simplest case first (N = 0 for the factorial problem) and then the more complicated cases, defined recursively. We know that the recursion will terminate because each time we invoke the subprogram we decrement N by one. Furthermore, we can apply the method of mathematical induction to prove that this function works: (1) Show it's true for zero; (2) Assume it's true for N - 1; (3) Then prove it's true for N. In most cases it's easy to apply mathematical induction to the proof of recursive subprograms.

Let's apply this general pattern to developing a procedure for sorting an array. The sorting method we'll program is due to C. A. Hoare, who dubbed his method "Quicksort." The method is well named, for it's outstandingly efficient. We'll explain later why this sorting method is so efficient. Our main objective now is to show how we can use the pattern of recursion to develop the algorithm.

We'll use a terminology that will allow us to sort an array or any subarray; let's call the subarray A[L..R]. Thus A has R - L + 1 components. Remembering our pattern for recursive solutions, let's isolate the simplest case. There are actually two simple cases for which we can write the solution straight off. One of these cases is degenerate: where L >= R. In this degenerate case we have an array with zero or one element and we don't have to take any action at all. The simplest nondegenerate case is L + 1 = R. In this case there are two components in the array and the sorting problem is trivial. Let's write a first cut at a sort procedure which sums up what we've discussed so far. The following top-level design appears effective if we can refine the English statements "Partition array into a left part and a right part; call SubSort to sort the left subarray; call SubSort to sort the right subarray."

```
procedure SubSort(L, R . Index);
    begin {SubSort}
        if L + 1 = R then {Array segment has 2 components}
            begin
                if A[L] > A[R] then
                    Swap(A[L], A[R])
            end
        else if L + 1 < R then {Segment has 3 or more components}
            begin
                Partition array into a left part and a right part;
                call SubSort to sort the left subarray;
                call SubSort to sort the right subarray
            end
    end {SubSort}
```

The thrust of SubSort should be familiar to you: break down the higher
order case (N >= 3) by recursive calls until the repetitive reduction of
order yields a case (N <= 2) for which there's a simple nonrecursive
solution. The specific strategy is to divide an array with more than 2
components into two subarrays and to keep dividing these subarrays until
eventually we have reduced the subarray length to two or fewer
components. We'll undertake the refinement in a moment. But first,
notice that we handle the simple cases correctly. If L >= R, the
procedure does nothing (as it should). We must always be sure to account
for these degenerate cases. If L + 1 = R, the procedure sorts the
two-component array.

Now let's refine the statement "Partition array into a left subarray
and a right subarray." It should be evident with a little thought that
we must so partition the array that all the components in the left
subarray are less than or equal to all the components in the right
subarray. Only then can we independently sort the left subarray and the
right subarray and have the consequence that the joint array is also
sorted. Here's how we might perform such a partition. Pick an component
(whose index we call M) near the middle of the array.

M := (L + R) div 2

(The partitioning component, A[M], is sometimes called the "pivot" item
because we have to exchange items--using the value A[M] as a
pivot--between the original right subarray and the original left
subarray.) Now follow this algorithm for the partition:

1. Scan the array from the left until finding an item A[I] > A[M].
2. Scan the array from the right until finding an item A[J] < A[M].
3. If I < J, then swap the items A[I] and A[J]
4. Continue scanning and swapping until the scan from the left and
the scan from the right meet each other.

Here's a procedure for carrying out this partitioning process:

```
procedure PartitionArray(L, R : Index);
   var
      PivotValue : Scalar;
      I, J       : Index;
   begin {PartitionArray}
      I := L;
      J := R;
      PivotValue := A[(L + R) div 2];
      repeat
         while A[I] < PivotValue do
            I := I + 1;
         while A[J] > PivotValue do
            J := J - 1;
         if I <= J then
            begin
               Swap(A[I], A[J]);
               I := I + 1;
               J := J - 1
            end
      until I > J
   end {PartitionArray}
```

The complete procedure, QuickSort, appears on page 182. Assume the
following global definitions and declaration:

```
type
   Index  = 1..N;
   Scalar = {Some scalar type}
var
   A : array[Index] of Scalar
```

Quicksort accesses A as a global variable. Note that we found it
convenient in assembling QuickSort to nest PartitionArray inside
Subsort. This convenience stems from both procedures' using the same
local variables, I and J.

QuickSort is an exceptionally fast sorting algorithm--faster, for
example, than the algorithm on page 131. Many sorting algorithms work by
comparing pairs of items and then exchanging these items if they're out
of order. It doesn't take the processor any longer to swap items over a
long distance than over a short distance. Thus, long-distance swaps are
potentially more efficient than short-distance swaps. There's an
algorithm called BubbleSort, for example, that sorts by comparing each
adjacent pair of items and exchanging them if they're out of order.
BubbleSort exchanges pairs of items the minimum distance possible.
Consequently, BubbleSort usually has to make many exchanges to effect a
complete sort. The optimizing trick is to find two widely separated
items that ought to be exchanged. The efficiency of QuickSort stems from
the fact that, on the average, QuickSort swaps widely separated items,
resulting in fewer swaps to sort the whole array. If you examine our
English description of PartitionArray, you'll see why this is so: the
search for swappable items starts from opposite ends of the subarray.

```
procedure QuickSort;
    procedure Swap(var X, Y : Scalar);
        var
            Temp : Scalar;
        begin {Swap}
            Temp := X;
            X := Y;
            Y := Temp
        end; {Swap}

    procedure SubSort(L, R : Index);
        var
            I, J : Index;
        procedure PartitionArray(L, R : Index);
            var
                PivotValue : Scalar;
            begin {PartitionArray}
                I := L;
                J := R;
                PivotValue := A[(L + R) div 2];
                repeat
                    while A[I] < PivotValue do
                        I := I + 1;
                    while A[J] > PivotValue do
                        J := J - 1;
                    if I <= J then
                        begin
                            Swap(A[I], A[J]);
                            I := I + 1;
                            J := J - 1
                        end
                until I > J
            end; {PartitionArray}
        begin {SubSort}
            if L + 1 = R then {Array segment has 2 components}
                begin
                    if A[L] > A[R] then
                        Swap(A[L], A[R])
                end
            else if L + 1 < R then {Segment has 3 or more components}
                begin
                    PartitionArray(L, R);
                    SubSort(L, J);
                    SubSort(I, R)
                end
        end; {SubSort}

    begin {QuickSort}
        SubSort(1, N)
    end {QuickSort}
```

If we had space to show you a nonrecursive development and implementation of QuickSort, you'd see that our recursive version is easier to develop, program, and read.

In summary, recursive subprograms are often easier to design, program, understand, and prove correct. Thinking recursively is a good top-down technique. It helps you to break the problem into the simplest case and a complex case--which in turn is broken recursively into simpler cases.


## SUBPROGRAM DIRECTIVES


There's one aspect of subprograms we haven't discussed yet, namely, that Pascal permits the programmer to substitute some form of "directive" for the subprogram block. In BNF notation:

```
<procedure declaration> ::=
    <procedure heading>;
        <procedure block> | <directive>
```

There's a similar definition for function declarations.

The full set of directives available depends on your particular Pascal implementation; but all implementations should provide the facility of a "forward" directive. The forward directive allows subprogram calls to precede the subprograms's full declaration in the program text. The programmer may have aesthetic or organizational motives for using a forward directive. A forward directive is absolutely necessary for declaring mutually recursive subprograms. Mutually recursive subprograms are subprograms that call each other. Suppose A and B are mutually recursive. It's impossible for A's declaration to precede B's invocation of A and for B's declaration to precede A's invocation of B. But Pascal has a rule that the definition or declaration of an object must precede its use. (We discuss the only exception to this rule in chapter 9.) The way out of this mutual impasse is illustrated in the following text:

```
procedure A(X, Y : real);
    forward;

function B(Z : real) : real;
    var
        U, V : real;
    begin {B}
    .  .  .
        A(U, V);
    .  .  .
    end; {B}
```

```
procedure A; {which has been forward declared}
   var
      W : real;
   begin {A}
   .  .  .
   Y := B(W)/X;
   .  .  .
   end; {B}
```

Note the following:

**1.** The forward declaration consists of the subprogram heading followed by the directive "forward": **procedure** A(X, Y : real); forward.

**2.** In the subsequent subprogram declaration, one omits the formal parameter list: **procedure** A; {which has been forward declared}. The comment is not required, of course; but it's helpful.

**3.** The forward declaration and the subprogram declaration are local to the same block.

**4.** The forward declaration (which is followed by the subprogram declaration) is the defining occurrence of the subprogram.

Some implementations provide directives for using external subprograms. These directives may take forms like "External," "Extern," or "Fortran" (in the case of Fortran subroutines). To use an external subroutine one gives the subprogram heading as usual with the block replaced by the appropriate directive. For example:

**procedure** PlotGraph(X, Y : real); Fortran


## BLOCK STRUCTURE AND SCOPE OF IDENTIFIERS


Every Pascal program is composed of one or more headings and associated blocks. There is always a program heading and a program block:

```
<program heading>;
<block>.
```

where

```
<block> ::=
<label declaration part>
<constant definition part>
<type definition part>
<variable declaration part>
<procedure and function declaration part>
<statement part>
```

Every part of a block except the statement part can be empty. But in all
but the simplest programs most of the parts will not be empty; in
particular, in any program of reasonable complexity and size, the
procedure and function declaration part will not be empty. Suppose the
procedure declaration part is not empty; its BNF definition is:

    <procedure heading>;
        <block>

The program block can contain many of these procedure declarations.
Furthermore, the block in a procedure declaration has the same
definition as a program block: it's a true program block within a
program block. Therefore, each procedure block can contain more
procedure blocks. Here's a possibility for the spread of this recursive
structure:

    <P program heading>;

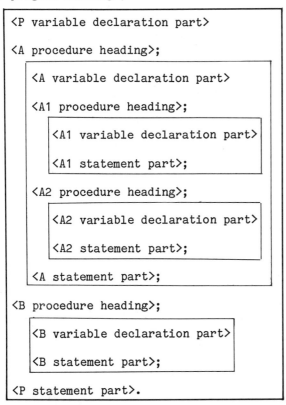

Notice that we have drawn boxes around the program and procedure
blocks to make apparent the block structure of this typical Pascal
program. (We have simplified matters somewhat by not showing label,
constant, and type definitions; but our discussion about scope applies

equally to these objects.) The blocks are either nested entirely inside
each other or they're completely disjoint; but blocks cannot overlap in
any other way. The A and B blocks are completely disjoint; so are the A1
and A2 blocks. A1 is nested inside A which is nested inside P. The
program creates the outermost block; and each subprogram declaration
creates another (nested) block.

A question we naturally ask about this structure is, "what is the
scope of the variables and procedures?" For example, can the A statement
part refer to variables declared in the A2 variable declaration part?
(No.) Can the A2 statement part invoke the B procedure? (Yes.) Can the
A2 statement part refer to variables declared in the B variable
declaration part? (No.) Can the P statement part invoke the A1
procedure? (No.) These are the kinds of questions we answer in this
section. If you already know the answers you might want to skip right to
the end of this section where we give some reasons for constructing
programs in this block structure.

**Definition of Scope**: The "scope" of an object (label, constant, type,
variable, or subprogram) is the range of the program text in which that
particular object is known and can be used. This range is the particular
block in which the object has its defining occurrence (i.e., the block
where the object is defined or declared) and all blocks internal to that
block **except** if an internal block defines or declares any object with
the same identifier, that block and all blocks internal to it are
excluded from the scope of the identifier's earlier definition or
declaration.

For example, if X has a defining occurrence in the variable
declaration part of A:

**var**
    X : real

then the scope of X is the blocks A, A1, and A2; and X as such does not
exist outside the A block at all. However, if X has a further defining
occurrence in the variable declaration part of A1:

**var**
    X : **packed array**[1..3] **of** char

then A1 is excluded from the scope of the defining occurrence of X in A.
The result is that A's X has the scope A and A2; and A1's X has the
scope A1. The two Xs are obviously different; but they would be
different variables even if both were declared to be real.

An interesting aspect of this block structure is that the more nested
a subprogram is, the more identifiers it potentially has access to. Does
it make sense to you that more subordinate subprograms can potentially
access more program objects? Remember the idea of information hiding:
the details which outer blocks don't have a "need to know" are hidden
inside the inner blocks. When an outer block delegates a task to an
inner block, the inner block must have the resources it might need to do
its job (global labels, constants, types, variables, and subprograms) as

well as the ability to create new resources which outer blocks couldn't
care less about. It does seem to make sense; but some beginning
programmers are surprised to learn that the most humble nested procedure
has the power to refer to and alter the largest number of objects. This
"power of access" is dangerous only if nested subprograms are "disloyal,
sloppy, or ignorant." It's essential that subprograms observe a proper
discipline and protocol when accessing global variables. For example,
except in the case of very large data structures, which it would be too
burdensome to copy, functions should not access any global variables.

The only way a subprogram can lose the potential to refer to an
entity defined or declared in an external block is for the subprogram to
redefine or redeclare the identifier associated with the entity.

Suppose that you're reading a program and encounter a statement that
refers to a variable X which has several defining occurrences in the
text. How do you establish which defining occurrence corresponds to the
present use of X? Of course, type compatibility may give you a vital
clue; but that's not the rigorous way. What you must do is find the
smallest block enclosing one declaration of X and the statement
containing the occurrence of X. That's the declaration which corresponds
to the present use of X. If there's a type incompatibility between the
use of X and the declaration of X so found, then the program is in
error.

We have defined and illustrated scope rules in terms of the static
text; but these rules also help describe a dynamic aspect of the
program, namely, the lifetime of local variables. A variable exists
during, and only during, the entire execution process of the block in
which it's declared. Therefore, the processor creates a subprogram's
local variables at the invocation of the subprogram and releases the
storage for these variables at the termination of the subprogram. This
means that it's physically impossible for the calling segment to refer
to variables local to the called procedure since the processor does not
create the variables until it executes the procedure call statement and
it destroys the variables before it returns control to the calling
segment.

The restricted life of subprogram variables can result in memory
savings: a local declaration results in memory being allocated only
during the time it's needed. Therefore, two subprograms that run in
succession can use the same storage locations for their local variables.
To maximize this kind of memory savings, declare variables as local to
their actual use as possible. This also improves the readability of
programs; one does not want to read definitions and declarations before
they're required. (Remember information hiding?)

Here's an example on which you can check your understanding of block structure and scope rules:

```
program Prog;

type
   Index    = 1..18;
   String18 = packed array[Index] of char;
var
   Title, Subtitle : String18;
   I, J            : Index;

procedure P(Title : String18);
   const
      Pitch = 10;
   var
      Temp : String18;
      I    : Index;

   function F(SubTitle : String18) : integer;
      var
         I    : Index;
      begin {F}
        F's statement part can use these identifiers:
         F's SubTitle (not the same variable as Prog's Subtitle);
         F's local I (not P's I or Prog's I);
         F (F can call itself);
         P (F can call P);
         Pitch;
         Temp;
         Prog's Title and J
      end; {F}

   begin {P}
      P's statement part can use these identifiers:
       P's Title (not the same variable as Prog's Title);
       Pitch;
       P's local I (but not Prog's I or F's I);
       Temp (note that P referred to String18 to declare Temp);
       P (P can call itself);
       F (P can call F);
       Prog's Subtitle and J
   end; {P}

begin {Prog}
  Prog's statement part can use these identifiers:
   It's own Title, SubTitle, I, and J;
   P (Prog can call P);
end. {Prog}
```

SOME TIPS ON WRITING SUBPROGRAMS


   Expert programmers use subprograms skillfully. One way to acquire
this skill is to read a lot of well written long programs. A definite
prerequisite to the skill is a thorough understanding of block structure
and identifier scope, the subject of the previous section. In addition
to these factors, we offer the following advice and tips:

   **1.** Avoid "overloading" identifiers. Although it's legal to redeclare
or redefine an identifier in a different block from the one where it has
another defining occurrence, "overloading" of an identifier might make
your program quite difficult to read and subject to misunderstanding.
   **2.** Nest a subprogram inside another block when its action is so
specialized that only the enclosing block is ever likely to refer to it.
   **3.** Nest a procedure inside another block when it's necessary to take
advantage of the nested procedure's consequent access to all the
identifiers of the enclosing block. This may be desirable when the
procedure would otherwise have so many parameters that it becomes
inconvenient to list them all.
   **4.** Nest a procedure inside another block in order to hide the nested
procedure from readers (or modifiers!) who do not have a need or desire
to know about the procedure.
   **5.** Remember that all the local variables of a subprogram are
undefined on each entry to the subprogram. There's no "carry-over" in
this respect from one call to another. Therefore, one of the first tasks
of a subprogram block is initialization of the local variables.
   **6.** Declare an identifier as local to its use as possible. This
usually means declaring it in the block where it's used. But if a
procedure requires "carry-over" of a value from one call to another,
then declare the variable in the innermost enclosing block that will
ensure existence of the variable between all the subject procedure's
calls. Declaring an identifier as close to its use as possible increases
program readability, minimizes the chances of other segments of code
using the identifier inadvertently, and minimizes the amount of storage
required for local variables.
   **7.** Finally, use functions and especially procedures to implement the
strategy of top-down design using step-wise refinement. Translate the
steps you isolate into procedures. Remember to limit the amount of text
in any one block to a graspable amount. (The amount of "one page" or
fifty lines is often suggested. This could be on the high side,
depending on the density of concepts in the text.)



EXERCISES


   **1.** Write a function which finds the length of a string stored in an
array of type = **array**[1..Length] **of** char. Count embedded blanks but not

external blanks. Thus ' Thank you!   ' should return 10. If you use a
value parameter explain why. If you use a variable parameter explain
why.

**2.** Write a function which finds the dot product of two arrays of real
variables. The dot product of A and B is:

A[1]*B[1] + A[2]*B[2] + ... + A[N]*B[N]

If you use a value parameter explain why. If you use a variable
parameter explain why.

**3.** Write a function that finds the norm of a vector. A vector is a
one-dimensional array. The norm of a vector is the square root of the
sum of the squares of the components of the vector. (The norm has the
physical interpretation of the length of a two- or three-dimensional
vector.) Write your subprogram so that it calls the previous function
(dot product) as a subprogram.

**4.** The following procedure reads a sequence of hexidecimal digits and
assigns the equivalent positive integer to the variable formal
parameter. Write a similar procedure to read a sequence of octal digits.
Then write a program that uses the procedure to read a sequence of octal
numbers, sums them, and prints out the sum in the form of an integer.

```
procedure ReadHex(var Number : integer);
   var
      Ch : char;
   begin {ReadHex}
      repeat
         read(Ch)
      until (Ch <> ' ');
      Number := 0;
      repeat
         if ('0' <= Ch) and (Ch <= '9') then
            Number := 16*Number + (ord(Ch) - ord('0'))
         else if ('A' <= Ch) and (Ch <= 'F') then
            Number := 16*Number + (ord(Ch) - ord('A') + 10)
         else
            writeln(Ch, ' is not a hexidecimal digit.');
         read(Ch)
      until not (('0' <= Ch) and (Ch <= '9'))
         and not (('A' <= Ch) and (Ch <= 'F'))
   end {ReadHex}
```

**5.** Another algorithm for sorting an array A[L..R] is:

a. Pick the middle component of the array: M = (L + R) **div** 2;
b. Sort subarray A[L..M];
c. Sort subarray A[(M + 1)..R];
d. Merge the two sorted subarrays into one sorted array.

Modeling your implementation on QuickSort, write a recursive procedure to implement the above algorithm. You may use an auxiliary array, Aux[L..M], if you wish.

This is a divide and conquer approach like QuickSort; but QuickSort is vastly more efficient. Can you see why? Nevertheless, the concept of merging sorted subsequences is an important idea in sorting files, and we'll meet the idea again in chapter 10.

# 8. Structured Data Type 2: The Record

In Chapter 6 we introduced the array, one of Pascal's structured data types. In some programming languages the array is the only structured data type available. One of the reasons Pascal is an improvement over many older languages is that it offers a richer repertoire of structured data types. Pascal offers, in addition to the array, the record, dynamic data structures, files, and sets. In this chapter we'll discuss the record data type. The record is a structure with <u>named</u> components; these components can be of <u>different</u> types.

The array is a <u>homogeneous</u> data structure: all of its component variables must be of the same data type, called the component type. The array is quite powerful and convenient for representing objects describable with a set of ordered variables all belonging to the same type. But many problems arise where we have to describe objects that have features or measurements describable only with variables belonging to differing data types. Therefore, we need a <u>heterogeneous</u> data type, a structured type whose components can belong to different types. The record data type fills this general need; it gathers together into one unit the heterogeneous variables applying to a single object. Here are some examples. Note how the reserved words **record** and **end** bracket each definition.

A <u>date</u> (e.g., 17 Feb 1980) is a single object describable with three variables: a small integer, a short character string, and a medium-sized integer:

```
type
   DateType =
      record
         Day    : 1..31;
         Month  : array[1..3] of char;
         Year   : 0..2100
      end;
var
   Today, MyAnniversary, RodsBirthday : DateType
```

One denotes an individual component of a record by the record variable identifier followed by the component's name. Thus we can write

```
if (Today.Day = 25) and (Today.Month = 'Dec') then
    writeln('Merry Christmas!')
```

and

```
RodsBirthday.Day := 4;
RodsBirthday.Month := 'Jan'
```

A <u>rational number</u> (e.g., 5/8) is a single numerical object that can be expressed as an integer or the quotient of two integers:

```
type
    RationalNumber =
        record
            Numerator : integer;
            Denominator : 1..maxint
        end
```

An <u>automobile</u> (e.g., 1974 grey 4 door Ford sedan, license number BCM 185) is a single object describable with several variables:

```
type
    Automobile =
        record
            Year    : 1950..1985;
            Color   : (Red, Brown, Green, Blue, Silver, Grey, White);
            NmbrOfDoors : 2..5;
            Manufacturer: packed array[1..12] of char;
            BodyStyle   : (Convertible, Sports, Sedan, Wagon);
            License     : array[1..8] of char;
            Owner       : Person
        end;
var
    StolenCar : array[1..N] of Automobile
```

We have introduced two new ideas in this example. Person, the type of owner, could be a previously defined record containing a person's name, address, and telephone number. Thus we can embed records within records. Second, StolenCar is an <u>array of records</u>; this is a common and useful data structure in Pascal.

How would you assign a license number to the Kth stolen car? Since the components of StolenCar are records of type Automobile, you denote the license component by the record variable's name, StolenCar[K], followed by the name of the component:

```
StolenCar[K].License := 'MEL 434 '
```

The components of a record may all belong to the same data type. In

that case the motive for using a record rather than an array might be
that the record has named rather than subscripted components. The
following is an example of a record with homogeneous components.

A complex number (e.g., 2 + 3i) is a single numerical object with two
real components:

```
type
    ComplexNumber =
        record
            Re, Im : real
        end;
var
    X, Y : ComplexNumber
```

The components of X and Y are X.Re, X.Im, Y.Re, and Y.Im.
{On the other hand, one could also express this idea as an array with
an enumerated index type:

```
type
    IndexType    = (Re, Im);
    ComplexNumber = array[IndexType] of real;
var
    X, Y : ComplexNumber
```

Then the components of X and Y are X[Re], X[Im], Y[Re], and Y[Im].}

Records can be passed as parameters to subprograms. This can be very
useful. For example, the following procedure computes the product of two
complex numbers and exports the result in the variable formal parameter
Z.

```
procedure Multiply(    X : ComplexNumber,
                  {by} Y : ComplexNumber,
                   var Z : ComplexNumber);
    {(a + bi)(c + di) = (ac - bd) + (ad + bc)i}
    begin
        Z.Re := X.Re*Y.Re - X.Im*Y.Im;
        Z.Im := X.Re*Y.Im + X.Im*Y.Re
    end {Multiply}
```

To illustrate the usefulness of the record data type, let's consider
a specific problem. Suppose we want to design a record system for a
mental health clinic. We'll have to keep essential records on the
patients who use the clinic's services. No doubt we'll want to include
data such as last name, first name, sex, age, marital status, whether or
not the patient has insurance, the name of the therapist, and perhaps
the primary diagnosis. Other information may be desirable (e.g., fee,
payment record, billing address); but this conglomeration of data will
more than illustrate our point. We could represent this patient data
with the following data type definition.

```
type
   String12 = array[1..12] of char;

   Patient  = record
                 LastName       : String12;
                 FirstName      : String12;
                 Sex            : (Male, Female);
                 Age            : 5..80;
                 MaritalStatus  : (single, married, divorced, widowed);
                 Insurance      : Boolean;
                 Therapist      : String12;
                 Diagnosis      : real {written as xxx.xx}
              end
```

This record type, named Patient, has eight components. We sometimes
refer to the components as __fields__. Notice that the type definition for
Patient specifies an identifier, called the __field identifier,__ and a data
type for each field. Thus the field identifier of the first field is
LastName and its data type is String12.

The Patient data structure should give you some idea of the
generality of the record data type. The data object Patient has
components belonging to these data types: array, user-defined scalar,
integer subrange, Boolean, and real. We can also nest records within
records within records. For example, we could declare a data type,
Appointment, as follows:

```
type
   Appointment =
      record
         Date  : DateType; {defined earlier as record}
         Hour  : 0..2400 {"military" time}
      end
```

and then include two new components in the Patient record.

```
Patient  = record
              LastName       : String12;
              FirstName      : String12;
              NextSession    : Appointment;
              PastSessions   : array[1..52] of Appointment
                     .
                     .
                     .
              Diagnosis      : real {written as xxx.xx}
           end
```

Once we've defined the Patient data type, we can declare variables
belonging to that data type.

```
var
   NewPatient    : Patient
   FreudsPatient : array[1..6] of Patient
```

and we can assign values to the individual fields of the record:

```
   NewPatient.LastName  := 'Ciradi       ';
   NewPatient.FirstName := 'Michael      ';
   NewPatient.Sex       := Male;
   NewPatient.Age       := 28
      .     .     .
   NewPatient.Therapist := 'None         ';
   NewPatient.Diagnosis := 0.0             {No diagnosis yet}
```

If we had included NextSession in the Patient record, we could assign a
date and time for the new patient's first session:

```
   NewPatient.NextSession.Date.Day   := 15;
   NewPatient.NextSession.Date.Month := 'Jun';
   NewPatient.NextSession.Date.Year  := 1981;
   NewPatient.NextSession.Hour        := 1100
```

Notice how we designated individual fields in the above assignments: we
wrote the name of the record variable followed by a period followed by
the field identifier of the component. In BNF notation we have this
definition:

```
   <field designator> ::= <record variable>.<field identifier>
```

Since NextSession is a component within NewPatient and also a record,
NewPatient.NextSession is a field identifier from the viewpoint of
NewPatient; but it's a record variable from the viewpoint of its data
type.

   **Note.** Contrast naming the components of a record with the way we
identify the components of an array. If we've declared an array called
Names, we can refer to the fourth component of the array by the
identifier Name[I] where I has the value 4; but we must refer to the
fourth component (or field) of the Patient record by the identifier
"NewPatient.Age." We shall go deeper into the reasons for this later.
For now just consider this: if we wrote "NewPatient.I" where I was
supposed to be a "record index" (there is no such thing) and not a
defined field identifier, what data type would NewPatient.I be? If I =
1, then NewPatient.I would be a string of length twelve--but if I = 6,
then NewPatient.I would be a Boolean variable! This approach to
identifying fields would not only defeat the compiler's attempt to
perform type checking, it would make the human being's job of
comprehending the program a record-keeping nightmare. **End of note.**

   After the clinic has completed its intake interview and psychological
evaluation of our new patient, we can selectively update the appropriate
fields:

```
NewPatient.Therapist := 'Freud     ';
NewPatient.Diagnosis := 301.4
```

**Psychiatric note:** 301.4 is the American Psychiatric Association's code for "obsessive compulsive personality disorder." **End note.**
   We can assign records as whole units:

```
FreudsPatient[5] := NewPatient
```

This statement assigns the value of every field in NewPatient to the corresponding field in FreudsPatient; it's equivalent to eight individual assignment statements, three of which are string assignments.
   As we already mentioned, we can form an array of records, an extremely useful data structure. For example, we can assign patients to psychotherapy groups. First, let's define a Group as an array of patients; then we can declare as many therapy groups as we need of type Group. The following structures define five therapy groups, each having up to twelve members.

```
type
    Group = array[1..12] of Patient;
var
    Psychodrama,
    Assertiveness,
    MixedSingles,
    MaleAlcoholics,
    WolfsGroup       : Group
```

With this structure in mind, we can assign a new patient to be the tenth member of the psychodrama group.

```
begin
    Psychodrama[10] := NewPatient;
    .     .      .
```

The following program fragment prints out the name of the therapist and all the members of the psychodrama group.

```
writeln(Psychodrama[1].Therapist);
writeln;
J := 1;
while (J <= 12) and (Psychodrama[J].LastName <> '      ') do
    begin
        writeln(Psychodrama[J].FirstName,' ',Psychodrama[J].LastName);
        J := J + 1
    end
```

where we have assumed that the patient records are arranged contiguously starting with the first component of the array and that empty records have blanks in the LastName component.

The sorting and searching operations we studied on arrays of simple variables are applicable to arrays of records--so long as the programmer specifies an appropriate field for the operation. For example, we could sort or search all the patient records using an appropriate field for the key. The mental health clinic would probably want all the Patient records sorted on the LastName field. We could search the records on particular keys to compile "statistics" on the clinic's patient population.

Assuming that all (N) of the Patient records are contained in one long array named Client, the following program fragment counts the number of patients carrying the primary diagnosis of alcoholism (the APA codes for alcoholism are 303.0, 303.1, 303.2, and 303.9; the other possible codes between 303.0 and 303.9 are unused).

```
Alcoholics := 0
for J := 1 to N do
   if (303 <= Client[J].Diagnosis) and
                (Client[J].Diagnosis < 304) then
       Alcoholics := Alcoholics + 1
```

## THE WITH STATEMENT

In the previous section you probably noticed the verbosity of the statements assigning values to the fields of NewPatient

```
NewPatient.LastName  := 'Ciradi      ';
NewPatient.FirstName := 'Michael     ';
NewPatient.Sex       := Male;
NewPatient.Age       := 28
   .        .        .
```

It's tedious to write and somewhat annoying to read the same record variable identifier, NewPatient, over and over again. We ought to be able to write NewPatient once at the beginning of our assignments and thereby allow each field identifier to become a full-fledged variable identifier. Pascal provides such a feature: the with statement. By means of the with statement we can simplify the above to

```
with NewPatient do
   begin
      LastName :=  'Ciradi     ';
      FirstName := 'Michael     ';
      Sex       := Male;
      Age       := 28;
        .        .        .
   end
```

The occurrence of the record variable NewPatient between **with** and **do** is equivalent to a defining occurrence of NewPatient's field identifiers as variable identifiers. The scope of the field-identifiers-qua-variable-identifiers is the statement which immediately follows the **do**. Normally, the field identifiers LastName, FirstName, and so on are <u>by themselves</u> no more variable identifiers than an array's index values 1, 2, ..., N are <u>by themselves</u> variable identifiers. But within the statement controlled by the with statement a field identifier alone (in the example, LastName, FirstName, and so on) may denote a variable of the indicated record (in the example, NewPatient).

The general form of the with statement is

**with** V1, V2, ..., VN **do**
   ⟨statement⟩

where the Vs are record variables. This statement is equivalent to

**with** V1 **do**
  **with** V2 **do**
     . . .
     **with** VN **do**
       ⟨statement⟩

Pascal's scope rules apply to this structure. Let's see the implication of these scope rules when we try to rewrite the Multiply procedure for complex numbers using the with statement. What follows is arrant nonsense.

```
procedure Multiply(    X : ComplexNumber,
                  {by} Y : ComplexNumber,
                  var  Z : ComplexNumber);
   {(a + bi)(c + di) = (ac - bd) + (ad + bc)i}
   begin
      with X, Y, Z do {ARRANT NONSENSE!}
         begin
            Re := Re*Re - Im*Im;
            Im := Re*Im + Im*Re
         end {with}
   end {Multiply}
```

Since there are three record variables with the same field identifiers Re and Im, how does the compiler know which record variable applies to each field identifier? It doesn't know, of course, what the author intended; but it applies the scope rules and decides that each Re and each Im denotes the corresponding field of Z, the innermost of the nested scopes. Thus the procedure as written yields the square of Z! This example should be a warning to the reader to use with statements--especially with statements that have multiple record variables--with circumspection. For this example you may use the with statement for either X or Y or Z. If you decide to use the with

statement for X, then the components of Y and Z must be referred to by
Y.Re, Y.Im, Z.Re, and Z.Im:

```
begin
   with X do
      begin
         Z.Re := Re*Y.Re - Im*Y.Im;
         Z.Im := Re*Y.Im + Im*Y.Re
      end {with}
end {Multiply}
```

Do you remember these assignments earlier in this section?

```
NewPatient.NextSession.Date.Day   := 15;
NewPatient.NextSession.Date.Month := 'Jun';
NewPatient.NextSession.Date.Year  := 1981
```

These assignments may be rewritten more compactly as

```
with NewPatient, NextSession, Date do
   begin
      Day   := 15;
      Month := 'Jun';
      Year  := 1981
   end
```

The following statements are semantically equivalent to the above
statement:

```
with NewPatient do
   begin
      NextSession.Date.Day   := 15;
      NextSession.Date.Month := 'Jun';
      NextSession.Date.Year  := 1981
   end
```

```
with NewPatient.NextSession do
   begin
      Date.Day   := 15;
      Date.Month := 'Jun';
      Date.Year  := 1981
   end
```

Which form should you use? Your choice should emphasize the program's
readability over your ease of writing it. The reasons for this are
economic as well as humane: more money is spent on debugging,
maintaining, and modifying existing programs than is spent on the first
writing of programs.

VARIANT RECORDS


Our descriptions of similar objects usually contain some identical
attributes; but these descriptions may also contain variant attributes.
To describe similar objects that may have some dissimilar attributes,
Pascal provides the <u>variant record</u>. The word "variant" is used here in
its sense of "a form or modification differing in some respects from
other forms of the same thing." To illustrate the record variant we'll
discuss an example from the population of patients. All patients have
some attributes in common: they have names, home addresses and phones,
ages, and next of kin; but some are inpatients and some are outpatients.
Inpatients have wards, resident physicians, and standard or special
hospital diets. Outpatients have day phones and appointments. Each
variant in the record is introduced by a case constant.

```
type
    String3  = packed array[1..2] of char;
    String10 = packed array[1..10] of char;
    String12 = packed array[1..12] of char;
    String30 = packed array[1..20] of char;
    AddressType =
      record
         Street    : String30;
         City      : String12;
         State     : String3;
         Zip       : integer
      end; {AddressType}
    Person =
      record
         LastName   : String12;
         FirstName  : String12;
         Address    : AddressType;
         HomePhone  : String10
      end; {Person}
    PatientRecord = {a variant record}
      record
         Patient   : Person;
         Age       : 1..110;
         NextOfKin : Person;
         case Hospitalized : Boolean of
            true:
               (Ward        : String3;
                ResidentDoc : String12;
                Diet        : (Standard, LowSodium, RestrictedCal));

            false:
               (DayPhone        : String10;
                NextAppointment : Appointment)
      end {PatientType}
```

There are several features worth noting about this structure:

**1.** The invariant part (called the "fixed part") always <u>precedes</u> the variant part. The fixed part in this example is composed of Patient, Age, NextOfKin. The variant part is the rest of the record.

**2.** "Hospitalized" is called the variant's "tag field"; Boolean is its tag type. Although the tag type is Boolean in this example, the tag type can be any ordinal type. The tag type must be an ordinal type <u>identifier</u>. Thus, if the tag's type were Status = (Inpatient, Outpatient, Expatient), you could not write

    **case** PresentStatus : (Inpatient, Outpatient, Expatient) **of**

for the first line of the variant. Instead, you would have to define Status earlier (as an ordinal type identifier) and then write

    **case** PresentStatus : Status **of**

**3.** The tag field (in the example, Hospitalized) is a bona fide field in the record. Assuming that ThisPatient has been declared to be of type PatientRecord, then the following statements are legal:

    ThisPatient.Hospitalized := true {an assignment to the tag field}

```
with ThisPatient do
   case Hospitalized of
      false:
         begin
            writeln('Home phone is ', Patient.HomePhone);
            writeln('Day phone is ', DayPhone)
         end;
      true:
         writeln('Ward is ', Ward,);
   end
```

The use of case statements to process variant records is very common and useful.

**4.** A change of variant occurs when and only when the processor assigns a different value to the tag field. Suppose that the value of ThisPatient.Hospitalized has been true, and then this assignment occurs

    ThisPatient.Hospitalized := false

At the moment of this assignment the fields associated with the past variant (Ward, ResidentDoc, etc.) are destroyed, and the fields associated with the Hospitalized = false variant (DayPhone, NextAppointment) are created (with undefined values). It's an error to refer to a field of the variant part that doesn't belong to the current variant. The case statement (see the example in 3 above) is a useful way

of avoiding such errors when processing variant records.
   **5.** Note the form of a variant:

                false:
                    (DayPhone        : String10;
                     NextAppointment : Appointment)

a tag-field value (false), followed by a <u>field list</u> enclosed in
parentheses. The tag-field value is sometimes called a case constant;
but you can't (and shouldn't) carry the analogy of the variant part and
a case statement very far. The variant selector (**case** Hospitalized **of**)
looks superficially like the beginning of a case statement; but the
variants of the variant part are considerably different in syntax and
meaning from the case list elements of a case statement. The variant's
field list defines the identifiers and types of components corresponding
to a particular tag field value; whereas the syntactical part in the
corresponding position in a case list element is a statement denoting an
algorithmic action. Note also the syntactical peculiarity of enclosing
the field lists in parentheses.
   **6.** A field list can be empty, signifying that the variant doesn't
need any fields in addition to the ones in the fixed part. For example,
if the hospital decides not to include any additional information on
outpatients (leaving this up to individual units or doctors), the
PatientRecord's variant part would look like this:

    **case** Hospitalized : Boolean **of**
        true:
            (Ward        : String3;
             ResidentDoc : String12;
             Diet        : (Standard, LowSodium, RestrictedCal));

        false:
            ( )

Thus, three additional fields are provided to describe the hospitalized
patient; but no additional fields are provided to describe the
outpatient. Parentheses must enclose every variant field list, even if a
field list is empty.
   **7.** It's permissible to have several tag-field values for the same
variant. For example, some psychiatric hospitals have day patients,
patients who spend their days at the hospital but sleep at home. The
same information is needed for inpatients and day patients. Assuming the
definition,

    **type**
        PatientType = (Inpatient, Daypatient, Outpatient, Expatient)

we could have the following variant record defintion:

```
type
    PatientRecord =
        record
            Patient   : Person;
            Age       : 1..110;
            NextOfKin : Person;
            case Care : PatientType of
                Inpatient, Daypatient:
                    (Ward          : String3;
                     ResidentDoc : String12;
                     Diet          : (Standard, LowSodium, RestrictedCal));

                Outpatient:
                    (DayPhone        : String10;
                     NextAppointment : Appointment);
                Expatient:
                    (KindOfDischarge : (Regular, Irregular, AMA);
                     DateOfDischarge : DateType)
        end {PatientType}
```

**8.** Note that the variant selector (**case** <tag field> <tag type> **of**) does not require a corresponding **end** as one might expect from the superficial similarity between the variant part and a case statement. The **case** in the variant part does not require a matching **end** because the **end** associated with **record** serves to terminate the variant part, which always follows the fixed part. There are never any fields after the variant part; therefore the end of the variant and the end of the record are synonomous, and one **end** suffices for both.

**9.** The field names in each variant must be unique identifiers throughout the <u>entire</u> record. Because a variant's field names are unique, they can be used in the program without reference to or support from the tag-field values. Therefore, the following references are syntactically correct.

```
with ThisPatient do
    begin
        Ward := '3DW';
        Diet := LowSodium
    end
```

and

```
writeln('Patient's day phone is', ThisPatient.DayPhone)
```

The use of a particular variant field name certainly implies a particular tag-field value; but some Pascal systems may not check that the reference to a variant field identifier is consistent with the tag-field value. Therefore, the preceding statements are acceptable syntactically; but they may be nonsense--that is, the first statement may assign a ward and diet to an outpatient, and the second statement

may print out the "day phone" of an inpatient. It's the responsibility
of the programmer to synchronize the tag-field values and the references
to field lists. For example, if a patient is being admitted to the
hospital, the tag-field value as well as the appropriate field
identifiers should be updated:

```
with ThisPatient do
   begin
      Hospitalized := true;
      Ward := '3DW';
      ResidentDoc := 'Meyer      ';
      Diet := LowSodium
   end
```

It's good practice to test the tag field rather than assume its value:

```
with ThisPatient do
   case Hospitalized of
      false:
            writeln('Patient's day phone is ', DayPhone);
      true:
         writeln('Patient is inpatient on ward ', Ward)
   end
```

As we mentioned in 3, the case statement is a common and useful way to
process variant records. Its systematic use can improve the security of
references to variant components.

10. If you examine the BNF definition of the record in the Appendix,
you'll see that the definition is recursive. That is, the variant
contains a field list which can contain another variant part. As an
example, consider the payment arrangements of the patient. The patient
may be personally responsible for paying the hospital, he may be a ward
of the state, or he may have hospital insurance. If he is personally
responsible, the hospital may require additional credit information. If
he has hospital insurance, the hospital will record the name of the
insurance company and the type of coverage. The following record
contains a nested variant record.

```
type
   BillToType = (Patient, State, Insurance);
   PatientRecord = {a variant record}
      record
         Patient   : Person;
         Age       : 1..110;
         NextOfKin : Person;
         case Hospitalized : Boolean of
            true:
               (Ward       : String3;
                ResidentDoc : String12;
                Diet        : (Standard, LowSodium, RestrictedCal);
```

```
                    case BillTo : BillToType of
                        Patient:
                            (CreditRating : CreditType);
                        State:
                            ( );
                        Insurance:
                            (Company  : String20;
                             Coverage : CoverageType));
                false:
                    (DayPhone        : String10;
                     NextAppointment : Appointment)
        end {PatientType}
```

Note the syntax for the embedded variant part. The embedded variant part
follows the fixed part of the Hospitalized = true variant; this follows
from the definition of a field list. Also note the parentheses in the
true variant; these parentheses also comply with the definition of a
field list.

There's one more topic to cover on variant records. If you examine
the definition of the variant part and the tag field in the Appendix on
the BNF description of Pascal, you'll see that the tag field is
optional!

```
<variant part> ::=
    case <tag field> <tag type> of
        <variant> {; <variant> }


<tag field> ::=
    <field identifier> : | <empty>
```

This may surprise you since we've been emphasizing the importance of
keeping the tag-field value up-to-date and the sound practice of basing
references to variant field identifiers on the current tag-field value.
Why, then, does Pascal make it possible to define a variant record
without a tag field? Because some situations don't strictly require a
tag field in the variant record. Here are two such situations:

**1.** The context of the program may unambiguously determine which
variant is intended.
**2.** The information that determines the variant is stored in another
place.

Both of these reasons imply that <u>eliminating</u> the storage for the tag
field and the overhead for maintaining and inspecting the tag field
value may be critical in some applications. Pascal is a practical
language with one eye on reliability through redundancy and another eye
on efficiency. Because Pascal is a practical programming tool it offers
a balance of compromises.

We suggest that you define all your variant records with tag fields,
until you find an imperative reason not to.

A PROGRAM TO CREATE A LINE INDEX


"**index**: a listing of names, places, and topics along with the numbers
of the pages or lines on which they are mentioned or discussed"


Suppose we require a program that will read a list of keywords, then
read a text, and then print out the following:

**1.** the same text with prefixed line numbers and,
**2.** following the text, an index of all the keywords with the numbers
of the lines on which the keywords can be found.

For example, this input (the integer 3 gives the number of keywords to
follow):

```
3
automata
computer
computers
Although there's an analogy between a cooking recipe and
a computer program, there are also distinct differences.
Programs for computers tend to be much longer and more
intricate than cooking recipes; and computer programs are
processed by ignorant and rigid automata, whereas cooking
recipes are usually processed by relatively perceptive,
versatile, and knowledgeable human beings. Therefore, the
author of a computer program must exercise a great deal
more care and precision in the preparation of his
instructions.
```

should produce this output:

```
01    Although there's an analogy between a cooking recipe and
02    a computer program, there are also distinct differences.
03    Programs for computers tend to be much longer and more
04    intricate than cooking recipes; and computer programs are
05    processed by ignorant and rigid automata, whereas cooking
06    recipes are usually processed by relatively perceptive,
07    versatile, and knowledgeable human beings. Therefore, the
08    author of a computer program must exercise a great deal
09    more care and precision in the preparation of his
10    instructions.

Line Index

AUTOMATA, 5
COMPUTER, 2, 4, 8
COMPUTERS, 3
```

The specification for this program suggests a loop that will read and process one line at a time. Accordingly, the top level might look like this:

```
Initialize the variables;
Read the keywords;
While there's any text remaining
    begin
        print the line number;
        read a line of text;
        print the line;
        for all the keywords
            check whether the keyword occurs on this line;
            if the keyword does occur on this line then
                store the line number for this word
    end
Print the index.
```

We may change our minds about some of this; but it gives us an initial grip on the problem. Everything looks straightforward enough so far.

Before we can refine this level, we must choose data structures to represent the input and output data. For each keyword we'll want to store the spelling, possibly the number of letters in the keyword, and, of course, the values we're looking for--the numbers of the lines that contain the keyword. This heterogeneous collection of data strongly suggests a record data structure for each keyword. Accordingly:

```
Word =
    record
        Length     : 1..MaxWordLength;
        Spelling   : array[1..MaxWordLength] of char;
        Occurrence : ?????
    end
```

How shall we represent an occurrence (a line number)? A straightforward approach would be an array of integers. We could fill in the components of the array with the numbers of the lines that contained the keyword. How many integer components would the Occurrence array require? Since a keyword could appear on every line, we would need as many components in the array as the number of lines of text. Furthermore, we would need an array like this for every keyword. If we had 100 keywords and 10,000 lines of text, we would require one Million components. That's one Million components of integer type. And that's a lot of random access memory. Of course, we could restrict the number of keywords on any one run. The user could develop his index with several passes. Or we could consider ten lines of text or even a page of text at a time. Most indexes are predicated on page occurrences, not line occurrences. That seems like a good solution--it would divide the number of components we need by about 50 (assuming 50 lines to a page). But is there a solution that doesn't require us to ask our client to change his specification?

We've been discussing the number of components needed to store the line numbers. But the subscripts of an array <u>are</u> numbers. So why not let the subscripts represent the line numbers; and then the components can simply be Boolean variables. Thus, if the 27th line contains the keyword, then

    Occurrence[27] := true

otherwise

    Occurrence[27] := false

With this understanding for the Occurrence array, we can represent a keyword as:

    Word =
        **record**
            Length      : 1..MaxWordLength;
            Spelling    : **array**[1..MaxWordLength] **of** char;
            Occurrence : **packed array**[1..MaxNmbrLines] **of** Boolean
        **end**

It's possible to pack eight Boolean variables into one byte of storage (one Boolean variable per bit). Admittedly, not every Pascal compiler will pack this tightly. Nevertheless, we've reduced the storage requirement substantially.

We're now ready to refine one of the lines in our top-level description: "Read the keywords." As we tackle the procedure for implementing this action we have to consider a problem that every automatic indexer must solve: how to deal with uppercase and lowercase letters. The human indexer recognizes computer, Computer, and COMPUTER as three instances of the <u>same</u> word; but the computer "sees" them as three <u>different</u> words. Here's a problem that the monotony of all uppercase letters circumvents. Therefore, we'll solve this problem in pattern recognition (for that's what it is) by converting all lowercase letters to uppercase letters before searching for keywords on a line. This suggests that we might as well store the keywords in uppercase form in the record. To this end we declare the following function for "capping" lowercase letters:

    **function** Cap(Ch : char) : char;
        **begin**
            **if** ('a' <= Ch) **and** (Ch <= 'z') **then**
                Cap := chr(ord(Ch) - 32))
                {ASCII only! More general conversions on pages 54 and 72}
            **else**
                Cap := Ch
        **end** {Cap}

Assuming the following declaration

```
var
    Keyword : array[1..MaxNmbrKeywords] of Word
```

here's the procedure to "Read the Keywords:"

```
procedure ReadKeywords;
    var
        I : 1..MaxNmbrKeywords;
        J : 1..MaxWordLength;
    begin {ReadKeywords}
        MinWordLength := MaxWordLength;
        for I := 1 to NmbrOfKeywords do
            with Keyword[I] do
                begin
                    J := 1;
                    Spelling[J] := ' ';
                    {The following assumes each keyword is flush left.}
                    while not eoln do
                        begin
                            read(Ch);
                            if J < MaxWordLength then
                                begin
                                    J := J + 1;
                                    Spelling[J] := Cap(Ch)
                                end
                        end; {while}
                    Length := J;
                    if Length < MinWordLength then
                        MinWordLength := Length;
                    readln
                end {for and with}
    end {ReadKeywords}
```

We've anticipated and solved two problems in this procedure without discussing them; so let's discuss them now.

First, why have we stored one leading blank at the beginning of each keyword? Because this leading blank is one way we'll avoid getting false matches of the keyword with embedded "keywords." For example, suppose that we're searching for the keyword "WORD" and that the text undergoing search is the procedure ReadKeywords (which you must imagine in all uppercase letters). The keyword "WORD" does not occur in the procedure; but if we searched for 'WORD' we'd get 11 different matches! The matches would occur on READKEY<u>WORD</u>S, MAXNMBRKEY<u>WORD</u>S, MAX<u>WORD</u>LENGTH, and so on. If we search for ' WORD' we won't get any of these false matches. However, we'll have to be careful when searching for a keyword at the very beginning of a line; we'll have to start the search on a new line with the <u>second</u> character in Spelling.

Second, why have we stored the minimum length of all the keywords in MinWordLength? We'll use this quantity for a test to avoid searching for keywords on lines that are too short to produce any matches. Actually,

the pitfall we must especially avoid is searching for keywords on lines
of length <u>zero</u>. These lines occur frequently in textfiles; they're blank
lines. One usually creates a blank line by executing "writeln," which
simply puts a line marker at the beginning of a line, resulting in a
line of zero length. We could simply make sure that a line has length
greater than zero before searching for keywords on it. By comparing the
line length with MinWordLength, we have a more efficient test that may
further reduce fruitless searching.

Now that we've refined the main data structure and designed a
procedure to read input data into this structure, we're ready for the
next step of refinement. Let's attack the central loop--the loop that
prints the line numbers, reads the lines of text, prints the lines, and
searches each line for keywords. When faced with a problem, try to think
of similar problems for which you know solutions. In Chapter 5 we saw a
problem quite similar to part of our current problem. That problem (page
100) was to add line numbers to a text while copying it from the input
file to the output file. The program to do this is on page 100. If you
examine this program, you'll see that most of it is directly applicable
to our current problem. The most crucial change we have to make is to
read the input into a line buffer while we're transferring the input to
the output. We'll call this array "LineBuffer." Later, of course, we'll
have to add the code to search for all the keywords on each line. Using
the heart of the program on page 100 for the heart of our present
program, the next refinement of the top level looks like this: (Notice
that we've replaced all the English sentences with procedure calls or
other Pascal statements.)

```
LineNumber := 0;
while not eof and (LineNumber < MaxNmbrLines) do
   begin {while not eof}
      LineNumber := LineNumber + 1;
      write(LineNumber :5, ' ':3);
      Cursor := 0;
      while not eoln do
         begin
            read(Ch);
            write(Ch);
            Cursor := Cursor + 1;
            LineBuffer(Cursor) := Cap(Ch)
         end;
      readln;
      writeln;
      LineBuffer(Cursor + 1) := ' '; {' ': word separator}
      LineLength := Cursor + 1;
      if LineLength >= MinWordLength then
         SearchLineForKeys(LineNumber)
      else
         for I := 1 to NmbrOfKeywords do
            Keyword[I].Occurrence[LineNumber] := False
   end {while not eof}
```

The previous code capitalizes all the letters assigned to LineBuffer. Since ReadKeywords capitalizes the keywords, the search for keywords on the line stored in LineBuffer will produce matches independently of the original case of letters. Note that we stored a blank in LineBuffer at the end of the line. This extension of the line with a blank in LineBuffer is essential to the operation of the search procedure, as you will shortly see.

We're now ready to refine the procedure SearchLineForKeys. Once again we'll exploit an earlier solution to a similar problem. The similar problem was to find a specified pattern in an array of characters. The solution to that problem can be found on page 142. That particular solution is cast in the form of a function returning the value of the index where the pattern begins. While this form is not appropriate to our present problem, the search algorithm, two nested repeat loops, is. Here's the search procedure for the present problem, borrowing liberally from the function on page 142.

```
procedure SearchLineForKeys(LineNumber : LineNumType);
   var
      I                : 1..MaxNmbrKeywords;
      J                : 0..MaxWordLength;
      K                : 0..MaxLineLength;
      Match            : Boolean;
      RealMatch        : Boolean;
   begin {SearchLineForKeys}
      for I := 1 to NmbrOfKeywords do
         with Keyword[I] do
            begin
               J := 1; {Skip leading blank for first match on new line}
               K :  0;
               repeat
                  repeat
                     J := J + 1;
                     Match := (Spelling[J] = LineBuffer[J + K - 1])
                  until not Match or (J = Length);
                  RealMatch := Match and
                  ((LineBuffer[J+K] < 'A') or (LineBuffer[J+K] > 'Z'));
                  J := 0;
                  K := K + 1
               until RealMatch or (K + Length > LineLength);
               Occurrence[LineNumber] := RealMatch
            end
   end {SearchLnForKeys}
```

What's the distinction between "Match" and "RealMatch?" Suppose that the Keyword is ' CH'; then we could get matches on ' CHR' and ' CHAR'. In order to distinguish real matches we have to eliminate these false matches. The false matches are characterized by letters following the embedded "keyword." The expression for RealMatch rules out those cases where Match is true but the next character in the line buffer is a

<u>letter</u>. This explanation also clarifies our storing a blank in the line
buffer following the line. In case the keyword occurs at the very end of
a line, we must make sure that the <u>next</u> character is not a letter. We
used a blank for that purpose; but any nonletter would have served.
    The print procedure, PrintKeywords, is relatively straightforward.
Here's the complete program for producing a line index.

```pascal
program LineIndexer(input, output);

const
    MaxWordLength   = 16;
    MaxLineLength   = 137; {Maximum line length + 1 for line separator}
    MaxNmbrKeywords = 100;
    MaxNmbrLines    = 10000;

type
    LineNumType = 0..MaxNmbrLines;
    Word =
        record
            Length     : 1..MaxWordLength;
            Spelling   : array[1..MaxWordLength] of char;
            Occurrence : packed array[1..MaxNmbrLines] of Boolean
        end;
var
    Ch              : char;
    Cursor          : 0..MaxLineLength;
    I               : 1..MaxNmbrKeywords;
    J               : 0..MaxWordLength;
    Keyword         : array[1..MaxNmbrKeywords] of Word;
    LineBuffer      : array[1..MaxLineLength] of char;
    LineLength      : LineNumType;
    LineNumber      : 0..MaxNmbrLines;
    MinWordLength   : 1..MaxWordLength;
    NmbrOfKeywords  : 1..MaxNmbrKeywords;
    N, K            : integer; {used for reading number of key words}

function Cap(Ch : char) : char;
    begin
        if ('a' <= Ch) and (Ch <= 'z') then
            Cap := chr(ord(Ch) - 32)
            {ASCII only! More general conversions on pages 54 and 72}
        else
            Cap := Ch
    end; {Cap}

procedure ReadKeywords;
    begin {ReadKeywords}
        MinWordLength := MaxWordLength;
        for I := 1 to NmbrOfKeywords do
            with Keyword[I] do
```

```
            begin
              J := 1,
              Spelling[J] := ' ';
              {The following assumes each keyword is flush left.}
              while not eoln do
                 begin
                    read(Ch);
                    if J < MaxWordLength then
                       begin
                          J := J + 1;
                          Spelling[J] := Cap(Ch)
                       end
                 end; {while}
              Length := J;
              if Length < MinWordLength then
                 MinWordLength := Length;
              readln
            end {for and with}
    end; {ReadKeywords}

procedure SearchLineForKeys(LineNumber : LineNumType);
    var
       K            : 0..MaxLineLength;
       Match        : Boolean;
       RealMatch    : Boolean;
    begin {SearchLineForKeys}
       for I := 1 to NmbrOfKeywords do
          with Keyword[I] do
             begin
                J := 1; {Skip leading blank for first match on new line}
                K := 0;
                repeat
                   repeat
                      J := J + 1;
                      Match := (Spelling[J] = LineBuffer[J + K - 1])
                   until not Match or (J = Length);
                   RealMatch := Match and
                   ((LineBuffer[J+K] < 'A') or (LineBuffer[J+K] > 'Z'));
                   J := 0;
                   K := K + 1
                until RealMatch or (K + Length > LineLength);
                Occurrence[LineNumber] := RealMatch
             end {for and with}
    end; {SearchLineForKeys}

procedure PrintKeywords;
    var
       L : 1..MaxNmbrLines;
       M : 0..6;
       Q : 0..MaxNmbrLines;
```

```
begin {PrintKeywords}
   writeln;
   writeln('Line Index');
   writeln;
   for I := 1 to NmbrOfKeywords do
      with Keyword[I] do
         begin
            for J := 2 to Length do
               write(Spelling[J]);
            for L := 1 to LineNumber do
               if Occurrence[L] then
                  begin
                     M := 0;
                     Q := L;
                     while Q > 0 do
                        begin
                           Q := Q div 10;
                           M := M + 1
                        end;
                     write(', ', L : M)
                  end;
            writeln
         end
end; {PrintKeywords}

begin {LineIndexer}
   readln(N); {N should equal the number of key words.}
   if N < 1 then
      writeln('The number of key words must exceed zero.')
   else
      begin
         if N > MaxNmbrKeywords then
            begin
               for K := 1 to N - MaxNmbrKeywords do
                  readln; {Skip the excess words and continue}
               NmbrOfKeywords := MaxNmbrKeywords
            end
         else
            NmbrOfKeywords := N;
         ReadKeywords;
         LineNumber := 0;
         while not eof and (LineNumber < MaxNmbrLines) do
            begin {while not eof}
               LineNumber := LineNumber + 1;
               write(LineNumber : 5, ' ': 3);
               Cursor := 0;
```

```
                while not eoln do
                    begin
                        read(Ch);
                        write(Ch);
                        Cursor := Cursor + 1;
                        LineBuffer[Cursor] := Cap(Ch)
                    end;
                readln;
                writeln;
                LineBuffer[Cursor + 1] := ' '; {' ': word separator}
                LineLength := Cursor + 1;
                if LineLength >= MinWordLength then
                    SearchLineForKeys(LineNumber)
                else
                    for I := 1 to NmbrOfKeyWords do
                        Keyword[I].Occurrence[LineNumber] := false
            end; {while not eof}
        PrintKeywords;
    end {else}
end. {LineIndexer}
```

EXERCISES

**1.** Define a record data type, PersonalData, with components last name, first name, social security number, data of birth, number of dependents, and marital status (single, married, divorced, widowed, remarried).

**2.** Declare a variable MyPersonalData of type PersonalData and assign the appropriate values to the components of this variable. Make the assignments with and without a **with** statement.

**3.** Consider problem 1 again. If the marital status is single, provide a field that indicates whether the individual has established an independent residence. If the marital status is not single, provide a field for the data of marriage and the name of spouse. If the marital status is divorced provide a field for the date of the divorce. If the status is widowed, provide a field for the date of the spouse's death. If the status is remarried, provide a field for the date of the previous marriage and its termination as well as a field for the date of the current marriage and the name of the current spouse.

**4.** Assuming the type definition, DateType,

   **a.** write a procedure to advance the date by 24 hours. Be sure to handle the number of days in February correctly;
   **b.** Write a procedure to advance the date by nine months.

```
DateType =
    record
        Day   : 1..31;
        Month : 1..12;
        Year  : 0..2000
    end
```

**5.** A record can represent a radar measurement:

```
RadarTarget =
    record
        Range     : real;
        Azimuth   : real;
        Elevation : real
    end
```

Write a procedure that converts a radar measurement to Cartesian coordinates. The conversion equations are:

```
X := Range*cos(Elevation)*cos(Azimuth);
Y := Range*cos(Elevation)*sin(Azimuth);
Z := Range*sin(Elevation
```

Assume that the Cartesian coordinates are components of a record defined as:

```
record
    X, Y, Z : real
end
```

**6.** Assume that a record variable named Target contains the Cartesian coordinates of an object. Write a function that receives the record Target as a parameter and returns the range to the target. The range can be computed from

```
Range := sqrt(sqr(X) + sqr(Y) + sqr(z))
```

**7.** On page 192 we defined a data type for representing rational numbers. Write a procedure that reduces a rational number to its lowest terms. A rational number is reduced to its lowest terms by removing common factors from its numerator and denominator. An effective way to do this is to use Euclid's algorithm to calculate the greatest common factor of numerator and denominator and then dividing both numerator and denominator by this factor. There are versions of Euclid's algorithm in chapters 2 and 7.

# 9. Dynamically Allocated Data Structures

THE NEED FOR DYNAMIC VARIABLES

In the two structured data types we've met so far, the number of component variables and the structuring method were <u>static</u>. The exception, you might object, is variant records. However, the programmer must completely spell out the variations ahead of time. In effect, the variant record is just a union of static data structures. The variation comes about through selection of predeclared objects, not construction of undeclared ones. Does Pascal provide a facility for dynamic data strucures--data structures whose size can expand or contract and whose actual structuring method is flexible, not fixed? The answer is yes. This facility is provided by one new data type, the <u>pointer</u>, which can link the dynamic components into a structure, and two new procedures, <u>new</u> and <u>dispose</u>, which can dynamically allocate and deallocate the components themselves. Before we describe these new facilities, let's motivate their introduction.

Consider the limitations of a Pascal array. Its size is fixed by the size of its declared index type; its structure is fixed by static associations among its components. By the latter we mean, for example, that A[1] precedes A[2], A[2] precedes A[3],..., and A[N - 1] precedes A[N]; i.e., the structure (static) is A[1], A[2], A[3],... A[N - 1], A[N]. If this structure does not suit us; if, for example, we want to change the <u>structure</u> to A[K], A[K + 1], A[K + 2],... A[N], A[1], A[2],... A[K - 1], we would be unable to do so. Of course, we could exchange the <u>values</u> in the array so that what was in A[K] was assigned to A[1] and so on. But notice that this involves exchanging <u>every</u> value in the array. What we wanted to do was much simpler: we merely wanted to make the substructure A[K..N] precede rather than follow A[1..K - 1].

For another example, assume that the following text is stored in an array:

Fourscore and seven years ago our fathers started a new country, born in liberty, and dedicated to the proposition that all men are created equal. Now we are engaged...

and that we wanted to modify this text to Lincoln's actual version:

> Fourscore and seven years ago our fathers brought forth on this
> continent a new nation, conceived in liberty, and dedicated to the
> proposition that all men are created equal. Now we are engaged...

In order to replace the incorrect text, we must shift all the
chararacters "in liberty...equal." toward the end of the array (to make
room for the additional text). The shifting process does not seem too
laborious here; but what if we were dealing with the whole Gettysburg
address and had to shift all of its text? What if we were dealing with a
whole book and wanted to insert one new line in the first paragraph?
Another problem can occur: what if the declared array is not large
enough to contain the inserted words? Obviously, we have unpleasant
difficulties when we want to insert data in an array structure. Deleting
characters from an array of text leads to other difficulties: we have to
make a "hole" in the array and then mark the hole. We can close up the
text to eliminate the hole in the middle; but then we create a hole at
the end. This storage is wasted. It would be desirable to return the
memory cells no longer needed to the general storage available for other
variables. By means of the standard procedures new and dispose, we can
create storage locations when we need them and "recyle" them when we no
longer need them.
     With the facilities of the data type pointer and the procedure new,
we can edit the Gettysburg address as shown in Figure 9.1 (a) and (b).
(In the figures in this chapter, the arrows represent pointers.) The
pointers link the components together to form a structure. The structure
is composed of chained records (Chunks) with this definition:

```
type
    Chunk =
        record
            Phrase : packed array[1..N] of char;
            Next   : Pointer {points to the next chunk}
        end
```

where Next, a pointer data type, addresses or otherwise indicates the
location of the next chunk.
     Notice the process by which we edit the text. We change the text in
the array part of the second record from "started a new country, born in
liberty, " to "brought forth on this continent a new "; and we create a
new record for the text "nation, conceived in liberty, " which won't fit
in the existing records. But there's another change we have to make to
the second record: redirect its pointer so that it points to the new
record which contains "nation, conceived in liberty, ". However, we must
be very careful about the sequence in which we assign values to
pointers. First, we must assign the current value of the pointer in the
second record to the pointer in the new record (so that the new record's
pointer field points to the record which contains "and dedicated to the
..."); and then we assign a value to the pointer in the second record

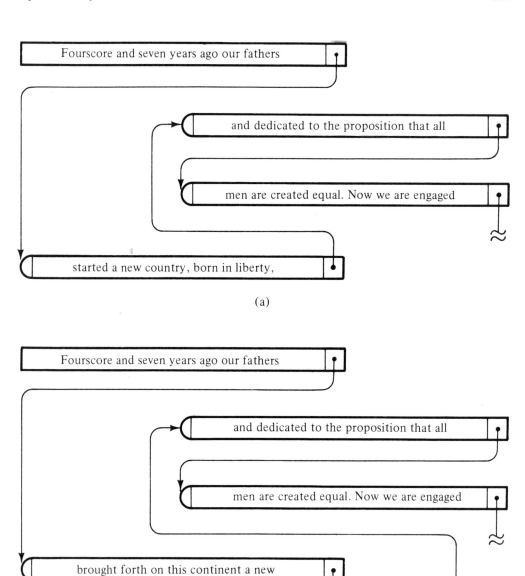

Fourscore and seven years ago our fathers

and dedicated to the proposition that all

men are created equal. Now we are engaged

started a new country, born in liberty,

(a)

Fourscore and seven years ago our fathers

and dedicated to the proposition that all

men are created equal. Now we are engaged

brought forth on this continent a new

nation, conceived in liberty,

(b)

**Figure 9.1** (a) Text before editing    (b) Text after editing

that makes it point to the new record. If we didn't follow this sequence of pointer assignments, we could wipe out the reference to the record that contains "and dedicated to the proposition that all " and lose that record and every record in the rest of the chain.

Let's review the steps:

**1.** Access the second record and change "started a new country, born in liberty, " to "brought forth on this continent a new ".

**2.** Recognize that the text requires more memory locations; therefore create a new record with the procedure new(P). This procedure creates a new record containing an array field for more text and a pointer field for linking the record to the next record in the chain. Both the array field and the pointer field are undefined. The procedure new(P) also assigns a pointer value to the pointer variable P. This pointer value points to the newly created record. You may think of this pointer value as the address of the newly created record. Because the new record has no identifier, this is the <u>only</u> way we can reference the newly created record--by the value of the pointer (stored initially in the variable P).

**3.** Assign the value "nation, conceived in liberty, " to the array field of the new record.

**4.** Assign the value of the pointer variable in the second record to the pointer variable (Next) in the new record.

**5.** Assign the value of P to the pointer variable in the second record.

Steps 4 and 5 link the new record into the structure.

## POINTER VARIABLES AND REFERENCED VARIABLES

A pointer variable consists of a set of values pointing to variables of a defined type. The cardinality of a pointer type is "unbounded"; in practice this means that the number of values belonging to the data type is undefined and limited only by the memory available for dynamic variables and their pointers. Every time the program invokes the standard procedure new, the processor creates a new pointer value--up to the point of exhaustion of the "heap" memory, the part of the memory from which the processor creates dynamic variables. The only operations available on pointer variables are assignment and the tests for equality and inequality (but not < or >).

Pointer variables can be passed to subprograms as parameters. Because the pointer type is simple (has no components), the result type of a function can be a pointer type. For example,

**function** FindWord(Word : String12; Start : Pointer) : Pointer

(where "Pointer" is a pointer type identifier) is a legal function heading. This function accepts two parameters, a target word and a pointer to the record in a linked chain where search for the word should begin. If Word = 'proposition ' and Start pointed at the first record in Figure 9.1 (b), then the function would return the pointer that points to the fourth record in Figure 9.1 (b).

Every dynamic data structure must have one or more terminal components. See Figure 9.2, which illustrates (a) a linear linked list and (b) a binary tree. The binary tree structure has many terminal components or "leaves." These components have pointer variables. What value should you assign to a pointer variable that currently points to no component? If we gave the target word "nation," for example, to the function FindWord and started the search at the first record in 9.1 (a), what value should FindWord return? To deal with situations like these, Pascal provides the standard pointer value **nil** for every pointer type. (The boldface type indicates that nil is a reserved word. But we shall not regularly boldface it in prose text.) A pointer variable with the value nil points nowhere.

We have two ways of indicating pointers with nil values in the figures in this section. One way is to print **nil** in the pointer field of the dynamic variable. This is the way we used in Figure 9.2 (a). The trouble with this way is that we get tired of printing **nil**s on the leaves of trees. Therefore, we provide a second way of indicating a nil value: simply make a large dot in the pointer field. This is the way we used in Figure 9.2 (b).

There's a difference between an undefined pointer variable and a pointer variable with the value nil. (In the figures in this section, we'll indicate an undefined pointer with a "?" in the pointer field.) Of course, it's always an error to try to use an undefined variable. It's not an error to use the basic operations on a pointer variable whose value is nil. In fact, the way to detect the end of list or a leaf of a tree, is to test whether the pointer field equals nil. It is an error, however, to try to "de-reference" a pointer variable whose value is nil. You "de-reference" a pointer variable by referring to the variable to which it points. You obviously commit an error if you try to de-reference a pointer variable whose value is undefined or nil.

The following is an example of the definition of a pointer data type and the data type referenced by the pointer, followed by the declaration of some pointer variables:

```
type
    Pointer = ^Item;
    KeyType = 1..maxint; {For example}
    Item =
        record
            Key       : KeyType;
            OtherData : {Whatever you wish};
            Next      : Pointer
        end;
var
    First, Last, Ptr : Pointer
```

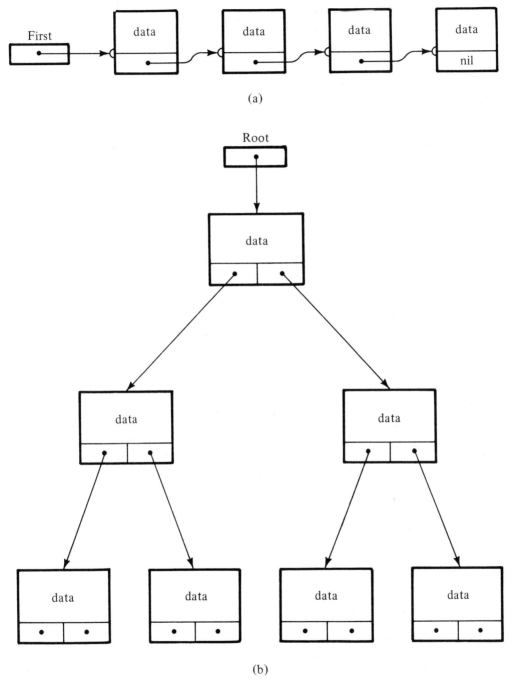

(a)

(b)

**Figure 9.2** (a) linear linked list  (b) binary tree

There are several points worth mentioning about this definition and declaration:

**1.** The word Pointer is not part of the Pascal standard vocabulary; it's a user-defined identifier. Another commonly used identifier for the pointer data type is "Link." You can use any legal identifier for the pointer type. The standard part is the "^" which you have not seen heretofore. (Some Pascal compilers may also allow "@" for those computers without the arrowhead character.) In BNF:

    <pointer type> ::= ^<type identifier>

You can read "P = ^T" as "P is a pointer (type) which points at variables of type T." That is, read ^ as "points at."

**2.** There is an oddity in the type definition which you may not have noticed: In the definition

    Pointer = ^Item

there is a reference to an identifier before it's been defined. This is forbidden in Pascal except for pointers and the data types to which they point. There's no way around having to use one or the other before it's been defined. For example, if we had placed the Item definition first, then the declaration "Next : Pointer" would have referred to Pointer before its definition. Pascal recognizes the problem and allows you to write "P = ^T" before defining T.

**3.** Every time the processor executes new(Ptr) it creates one of the variables to which Ptr points (i.e., a variable of type Item) and assigns to Ptr a value pointing to the new variable. But the processor does not automatically create a pointer variable in which to store the new pointer value. Therefore, the standard programming practice is to define the data type to which Ptr points to be a record with at least one pointer field. (As we have done with Item--see the component Next.) This way the processor creates pointer variables at the same rate that it creates pointer values. Consequently, we have an alternative definition of a pointer variable (but see 4):

"A pointer variable is a field in a record whose value addresses (points to) the location of some other record."

**4.** The preceding definition does not account for all pointer variables. We always declare one or more static pointer variables like First, Last, and Ptr. We require at least one such pointer variable to use as the first argument of new. And we usually declare other static pointer variables to point to, for example, the first item in a list (First), the last item in a list (Last), the first node of a tree (Root), and so on. Note that we declare these static pointer variables just as we do any other static variable. First, Last, and Ptr are not embedded in records.

**5.** Note that we haven't declared any variables of type Item in the above example. This is because variables of type Item are dynamic. We don't create dynamic variables by declaration; we create them by invoking the procedure new. The following definitions and declarations,

```
type
    KeyType = 1..maxint; {For example}
    StaticItem =
        record
            Key       : KeyType;
            OtherData : {Whatever you wish};
        end;
var
    StaticList : array[1..100] of StaticItem
```

create a "static list" of 100 variables of type StaticItem; whereas the definitions of Pointer and Item, the declaration of variables of type Pointer, and appropriate invocations of new(Ptr) and assignments to Next fields can create a dynamic list of unbounded length. We will now show you how to create such a list.

Since variables of type Item haven't identifiers, how do we refer to them? If P is a pointer variable bound to variables of type T, then P^ denotes the variable of type T currently referred to by P. Thus, in the example,

First^ denotes the variable of type Item referenced by First;
First^.Key denotes the Key field of the variable referenced by First;
Last^.Next denotes the pointer field of variable referenced by Last.

If Last does point to the last item, then Last^.Next should equal nil. If we've just invoked new(Ptr), then Ptr^.Next denotes the pointer field of the newly created variable of type Item.

To illustrate how to program a simple dynamic list, we will solve a somewhat academic problem: read an unknown number of integers from the input file and print them on the output file in exactly the opposite order. Thus the first number in should be the last out and the last item in should be the first out. Accordingly, this is called a FILO or LIFO list. Thus each new number we read should be stored first in the list. The heart of the program is two loops--a loop to read the numbers:

```
initialize the pointer variable First
read first number;
while there are any numbers remaining
   begin
      create a new variable to store number and pointer;
      store the last number read in the new variable;
      link the new variable into the front of the list:
         let the new variable point to the previous first variable;
         let First point to the new variable;
      read the next number
   end
```

and a loop to write the numbers in the reverse order:

> initialize the pointer variable Ptr to point at the first record in
> the list;
> while there are any items left in the list
>   begin
>     output the number in the record pointed at by Ptr;
>     advance Ptr to point at the next record in the list
>   end

Here's the complete program. Be sure that you can correlate the English
statements with the Pascal code.

```pascal
program ReverseSequence(input, output);
type
   Pointer = ^Cell;
   Cell =
      record
         Number : integer;
         Next   : Pointer
      end;
var
   Int         : integer;
   First, Ptr : Pointer;
begin
   First := nil;
   read(Int);
   while not eof do
      begin
         new(Ptr);
         Ptr^.Number := Int;
         Ptr^.Next := First;
         First := Ptr;
         read(Int)
      end;
   Ptr := First;
   while Ptr <> nil do
      begin
         write(Ptr^.Number);
         Ptr := Ptr^.Next
      end
end.
```

Note how we refine the statement "advance Ptr to point at the next
record in the list:"

> Ptr := Ptr^.Next

If Ptr points to a certain component in a list, after the above
assignment statement, Ptr points to that component's successor in the
list.

IMPLEMENTING STACKS WITH ARRAYS VERSUS
   IMPLEMENTING STACKS WITH DYNAMIC VARIABLES


One does not go very far in programming before encountering the data
structure known as a __stack__. A stack is a list which grows and contracts
in a specified way: items are added to and taken from the same end of
the list. A poker player often stacks his chips. When he wins a chip he
places it on top of the stack; when he bets a chip he takes it from the
top of the stack. Notice that the stack is a LIFO structure; the last
item in is the first out. Stacks are useful in certain kinds of
arithmetic used in both hand calculators and some computers. All
Hewlett-Packard calculators, for example, have a stack to carry out
their postfix (reverse Polish) arithmetic. If you've ever used one of
these calculators you're already familiar with the convenience of
postfix notation and stack storage which eliminate parentheses from
complicated expressions. In postfix notation, one enters the operator
__after__ the operands. Thus:

    X + Y becomes XY+
    (A + B)/(C - D) becomes AB + CD - /

The stack is used to store operands and intermediate results. When the
user enters an operand, or an intermediate result becomes available, the
processor automatically "pushes" it on the stack. When the user enters
an __operator,__ the processor "pops" the top item from the stack to use as
the first operand and then "pops" the new top item to use as the second
operand. Then the processor pushes the result of the operation on the
top of the stack.

As another example, suppose you're writing a program to format
unformatted Pascal programs (like the ones in the exercises on page 39).
One of the things you should do is align every **end** with its
corresponding **record, begin,** or **case.** How can you store and retrieve the
margins for the **end**s? One way is to build a stack structure called
EndMargin. After you calculate the margin for **record, begin,** or **case,**
push this margin onto EndMargin. (However, a **case** __within__ a record does
not have its own end; so don't push its margin onto EndMargin.) Then,
whenever you encounter an **end** in the input stream of tokens, pop the
EndMargin stack and use this value for the margin.

We can easily implement a stack of __fixed__ maximum length by using an
array to store the stacked items.

    **type**
        StackType : **array**[1..LastCell] **of** Items;
        IndexType : 0..LastCell {0 indicates an empty stack}

In the following subprograms, the value of Index refers to the top of
the stack (i.e., the last item pushed on the stack) except when the
stack is empty. When the stack is empty, Index is 0. Special action must
be taken when the caller tries to pop an item from an empty stack or
push an item on a full stack. The stack is full when Index = LastCell.

We'll assume that Stack is a global variable of type StackType. If there's more than one variable of type StackType, then the stack variable has to be passed to the following subprograms as a parameter.

The first subprogram we'll need is one that initializes the stack:

```
procedure InitializeStack;
   begin
      Index := 0
   end {InitializeStack}
```

We'll need a procedure for adding items to the stack:

```
procedure Push(X : Items);
   begin
      if Index < LastCell then
         begin
            Index := Index + 1;
            Stack[Index] := X
         end
      else
         StackOverflow {takes action that depends on application}
   end {Push}
```

We'll need a procedure for looking at the last item pushed on the stack:

```
procedure Top(var X : Items);
   begin
      if Index > 0 then
         X := Stack[Index]
      else
         StackUnderflow; {takes action that depends on application}
   end {Top}
```

We'll need a procedure for "popping" (observing and deleting) the top item on the stack:

```
procedure Pop(var X : Items);
   begin
      if Index > 0 then
         begin
            X := Stack[Index];
            Index := Index - 1
         end
      else
         StackUnderflow
   end {Pop}
```

And we may need a function for ascertaining the stack's state

```
type
   StateType = (Empty, Full, NeitherEmptyNorFull)
```

```
function StackState : StateType;
   begin
      if Index = 0 then
         StackState := Empty
      else if Index := LastCell then
         StackState := Full
      else
         StackState := NeitherEmptyNorFull
   end {StackState}
```

For comparison with the array implementation of a stack, we'll program a dynamic stack. The dynamic stack has only two states: (empty, not empty). We'll use the same names for the procedures so that you can compare the two implementations subprogram by subprogram. Assume the following global definitions and declaration:

```
type
   Pointer = ^StackCell;
   StackCell =
      record
         Data : Items;
         Next : Pointer
      end;
var
   Top : Pointer
```

The pointer Top will always point to the top cell of the stack; i.e., the last item pushed on the stack. Suppose that Items = integer and that first 1, then 2, and then 3 have been pushed onto the stack. Then the stack would look like Figure 9.3.

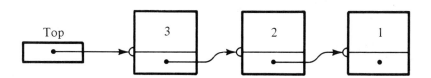

**Figure 9.3** Stack containing 3, 2, 1

Initialization is just as simple as before:

```
procedure InitializeStack;
   begin
      Top := nil
   end {InitializeStack}
```

Notice that instead of checking whether the stack storage has been exhausted, the dynamic Push procedure just blithely allocates more space.

```
procedure Push(X : Items);
    var
        Ptr : Pointer;
    begin
        new(Ptr);
        Ptr^.Data := X;
        Ptr^.Next := Top;
        Top := Ptr
    end {Push}
```

The execution of Push(4) would turn the stack in Figure 9.3 into the
stack in Figure 9.4.

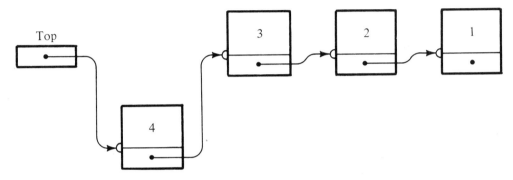

**Figure 9.4** Pushing 4 on stack in 9.3

```
procedure LastIn(var X : Items); {Functionally like Top on page 228}
    begin
        if Top <> nil then
            X := Top^.Data
        else
            StackUnderflow
    end {LastIn}

procedure Pop(var X : Items);
    var
        PoppedItem : Pointer;
    begin
        if Top <> nil then
            begin
                PoppedItem := Top;
                X := PoppedItem^.Data;
                Top := PoppedItem^.Next;
                dispose(PoppedItem)
            end
        else
            StackUnderflow
    end {Pop}
```

Notice that we programmed LastIn and Pop to return the _data_ stored in the top cell rather than a pointer to the cell. Whether we return only the data (which could be a record), or a pointer to the record in which we stored the data, depends on the application. Of course, if we returned a pointer to the stack cell, then we would have to eliminate the dispose statement in the Pop procedure.

The function for returning the state of a dynamic stack should have a name appropriate to its values. Therefore:

```
function StackIsEmpty : Boolean;
   begin
      StackIsEmpty := Top = nil
   end
```

To illustrate the use of these subprograms we'll apply them to the ReverseSequence problem given earlier in the chapter. Note that we can use the StackCell data type and the subprograms exactly as written; all we have to do to adapt the previous code is to define Items to be of type integer.

```
program ReverseSequence(input, output);

type
   Items = integer;
   Pointer = ^StackCell;
   StackCell =
      record
         Data : Items;
         Next : Pointer
      end;
var
   Top : Pointer;
   Int : integer;

procedure InitializeStack;
   begin
      Top := nil
   end; {InitializeStack}

procedure Push(X : Items);
   var
      Ptr : Pointer;
   begin
      new(Ptr);
      Ptr^.Data := X;
      Ptr^.Next := Top;
      Top := Ptr
   end; {Push}
```

```
procedure Pop(var X : Items);
   var
      PoppedItem : Pointer;
   begin
      if Top <> nil then
         begin
            PoppedItem := Top;
            X := PoppedItem^.Data;
            Top := PoppedItem^.Next;
            dispose(PoppedItem)
         end
      else
         StackUnderflow
   end; {Pop}

function StackIsEmpty : Boolean;
   begin
      StackIsEmpty := Top = nil
   end;

begin
   InitializeStack;
   read(Int);
   while not eof do
      begin
         Push(Int);
         read(Int)
      end;

   while StackIsEmpty = false do
      begin
         Pop(Int);
         write(Int)
      end
end.
```

This problem would have been awkward with an array implementation of the stack because we don't know how many integers the program has to read; hence we don't know what size to make the array.

IMPLEMENTING QUEUES WITH DYNAMIC VARIABLES

**"queue**  noun: a waiting line"

**"queue**  verb: to line up or wait in a queue"

Another useful data structure is the queue, a first in, first served structure. Senior items are served from the front of the queue; and newcomers are queued at the rear. We're all familiar with queues, having stood in them for registration in courses. The queue structure would be appropriate, for example, for patients on a waiting list who are waiting to be assigned to a therapist.

The representation of a queue with an array is somewhat more difficult than a stack. Besides having to keep track of both the front and rear of the queue, the programmer must deal with the fact that the whole queue can migrate to one end of the array. Because of this migration, the most efficient way to program a queue using an array is to regard the last component in the array as the predecessor of the first component; i.e., to regard the array as being wrapped around in a circular structure. This deals with the migration problem; but it does not deal with the insecurity that the length of the required queue may exceed the length of the array. (This same kind of insecurity hangs over an array implementation of a stack.) Because the dynamic implementation is more secure and more straightforward than the array implementation, we shall not show an array implementation of a queue.

We'll program the four procedures and one function required to initialize, manipulate, and inspect a queue, just as we did in the last section for a stack. This time we'll need two pointers, one to point to the front of the queue and one to point to the rear of the queue.

```
type
    Pointer = ^QueueCell;
    QueueCell =
        record
            Data : Items;
            Next : Pointer
        end;
var
    Front, Rear : Pointer
```

Figure 9.5 illustrates a queue that stores characters.

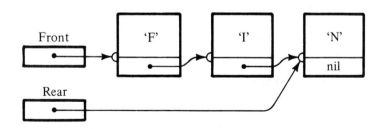

**Figure 9.5**  A queue storing characters

The procedure for initializing a queue is hardly more complex than the one for initializing a stack.

```
procedure InitializeQueue;
   begin
      Front := nil;
      Rear  := nil
   end {InitializeStack}
```

Figure 9.6 illustrates the extension of the queue in Figure 9.5. Since queue is a perfectly respectable verb meaning to form a queue or to put or get in a queue, we shall name the procedure for adding an item to a queue simply "Queue." Note that Queue requires a special action if Front is nil. Refer to Figure 9.6 as you study this procedure; this figure illustrates the stages in queuing another item in a nonempty queue. We suggest that you draw sketches like those in Figure 9.6 for all your list manipulations until you're fully confident of the meaning of all the assigning and linking statements. These sketches can help you avoid errors. Start practicing now by making a sketch of the situation when Front is nil; relate your sketch to the procedure's actions when Front is nil.

```
procedure Queue(X : Items);
   var
      Ptr : Pointer;
   begin
      new(Ptr);
      Ptr^.Data := X;
      Ptr^.Next := nil; {not necessary is some applications}
      if Front = nil then
         Front := Ptr
      else
         Rear^.Next := Ptr;
      Rear := Ptr
   end {Queue}

procedure Look(var X : Items);
   begin
      if Front = nil then
         QueueEmpty
      else
         X := Front^.Data
   end {Look}

procedure Serve(var X : Items);
   var
      ServedItem : Pointer;
   begin
      if Front = nil then
         QueueEmpty
```

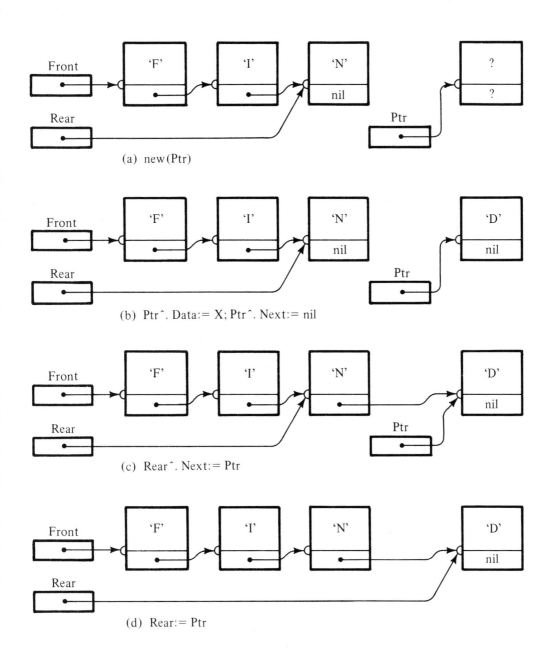

(a) new(Ptr)

(b) Ptr^. Data:= X; Ptr^. Next:= nil

(c) Rear^. Next:= Ptr

(d) Rear:= Ptr

**Figure 9.6**  Stages in queuing another item

```
    else
        begin
            ServedItem := Front;
            X := ServedItem^.Data;
            Front := Front^.Next;
            if Front = nil then
                Rear := nil;
            dispose(ServedItem)
        end
end {Serve}
```

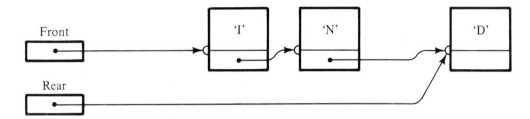

**Figure 9.7** Result of serving front item in Figure 9.6 (d)

Figure 9.7 shows the result of serving the item at the front of the
queue in Figure 9.6 (d). Note that we define a temporary pointer
variable, ServedItem, that continues to point at the record storing 'F'
after the Front pointer has been redirected to point at the record
storing 'I'. It's necessary to retain this reference to the former front
item so that we can dispose of it after serving its data and redirecting
Front to the next item in the queue.

```
    function QueueIsEmpty : Boolean;
        begin
            QueueIsEmpty := Front = nil
        end {QueueIsEmpty}
```

To illustrate the application of these subprograms we'll solve the
following problem. Copy the text on the input file onto the output file,
while preserving the line structure of the input file and prefixing each
line with the number of characters on the line. There's no limitation to
the number of characters on a line.

We can't write the input file directly onto the output file because
we have to prefix each written line with its character count. We can't
buffer the lines in an array because the line length is unbounded. We
can't use a dynamic stack because we must preserve the order of the
characters. That leaves us with a dynamic queue. (One could use an
internal file--but we haven't covered internal files yet!)

The program follows. It is built on a familiar and useful paradigm:
the program for copying text from the input to the output (page 75).

```pascal
program CopyWithPrefixedCharCount(input, output);

type
   Items    = char;
   Pointer = ^QueueCell;
   QueueCell =
      record
         Data : Items;
         Next : Pointer
      end;
var
   Front, Rear : Pointer
   Ch          : char;
   CharCount   : integer;

procedure InitializeQueue;
   ***Declare exactly as above.***

procedure Queue(X : Items);
   ***Declare exactly as above.***

procedure Serve(var X : Items);
   ***Declare exactly as above.***

function QueueIsEmpty : Boolean;
   ***Declare exactly as above.***

begin
   InitializeQueue;
   while not eof do
      begin
         CharCount := 0;
         while not eoln do
            begin
               CharCount := CharCount + 1;
               read(Ch);
               Queue(Ch)
            end;
         write(CharCount);
         write(' ');
         while not QueueIsEmpty do
            begin
               Serve(Ch);
               write(Ch)
            end;
         readln;
         writeln
      end
end.
```

BINARY SEARCH TREES

In our discussion of linked lists we gave two examples: stacks and queues. We did not program an ordered linked list, an omission you may have noted with disappointment. There was a good reason for our omission: even when it's ordered, we can conduct only linear searches on a linked list. This is a significant disadvantage of the linked list; the main reason for ordering items is to facilitate their rapid retrieval by binary search. In this section we discuss the <u>binary search tree</u>, a dynamic data structure that allows efficient binary search. The binary search tree has some of the characteristics of an ordered array, but like all dynamic data structures it allocates memory as needed and permits the insertion of new records without requiring a major reorganization of the existing data.

The idea of the binary search tree is to provide each record with <u>two</u> pointers, the left one leading to records with smaller keys and the right one leading to records with larger keys. Figure 9.8 illustrates a binary search tree whose keys are integers. This figure observes the convention of drawing trees "upside down", with the root at the top of the page and leaves at the bottom. Without some convention of orientation, the directions "left" and "right" would be ambiguous.

We built the search tree in Figure 9.8 from the following sequence of numbers:

57  48  76  53  25  87  70  73  51  37  95  17  55  84  66

The topmost node in the tree is called the root. The root is unique in that we can reach all the other nodes in the tree from the root. Note that the tree is composed of its root and two disjoint subtrees, a left subtree and a right subtree. The values of all the keys in the left subtree are less than the value of the key in the root; and the value of the key in the root is less than the values of all the keys in the right subtree. You can verify this easily in the binary search tree in Figure 9.8.

Binary search trees are recursive structures: every subtree of a binary search tree is also a binary search tree. Thus the left subtree of the whole tree (Figure 9.8) is also a binary search tree; its root key (48) is greater than all the keys in its left subtree (17, 25, 37) and less than all the keys in its right subtree (51, 53, 55). Because of the recursive structure of binary search trees, recursive subprograms are particularly appropriate for processing them. We'll demonstrate recursive processing of a binary search tree in a moment.

Note that we finally reach nodes in Figure 9.8 that are <u>terminal nodes</u> or <u>leaves</u>. The key values of the leaves in Figure 9.8 are 17, 37, 51, 55, 66, 73, 84, and 95. There are three kinds of nodes in a tree: the Root, intermediate nodes, and terminal nodes or leaves. The intermediate nodes in Figure 9.8 have the key values 25, 48, 53, 70, 76, and 87.

The terminal nodes are also binary search trees. (We want them to be

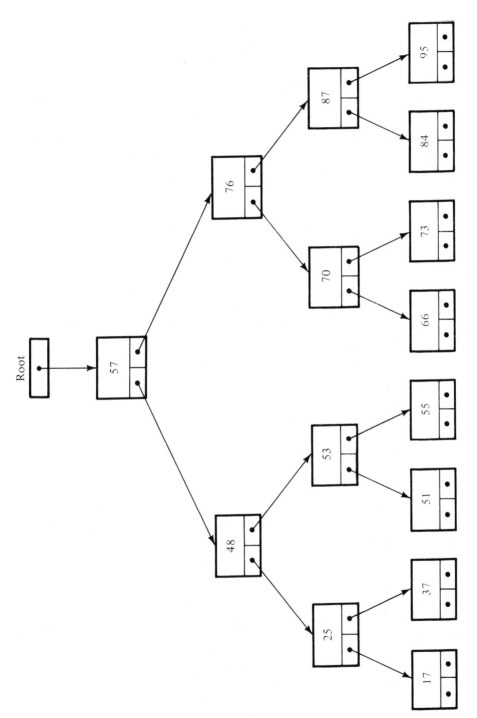

**Figure 9.8** Balanced binary search tree

so that our definition of a binary search tree applies everywhere in a
tree.) But the leaf subtrees have nil left and right pointers--that is,
the leaves have empty left and right subtrees. Our definition of a
binary search tree allows for empty subtrees:

**Definition**: A <u>binary search tree</u> T is a finite set of nodes that is
either empty or consists of a root-node with two disjoint binary search
trees called the left subtree and the right subtree and--

> 1. all keys in the left subtree of T are less than the key in the
> root-node T;
> 2. all keys in the right subtree of T are greater than the key in the
> root-node T;
> 3. the left and right subtrees of T are binary search trees.

Recursive definitions can give one a dizzy sense of circularity; but
they're quite useful with a recursive language like Pascal.

Exploiting the preceding definition, we'll develop a recursive
function for searching for a key in a binary search tree like the one in
Figure 9.8 or the one in Figure 9.9. One invokes this function with the
number sought and a pointer to the node where one wants the search to
begin. The function returns a pointer to the node where the number was
found. If the number was not present in the tree, the function returns
the value nil. The Root of the tree is the appropriate node at which to
start the search; for the tree's Root is the one node from which all
other nodes can be reached. Thus, to search for the node with the key
66, one would invoke the function with this function designator:

... Find(66, Root) ...

Here's the function in mixed English-Pascal notation:

```
function Find(Number : integer;
              {in} Subtree : Pointer) : Pointer;
   begin
      If Subtree is empty then
         Find := nil
      else if Number is less than Subtree's Key then
         Find Number in Subtree's Left subtree
      else if Number is greater than Subtree's Key then
         Find Number in Subtree's Right subtree
      else Number is equal to Subtree's Key so
         Find := Subtree
   end
```

where we've assumed the following definitions and declaration:

```
type
   Pointer = ^Node;
```

```
      Node =
         record
            Key   : integer;
            Left  : Pointer;
            Right : Pointer
         end;
var
   Root : Pointer
```

Here's the function in pure Pascal:

```
function Find(Number : integer;
              {in} Subtree : Pointer) : Pointer;

   begin
      if Subtree = nil then
         Find := nil
      else if Number < Subtree^.Key then
         Find := Find(Number, {in} Subtree^.Left)
      else if Number > Subtree^.Key then
         Find := Find(Number, {in} Subtree^.Right)
      else {Number is equal to this Subtree's root key so}
         Find := Subtree
   end
```

This search algorithm is efficient because the comparison of the sought number with the key at each node roughly halves the number of nodes remaining to be searched. At least this is true if the binary search tree is balanced. One is not always so lucky, however, to have an exactly balanced search tree like the one in figure 9.8. Later we'll discuss unbalanced search trees; i.e., trees whose left and right subtrees do not have the same number of nodes.

Our next task is to explain how to build a search tree from a file of data. Before showing you the procedures for building a search tree, we'll talk you through the initial steps of building the tree in Figure 9.8. This should help you to understand the subsequent code.

One starts with an empty tree. Initially, only the Root (a static pointer) exists, and its value is nil. We read the integer 57 and then start searching at Root for the appropriate place to insert this new key. Finding Root = nil, we create a new node, assign the pointer to this node to Root, assign 57 to the new node's Key field, and assign nil to the new node's left and right pointer variables. Next we read 48 and start searching at Root for the place to insert 48. Finding that Root points to a node whose key is 57, we compare the new key to 57 and decide that the new key is smaller. Consequently, we continue along the left pointer leading from the node with key = 57 to nodes with smaller keys. Finding that the left pointer is nil, we create a new node, assign the pointer to this new node to the left pointer variable in the node whose key is 57, assign 48 to the new node's key field, and assign nil to the new node's left and right pointer variables. Next we read 76 and start searching again at Root. Finding that Root points to a record whose key is 57, we compare the new key to 57 and decide that the new key is larger. Consequently, we continue along the <u>right</u> pointer leading from 57 to nodes with larger keys. Finding that the right pointer is nil, we create a new node, assign the pointer to this new node to the right pointer variable in the node whose key is 57, assign 76 to the new node's key field, and assign nil to the new nodes's left and right pointer variables. Next we read 53 and start searching at Root for the place to insert this key. Finding that Root points to a node whose key is 57, we compare the new key to 57 and decide that the new key is smaller. Consequently, we continue along the <u>left</u> pointer leading from 57 to nodes with smaller keys. Finding that the Root's left pointer points to a node whose key is 48, we compare the new key to 48 and decide that the new key is larger. Consequently we continue along the <u>right</u> pointer leading from 48 to nodes with larger keys. Finding that the right pointer is nil, we create a new node, assign the pointer to this new node to the right pointer variable in the node whose key is 48, assign 53 to the new node's key field, and assign nil to the new node's left and right pointer variables. Next we read 25...and so on.

We're now ready to show you a procedure to build a tree. Perhaps you noticed that construction of the tree involved searching the tree. In fact, each addition of a record to the tree was really a search followed by an insertion when the search found a node whose selected subtree was empty. Therefore, the procedure BuildTree calls another procedure named SearchAndInsert. Here's SearchAndInsert, followed by BuildTree. SearchAndInsert inserts one key in a specified subtree.

```
procedure SearchAndInsert(NewKey : integer;
                          {in} var Subtree : Pointer);
begin
    if Subtree = nil then
        begin
            new(Subtree);
            with Subtree^ do
                begin
                    Key := NewKey;
                    Left  := nil;
                    Right := nil
                end {with}
        end {then statement}
    else
        begin
            if NewKey < Subtree^.Key then
                SearchAndInsert(NewKey, {in} Subtree^.Left)
            else if NewKey > Subtree^.Key then
                SearchAndInsert(NewKey, {in} Subtree^.Right)
            else
                writeln(NewKey, ' is a duplicate entry.')
        end
end {SearchAndInsert}
```

```
procedure BuildTree;
   begin
      Root := nil;
      while not eof do
         begin
            read(NewKey);
            SearchAndInsert(NewKey, {starting at} Root)
         end
   end {BuildTree}
```

How does the pointer to a subtree actually get assigned to its parent
node's pointer variable? This is done through the mechanism of the
variable formal parameter in SearchAndInsert. Let's take as an example
the placement of the first key in the initially empty tree. BuildTree
reads the new key and then calls SearchAndInsert with the actual
parameters NewKey and Root. Note that NewKey is a value parameter, but
Root is a variable parameter. Thus, when SearchAndInsert operates on the
variable formal parameter Subtree, it simultaneously operates on the
corresponding actual parameter Root. Note what happens when
SearchAndInsert executes its statements. SubTree (same as Root) is nil,
so the procedure executes its then statement whose first statement is

```
new(Subtree)
```

which for this call is just the same as new(Root). And remember that
new(P) assigns to P the pointer to the new variable to which P is bound.
Thus the statement new(Subtree) assigns the pointer to the pointer
variable in the parent node.

Take as a second example the placement of the next NewKey, 48, in the
tree. This time BuildTree calls SearchAndInsert with the parameters 48
and Root, and this time Root is not nil. Therefore, SearchAndInsert
executes its else statement. Since NewKey (48) is less than Subtree^.Key
(57), SearchAndInsert invokes itself with the parameters 48 and
Subtree^.Left. On this recursive invocation, Subtree^.Left is nil, and
so SearchAndInsert executes its then statement whose first statement is

```
new(Subtree)
```

which for this call is just the same as new(Subtree^.Left) or
new(Root^.Left). Thus the statement new(Subtree) assigns the pointer
(that points to the new node containing the key 48) to the left pointer
variable in Root. It gets confusing for us human beings to go much
further with this. But no mind. We'll let the computer take it from
here. Now we understand it but really can't do it well. (And the
computer can do it well but can't understand it.)

It's particulary easy to write recursive algorithms for processing
binary search trees. This is because binary search trees are recursive
data structures; it's natural to process them recursively (and sometimes
incredibly messy to process them iteratively). The following recursive
procedure prints out--in order--the keys in a binary search tree.

```
procedure PrintTree(Subtree : Pointer);
   begin
      if Subtree <> nil then
         with Subtree do
            begin
               PrintTree(Left);
               writeln(Key);
               PrintTree(Right)
            end
   end {PrintTree}
```

Notice the order of the statements: print the left subtree; print the node; print the right subtree. This sequence of actions results in printing the keys in an ordered sequence because all the keys in the left subtree are less than the key stored in the node and the key stored in the node is less than all the keys in the right subtree.

Being able to treat a subtree as a single object is a great mental advantage. In general, when you write an algorithm for a binary search tree think of it as having just three parts: a left subtree, a node, and a right subtree. And don't forget to provide for those situations where one or both of the subtrees are empty. Delegate to recursion all the messy details, namely, that the left subtree may have many nodes and subtrees and that the right subtree may have many nodes and subtrees.

To print all the keys in a tree, call PrintTree with the parameter Root.

PrintTree(Root) {Statement that prints entire tree}

Note that we have written PrintTree to print out keys. "Real" programs would, of course, store more data in a node than just a key. We have not burdened our demonstration programs with these touches of realism, the details of which you can easily add. A realistic (but not conceptually more complex) PrintTree would print out other data associated with the key as well as or even instead of the key.

Although our illustrations have been with numerically ordered integer keys, our subprograms and code will generally work with lexicographically ordered alphabetic keys.

Let's review the subprograms we've developed. BuildTree will build a binary search tree starting from scratch. SearchAndInsert inserts additional items into a binary search tree without requiring major reorganization of the tree. Find conducts an efficient binary search for a specified key. PrintTree will print out the whole tree (or any subpart of it) in the ordered sequence of the keys. This package of subprograms constitutes an efficient set of programming tools for sorting, storing, and retrieving data. Because the binary search tree is a dynamic data structure which grows to meet the current requirements, one does not have to define a priori the size of the data structure. Because of its general efficiency for sorting, storing, and retrieving objects, systems programmers often use a package conceptually like this one to write compilers and data base management systems.

With all these wonderful advantages, are there any drawbacks, pitfalls, or cautions to be raised? There's one potential problem to watch out for: the binary search tree can degenerate into a linear linked list if the input data are perfectly ordered. In fact, the more ordered the input data, the more unbalanced the binary search tree. To see why this is so, assume a short sequence of ordered keys and consider where BuildTree places them. If the keys are in increasing order each successive key is placed in the right subtree of the preceding key. There will be **no** left subtrees and all the left pointers will be nil. In effect, all the left pointers are wasted. The procedure Find, for example, will still find a key; but it will find the key by inefficient linear searching.

In many problems data are known to arrive in a fairly random fashion. For example, the words in a piece of English text are lexicographically random. The social security numbers of individuals arranged in an alphabetical list are numerically random. The last names of individuals arranged in numerical order by social security numbers are lexicographically random. In these cases and many others like them you can reason that the data are in a fairly random sequence.

The following example should give you some insight into the effect of an unbalanced tree on search efficiency. This sequence of numbers was taken from a table of random numbers:

80  68  30  67  70  21  62  01  79  75  18  53  29  65  85

If we build a binary search tree with these integers, reading them in the order given, we obtain the tree illustrated in Figure 9.9. (It would be a good exercise for you to build this tree yourself.) Notice that the tree is unbalanced and that it requires **six** comparisons to find three of the keys (18, 53, and 65). The tree in Figure 9.9 has 15 nodes; so does the balanced tree in Figure 9.8. However, the maximum number of comparisons required to find a key in the balanced tree in Figure 9.8 is **four**. Furthermore, assuming that a search for all keys is equally likely, the average number of comparisons required to find a key in the balanced tree is 3.27; the average number of comparisons to find a key in the unbalanced tree is 4.07. On the average, then, search efficiency in the balanced tree is about 20% greater than search efficiency in this particular unbalanced tree. Although the search efficiency in the unbalanced tree is worse than the search efficiency in the balanced tree, it's still considerably better than search efficiency in a strictly linear list.

It's possible to build perfectly balanced trees; but the algorithms to do this are complicated. Professor Wirth (page 214, in "Algorithms + Data Structures = Programs") has shown that constructing a perfectly balanced tree instead of the "random" tree built by SearchAndInsert would produce an average reduction in search comparisons of about 39%. Usually, it's not worth it to try to achieve this level of improvement. Furthermore, there are several other techniques for improving search efficiency. For comparison of the balanced tree, our particular unbalanced tree, and a linear list, we offer the following table.

| Search Structure | Average Search Comparisons | Worst Case Search Comparisons |
|---|---|---|
| Balanced Tree | 3.27 | 4.00 |
| Unbalanced* Tree | 4.07 | 6.00 |
| Linear List | 8.00 | 15.00 |

*A particular example of an unbalanced tree. See Figure 9.9.

There are several techniques for improving the efficiency of binary search trees. For example, items that you know will be referred to frequently can be read into the tree earlier and hence appear nearer to the tree's root. Another technique is to keep a count in each node of the number of references to it. Infrequently referred to intermediate nodes can be deleted from the tree and reinserted. The deletion and reinsertion moves the item to a terminal node and generally further from the root. By this mechanism, more frequently accessed items migrate to the top.

We mentioned deletion of a node in the previous paragraph; but we haven't developed an algorithm for deleting a node from a binary search tree. Our tree-nursery package provides for growing trees but not for shrinking or pruning them. Deletion of a terminal node or any node with only one active pointer is simple; but deletion of an internal node with two active pointers is not so simple. Professor Wirth develops an algorithm for deleting nodes with a specified key on pages 210-211 of the previously mentioned book. (We heartily recommend this book. It provides a more advanced treatment of many topics in this book and covers many other topics as well. It's the perfect successor to this book. Written by the main creator of Pascal, it uses that language for the development of all its data structures and algorithms.)

## STORAGE FOR DYNAMIC VARIABLES

We started this chapter by stating that static structures like arrays are inconvenient for some problems because we can't increase the size of the structure dynamically (i.e., during the execution of the program). In this section we want to make a few concluding remarks about static storage versus dynamic storage and about allocating and disposing of dynamic storage for variant records.

Variables declared at the level of the main program are created at the initiation of the main program and exist throughout the execution of

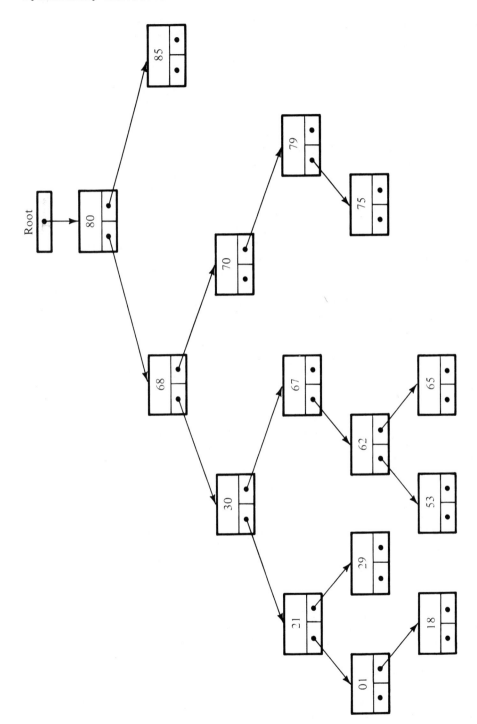

**Figure 9.9** Unbalanced binary search tree

the entire program. For that reason alone, the programmer should use local variables whenever their temporal existence during a block's activation is satisfactory. Subprogram blocks--procedure blocks and function blocks--use a stack for the storage of the return address, parameters (if any), local variables (if any), and the function's result (if we're dealing with a function). When the processor activates a subprogram, it uses a "stack frame" at the top of the stack for the subprogram data (return address, parameters, local variables, and function result). The processor releases this stack frame upon termination of the subprogram and return to the calling sequence. Note that subprogram local variables are "moderately dynamic" because they may be created and destroyed many times during the execution of the program; however, they are officially called static variables.

Dynamic variables, on the other hand, are created from and recycled to a storage area called the heap. The existence of a dynamic variable has no correspondence to the static block structure of the program. If new(P) is invoked during a subprogram block's activation, the variable to which P points continues to exist after the deactivation of the subprogram block (unless, of course, dispose(P) has been executed.) Thus, new(P) creates a new variable from memory in the heap; and dispose(P) releases memory back to the heap. These allocations and deallocations are independent of the block structure of the program. Local variables, on the other hand, have an existence strictly correlated with the activation of the block in which they're declared.

The computer does not have two random access memories, one devoted to the stack and another to the heap. That would be inefficient. There's one area of random access memory for both the stack and the heap. Typically, the heap starts at the top of this area and grows downward and the stack starts at the bottom and grows upward. The program runs out of storage when these two areas meet and try to overlap. The error message printed in this case (e.g. "RUN TIME STACK OVERFLOW") may implicate excessive stack growth when the real culprit is excessive heap growth. The main lesson to learn from this paragraph is that the heap is not a second marvelous source of random access memory. If your computer won't hold an array large enough for your problem, it won't hold a linked list large enough either.

The variables created by new(P) can be variant records. Suppose that one knows at the time of execution of new(P) exactly which variant is needed and knows with certainty that this variant won't change for the entire lifetime of the record. Suppose, further, that this variant has fewer components than other variants. Is there any way to take advantage of this knowledge and create a record with the smaller variant? If there were a way, then we could save storage. If there is no way, then the variant record must be created with enough storage to accommodate the largest variant. The answer to the question is yes; Pascal provides a version of the procedure new() which allows one to specify the variant for which the record should be created. There's a matching version of dispose to destroy such a record. The idea is simply to specify the relevant tag-field value immediately after the pointer variable in the procedure statement new(). Here's an example:

```
type
    PartOfSpeech = (Article, Verb, Adverb, Noun, Adjective)
    TenseType = (Present, Past, Future, PresentPerfect, PastPerfect,
                 FuturePerfect);
    Pointer = ^Word;
    Word =
        record
            Spelling : packed array[1..12] of char;
            case Category : PartOfSpeech of
                Article:
                    (Definite : Boolean);
                Verb:
                    (Main       : Boolean;
                     Regular    : Boolean;
                     Tense      : TenseType;
                     Voice      : (Active, Passive);
                     Mood       : (Imperative, Subjunctive, Indicative);
                     Person     : (First, Second, Third);
                     Number     : (Singular, Plural);
                     case Transitive of
                         false:
                             ( );
                         true:
                             (Object : packed array[1..12] of char));
                Noun:
                    ET CETERA;
        end;
var
    P : Pointer
```

We don't have to complete this record to illustrate our point. Notice
the great difference in storage required for the variants Article and
Verb. Suppose that we have just read the definite article 'the' and want
to create storage for it. If we write "new(P)", the processor will
create a variable of type Word with enough storage for the largest
variant, Verb. This storage will be largely wasted. If we analyze the
part of speech before creating the new variable we can generate a
variant record of the appropriate size:

```
case Category of
    Article:
        begin
            new(P, Article);
            P^.Category := Article
        end;
    Verb:
        begin
            new(P, Verb);
            P^.Category := Verb
        end;
```

```
      Adverb:
        begin
          new(P, Adverb);
          P^.Category := Adverb
        end;
      Noun:
        ET CETERA;
  end
```

Note that we have assigned the appropriate tag-field value to the tag field in the above case statement. It's necessary for the programmer to do this because the procedure new(P, <tag-field value>) does not assign the tag field value for the programmer (even though it could).

The programmer can list several tag-field values in the new statement. For example, suppose that the program is creating storage for an intransitive verb. Intransitive verbs can be stored with less memory because no storage is required for the verb's object. Therefore, creating the variable with Transitive = false will save storage. One does this by listing in succession all the applicable tag-field values:

new(P, Verb, false)

In summary, new(P, T1, T2, ..., Tn) allocates a variant record variable with fixed variants corresponding to the listed tag-field values. The tag-field values must be listed in the same order as they occur in the record definition and none may be omitted--except trailing tag field values may be omitted. To dispose of a record so created, one must use the procedure dispose(P, T1, T2, ..., Tn) with the same set of tag-field values that were used to create the record.

WARNING: There are limitations on the operations that can be performed on a referenced variable that has been created by the special form of new:

It is an error to use these variables as operands in an expression.

It is an error to use these variables in an assignment statement.

It is an error to use these variables as actual parameters.

EXERCISES

1. In the line indexer program in chapter 8, we represented the occurrences of a given word on the sequence of lines as a packed array of Boolean variables. As an alternative we could use a linked list (a queue) for the numbers of the lines on which the word can be found. The new type definitions could be similar to the following:

```
type
   Pointer = ^QueueCell;
   QueueCell =
      record
         LineNumber : 0..MaxNmbrLines;
         Next       : Pointer
      end;

   QueueOfLineNumbers =
      record
         Front, Rear : Pointer
      end;

   Word =
      record
         Length     : 1..MaxWordLength;
         Spelling   : array[1..MaxWordLength] of char;
         Occurrence : QueueOfLineNumbers
      end
```

Reprogram LineIndexer with this alternative representation of
Occurrence. You can use the subprograms developed in this chapter for
operating on a queue. One of the changes you'll have to make is to
replace

```
   Occurrence[LineNumber] := RealMatch
```

with

```
   if RealMatch then
      Queue(LineNumber)
```

Be sure you make all the definitions and declarations clearly and
tersely.

**2.** Write a function that returns the Sum of all the integers stored
in a stack.

**3.** Write a program to evaluate a reverse Polish formula, using a
stack. Assume that the reverse Polish formula is available as a sequence
of symbols on the input file. Each symbol is either an operand (a value)
or an operator (+, -, *, /). The following algorithm may be used:
Examine the next symbol. If it's a value (number), push it onto the
stack. If it's an operator, pop the top two items off the stack, perform
the operation, and push the result back on the stack. When you've
finished reading and processing the last symbol on the input file, the
correct answer will be on top of the stack.

**4.** The line indexer program in chapter 8 used an array of words to
store the keywords. The search for occurrences of a keyword on a line

was conducted by taking each keyword in turn and checking whether it occurred on the current line. It would be more efficient to read the keywords into a binary search tree, and then process a line by reading it word by word, and searching the binary search tree for the occurrence of each word on the line. Reprogram LineIndexer using this more efficient approach. Be sure that the keywords are not submitted in ordered sequence.

5. By using a sentinel, we can increase the efficiency of the subprograms for finding a key or inserting a key in a binary search tree. If, instead of assigning **nil** to every leaf in the tree, we assign the pointer to the same, identical sentinel, then we can simplify the termination condition by assigning the value sought to the sentinel key field. For example, here's the resulting simplification of the procedure Find from page xxx:

```
function Find(Number : integer;
              {in} Subtree : Pointer) : Pointer;
  begin
    if Number < Subtree^.Key then
       Find := Find(Number; {in} Subtree^.Left)
    else if Number > Subtree^.Key then
       Find := Find(Number; {in} Subtree^.Right)
    else
       Find := Subtree
  end
```

The calling sequence must assign the number sought to the Sentinel's key field before each invocation of Find. For example, this calling sequence,

```
Sentinel^.Key := X;
Ptr := Find(X; Root)
```

results in Ptr containing a pointer to a node with Key = X. If Ptr = Sentinel, then the key cannot be found in the tree.

Make the required changes to BuildTree, SearchAndInsert, and PrintTree so that they use the Sentinel for termination rather than the value **nil.**

# 10. Structured Data Type 3: The File

WHY HAVE A SEQUENTIAL FILE DATA TYPE?

Pascal's sequential file data type is a perfect abstraction of magnetic tape storage, paper tape storage, or card deck storage. However, the abstraction is more general than these devices and can be used to represent other devices. Indeed, Pascal represents all its input and output operations as manipulations of sequential files. Let's examine the notion of a sequential file to see why it's so generally useful.

The structured data type "file" is an abbreviation for sequential file. It's unfortunate that Professor Wirth shortened "sequential file" to "file" rather than "sequence." The term "sequence" describes the data structure better than the term "file." In BNF notation a sequence of Items is simply:

    {Item}

Remember that the curly brackets signify the repetition of the enclosed symbol zero or more times. Here's a common sequence, the empty sequence:

    <>

(During this discussion we'll enclose sequences in angle brackets.) The empty sequence corresponds to a deck of unpunched cards, a reel of erased tape, or a console keyboard whose buttons have not been depressed. In fact, every storage tape that is not chockablock full can be divided into two parts: the written part followed by an empty sequence.

Suppose we are dealing with a sequence of characters. Then we can append one character to the above sequence and obtain this sequence:

    <M>

We can continue appending characters to the sequence and see it grow:

⟨My⟩, ⟨My ⟩, ⟨My d⟩, ⟨My do⟩, ⟨My dog⟩

Suppose that we have another sequence:

⟨, Spot⟩

and we want to concatenate the first and second sequences. If we're limited to the primitive operations of reading and appending one item at a time, then we have to concatenate the two sequences by getting each successive character from the second sequence and putting it at the end of the first sequence. In fact, there's a rule about putting items on files: you can put them only at the end of the existing nonempty sequence; in other words, at the beginning of the trailing empty sequence.

```
⟨, Spot⟩      ⟨My dog⟩
⟨, Spot⟩ --> ⟨My dog,⟩
⟨,_Spot⟩ --> ⟨My dog, ⟩
⟨, Spot⟩ --> ⟨My dog, S⟩
⟨, Spot⟩ --> ⟨My dog, Sp⟩
⟨, Spot⟩ --> ⟨My dog, Spo⟩
⟨, Spot⟩ --> ⟨My dog, Spot⟩
```

We picked a sequence of characters for our illustration; but a sequential file can consist of a sequence of components of any data type. The only limitations are that the components must all be of the same data type and components cannot be files themselves.

If we define a file as a sequence of **strings** (of length 6), then we can concatenate ⟨My dog⟩ and ⟨, Spot⟩ with one operation. Notice that we would still be getting and putting one item; but now the Item and file would be defined this way:

```
type
    Item = packed array[1..6] of char;
var
    F : file of Item
```

In the first example the Item and file were defined this way:

```
var
    G : file of char
```

The definition of a sequential file sounds something like the definition of an array: a file data type is a structured type consisting of a sequence of components all of the same type. But there are profound differences. The definition of a file does not define the number of its components--a file's size is theoretically unlimited. This corresponds to the abstract theory that the length of a sequence is unlimited and to the reality that most data processing centers have an unlimited supply of magnetic tape or disk storage. An array's size, on the other hand, is specified and strictly limited.

The file is a sequential access structure. To find the 5,000th component in a sequential file of 10,000 components, you have to reset the file to the beginning and read the 4,999 components that precede the 5,000th. To access the 5,000th component in an array A, you merely write A[5000]. Computing systems do have random-access files today; they correspond to the addressable disks available on the smallest as well as the largest computers. Standard Pascal does not provide a random-access file facility. Many of the extensions to standard Pascal do, however.

Sequential files are important for storing and archiving computer generated information. Sequential files represent the external memory of the computer (at least the sequential part of it). The external memory is very important because of the limitations and high cost of the computer's internal memory. The internal memory is volatile (loss of power may result in loss of internal data); precious (no user can occupy it for long); and relatively small (it cannot hold very large volumes of data). Therefore, files are very important.

It should be clear that the sequential file is a rather general data structure. A file of char (extended to include line markers and an end-of-file indicator) can accommodate all of the human being's communication with the computer and a great deal of the computer's communication with its peripheral devices.

## CREATING (WRITING) A FILE

Unlike the other data structures of Pascal, a sequential file can be in only one mode at a time: a write mode or a read mode. This is a logical abstraction of many of the devices we represent with sequential files. For example, a paper tape reader/punch is either reading a tape or punching a tape. One does not intermingle reading and punching a paper tape. An audio cassette player/recorder (these devices are sometimes used for external storage for personal computers) is either playing or recording. There are very complex problems of registration, positioning, and mode switching when one tries to intermingle reading and writing on the same run. When it isn't physically impossible, it's physically impractical. Therefore, our first point: a sequential file is either in the read mode or in the write mode—never both.

Before we talk about putting a file in the write mode and writing on it, we have to establish what part of the file is available for writing. Obviously, the whole file is never available: it's too big; it's theoretically of unlimited length. If we think of a physical device, for example a tape drive, then we can see that there's always just one little piece of the tape available: the little piece just under the recording head. But we don't want to get too specific and concrete: then our data abstraction won't lift us above the details we wish to avoid.

The abstraction we want is the following one. Whenever we declare a file variable we automatically create a little window on the file which

gives us access to exactly one component of the file. We call this
window the "buffer variable." What data type is the buffer variable?
Since it contains one component of the file, it has to be the data type
of the file components. Thus, the following declaration:

**var**
   F : **file of** T

automatically creates a buffer variable of type T. We denote the buffer
variable by this symbol:

  F^ {This is the way we denote the file buffer variable.}

Summarizing the buffer variable, we can directly access only one
component of the file variable at any time. We call this component the
current file component. Pascal represents the current file component by
the file's <u>buffer variable</u>. (See Figure 10.1.)

Although most of the examples in this chapter are relatively simple,
file buffer variables can represent sophisticated structured variables.
Here's an example.

**type**
    Status = (single, married);
    String = **packed array**[1..12] **of** char;
    Person =
      **record**
         LastName, FirstName : String;
         Age : 0..105;
         **case** MaritalStatus : Status **of**
            Single:
              ( );
            Married:
              (NameOfSpouse : String)
      **end;**
**var**
    Alumni : **file of** Person

The buffer variable is Alumni^; its type is Person, a variant record.

We will now describe how to create a file. Assume the following
declarations:

**var**
    Item : SomeType;
    F   : **file of** SomeType;
    Ch  : char

We initiate the process of generating a new file by invoking the
standard procedure <u>rewrite</u>. This procedure discards the current value of
F and makes the function eof(F) become true. In other words, the file
now contains the empty sequence. (This is like erasing and rewinding a

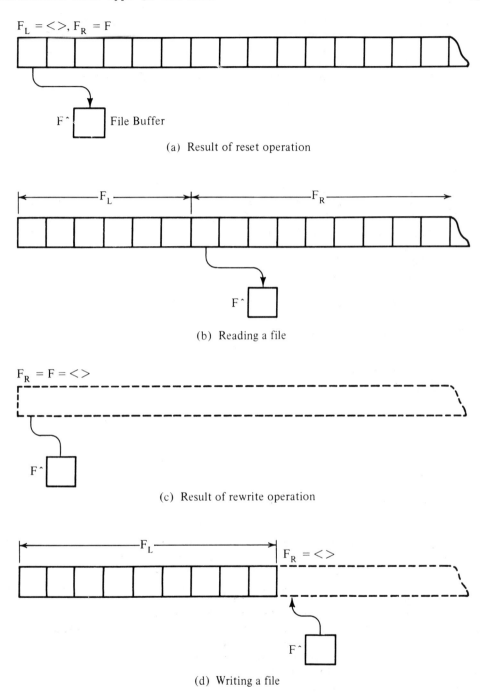

$F_L = <>, F_R = F$

$F\char`^$  File Buffer

(a) Result of reset operation

$F_L$    $F_R$

$F\char`^$

(b) Reading a file

$F_R = F = <>$

$F\char`^$

(c) Result of rewrite operation

$F_L$    $F_R = <>$

$F\char`^$

(d) Writing a file

**Figure** 10.1 Operations on a sequential file, $F = F_L F_R$

magnetic tape.) Obviously, you cannot apply the procedure rewrite to any
file that cannot be written upon (e.g., keyboard, card reader, paper
tape reader). Do not apply rewrite to the file output--the compiler
provides this operation for the programmer.

We append a new component to the end of the file F by assigning the
desired value of the component to the buffer variable F^ and then
calling the standard procedure put.

```
F^ := Item;
put(F)
```

If eof(F) is not true prior to the execution of put(F), an error will
occur. (Remember that rewrite(F) made eof(F) true.) Put(F) appends the
value of the buffer variable F^ to the file F. Executing put(F) leaves
eof(F) true and leaves the value of F^ undefined. Thus, executing two
put(F)s in succession, without an intervening assignment to F^,
constitutes an error.

The shorter way of writing the assignment to F^ and the subsequent
put(F) statement is

```
write(F, Item)    {This is equivalent to: F^ := Item; put(F)}
```

The following code copies the values of an array A onto the file F.

```
rewrite(F);
for J := 1 to N do
    begin
        F^ := A[J];
        put(F)
    end
```

INSPECTING (READING) A FILE


We initiate reading a file by calling the standard procedure reset.
This procedure resets the current position of the file to F's beginning
and assigns the first component of F to the buffer variable F^. If F is
empty, eof(F) will be true and F^ will be undefined. If eof(F) is false,
then the standard procedure get(F) advances the current file position to
the next component and assigns this component to the buffer variable F^.
If there is no next component, then execution of get(F) causes eof(F) to
become true and F^ to be undefined. An error will result if the
processor executes get(F) after eof(F) becomes false.

The following function illustrates the reading and processing of a
file. Notice that the file parameter F is a variable parameter. We
mentioned the requirement to pass file parameters as variable parameters
in chapter 7. If a file parameter were passed to a subprogram as a value
parameter, then the processor would have to make a copy of the complete

contents of the file upon activation of the subprogram. This could obviously be a very time-consuming operation. For this reason, Pascal stipulates that all file parameters should be variable parameters.

```
function TotalFile(var F : FileOfReals) : real;
    var
        Total, X : real;
    begin {TotalFile}
        Total := 0;
        reset(F);
        while not eof(F) do
            begin
                X := F^;
                Total := Total + X;
                get(F);
            end;
        TotalFile := Total
    end {TotalFile}
```

Pascal offers a shorter way of writing the statement that assigns the value of the file buffer to another variable and the statement that advances the current file position to the next component and assigns this component to the buffer variable:

```
read(F, Item)   {This is equivalent to: Item := F^; get(F)}
```

In general, use the write and read forms rather than the more primitive operations. There are situations, however, where the primitive operations are convenient: for example, get(F) allows you to "look ahead" without assignment to Item, but read(F, Item) does not.

## COPYING AND MODIFYING FILES

We already discussed copying textfiles in chapter 4. We will not repeat that discussion here.

Copying files is a frequent operation in data processing. For example, one rarely modifies an original file: if something went wrong during the modification, the entire data file could be destroyed. Therefore, one usually makes a copy of the file and performs the modification on the copy. If all goes well during the modification, then the modified copy may be substituted for the original file.

Furthermore, remember that it's not possible to alternate between reading and writing during the accessing of a sequential file: during a scan the file is either in the read mode or the write mode. Thus, we can't alter a single component of a file, leaving other components unwritten, by simply reading all the components before the target component and then rewriting just the target component. (This, of course, is perfectly feasible in an array.) To alter a certain component in a file, we must make a copy of the entire file, modifying the particular component as we are copying it.

As an example of file copying, let's consider the following situation: a retail business maintains the names and addresses of its customers on punched cards with this format:

        columns   1-15   last name
        columns  16-26   first name
        columns  27-30   title
        columns  31-51   street address
        columns  52-63   city
        columns  64-66   state
        columns  67-71   zip code

For example, here are a few cards:

Alexander       Donald       Dr   2832 Wilkerson Rd     Vienna       VA 22090
Blair-Smith     Charlene     Ms   3615 Hereford St      St. Louis    MO 63103
Costello        Michael      Mr   33 Aldenham Lane      Columbia     MD 21146

The company wants to convert the storage medium from punched cards to magnetic tape. We will write a program that reads the punched cards and creates a file (magnetic) of customers.

The appropriate algorithm for the program is an iterative loop:

**while not** eof(CardFile) **do begin**
    read all the fields of data (character by character) on this card;
    transfer these data to the new file's buffer variable;
    put the contents of the buffer variable on the new file;
    skip to the beginning of the next card or line
**end** {while loop}

We must refine this top-level statement by defining the data type to which we'll assign the card data. Often the first step in designing a program is defining the data structures. If we define the data structures carefully, the appropriate control structures will usually be obvious. We have a clear preference in this case: the customer data should be stored in records with seven fields:

```
type
   Records =
      record
         LastName   : packed array[1..15] of char;
         FirstName  : packed array[1..11] of char;
         Title      : packed array[1..4] of char;
         Street     : packed array[1..21] of char;
         City       : packed array[1..12] of char;
         State      : packed array[1..3] of char;
         ZipCode    : packed array[1..5] of char
      end
```

Accordingly, our file variable has the following declaration:

```
var
    RecordFile : file of Records
```

In the refinement of the pseudo code in the while loop, we must be suspicious about the completeness of the data on the cards. A card may be missing some fields of data or a card may terminate prematurely. For example, we want to store blanks in the new file's record fields for any card field data that is missing, and we have to monitor for a premature end of card (eoln before column 71). The following code illustrates our vigilant way of reading data from the first field on a card and storing it in the corresponding field of a record:

```
with RecordFile^ do
    begin
        LastName:= '               '; {15 blanks}
        J:= 0;
        while not eoln(CardFile) and (J < 15) do
            begin
                J:= J + 1;
                read(CardFile, Ch);
                LastName[J]:= Ch
            end;
        {Similar code for the other fields}
    end {with}
```

The complete program follows:

```
program CardsToRecords(CardFile, RecordFile, output);
    type
        Records =
            record
                LastName  : packed array[1..15] of char;
                FirstName : packed array[1..11] of char;
                Title     : packed array[1..4]  of char;
                Street    : packed array[1..21] of char;
                City      : packed array[1..12] of char;
                State     : packed array[1..3]  of char;
                ZipCode   : packed array[1..5]  of char
            end;
    var
        Ch : char;
        J  : 1..71;
        CardCount  : integer;
        CardFile   : text; {file of characters with eoln markers}
        RecordFile : file of Records;
begin
    reset(CardFile);
    rewrite(RecordFile);
```

```
{program CardsToRecords continued}
    CardCount:= 0;
    while not eof(CardFile) do
        begin
            with RecordFile^ do
                begin        {12345678901234567890 1--for counting blanks}
                    LastName := '                    ';
                    FirstName:= '            ';
                    Title    := '    ';
                    Street   := '                            ';
                    City     := '            ';
                    State    := '   ';
                    ZipCode  := '      ';
                    J:= 0;
                    while not eoln(CardFile) and (J < 15) do
                        begin
                            J:= J + 1;
                            read(CardFile, Ch);
                            LastName[J]:= Ch
                        end;
                    while not eoln(CardFile) and (J < 26) do
                        begin
                            J:= J + 1;
                            read(CardFile, Ch);
                            FirstName[J-15]:= Ch
                        end;
                    while not eoln(CardFile) and (J < 30) do
                        begin
                            J:= J + 1;
                            read(CardFile, Ch);
                            Title[J-26]:= Ch
                        end;
                    while not eoln(CardFile) and (J < 51) do
                        begin
                            J:= J + 1;
                            read(CardFile, Ch);
                            Street[J-30]:= Ch
                        end;
                    while not eoln(CardFile) and (J < 63) do
                        begin
                            J:= J + 1;
                            read(CardFile, Ch);
                            City[J-51]:= Ch
                        end;
                    while not eoln(CardFile) and (J < 66) do
                        begin
                            J:= J + 1;
                            read(CardFile, Ch);
                            State[J-63]:= Ch
                        end;
```

```
{program CardsToRecords continued}
                  while not eoln(CardFile) and (J < 71) do
                     begin
                        J:= J + 1;
                        read(CardFile, Ch);
                        ZipCode[J-66]:= Ch
                     end;
               end {with};
            CardCount:= CardCount + 1;
            put(RecordFile);
            readln(CardFile) {Skip to beginning of next card}
         end {while};
      writeln(CardCount, ' cards read and transferred to RecordFile.')
   end.
```

It's important to realize that the file this program creates <u>is not</u> a text file. It is a file of records, not a file of characters structured into lines by line markers. Therefore, the new file RecordFile cannot be read as a text file or printed out as a text file. A program on page 274 (Exercise 10) shows how to read and print the fields of RecordFile.

As a final example in this section, we'll quote a procedure from the British Standard Institution's proposed standard for Pascal. (I alluded to this proposal in the preface.) This procedure deals with a knotty logical problem that occurs if you want to append components to the end of a file when you're not already at the end of the file in the write state. To find the end of a file you have to inspect the file (read it) until you reach the end of the file (eof = true). The problem is that now you're where you want to be in the file--but you're in the wrong state! You're in the the read state; but you want to be in the write state. The following procedure enables you to append components to the file regardless of its current state. It does this by making two copies of the file. The procedure makes the second copy on the original file and puts you at the end of the file in the write state. The file to which you want to append components is named F. Assume that the declaration of F is nonlocal.

```
procedure Append(var F : IntFile);

   var
      G : IntFile;

   procedure Copy (var X, Y : IntFile);
      begin {Copy}
         reset(X);
         rewrite(Y);
         while not eof(X) do
            begin
               Y^ := X^;
               put(Y);
```

```
                         get(X)
                  end
            end;  {Copy}

         begin {Append}
            Copy(F, G);
            Copy(G, F)
         end {Append}
```

## MERGING AND SORTING FILES

The sorting methods we presented in previous chapters (pages 131 and 182) are applicable when all the data will fit simultaneously in the computer's internal memory. Thus, those methods are applicable to sorting arrays. But when the data is stored on a sequential file and won't fit in the computer's internal memory, we must use a sorting method applicable to a data structure where only one component is available at a time.

A useful auxiliary process in sorting sequential files is _merging_. Merging two ordered sequences means combining the ordered sequences (or "runs") into a single ordered sequence. For example, consider the following sequences of integers:

```
   Sequence F: 06 12 18 25 29 67
   Sequence G: 11 23 37 42 48 52
```

Merging these sequences results in this third sequence:

```
   Sequence H: 06 11 12 18 23 25 29 37 42 48 52 67
```

which we form by repeatedly selecting the smaller component of the two currently accessible components. The following procedure carries out the merging process:

```
procedure Merge1and2on3(var F, G, H : IntFile);
   begin
      reset(F);
      reset(G);
      rewrite(H);
      while not eof(F) and not eof(G) do
         begin
            if F^ < G^ then
               begin
                  H^ := F^;
                  get(F)
               end
            else
```

```
            begin
                H^ := G^;
                get(G)
            end;
        put(H);
    end;

    while not eof(F) do {write tail of F onto H}
        begin
            H^ := F^;
            put(H);
            get(F)
        end;
    while not eof(G) do {write tail of G onto H}
        begin
            H^ := G^;
            put(H);
            get(G)
        end
end
```

Let's consider how the above procedure (modified to accommodate the appropriate file type) might be used in a data processing application. Suppose that the retail business referred to earlier maintains their CustomerFile by periodically adding new customers to the file. Once a month, for example, they could enter their new customers' names and addresses into the computer's internal memory and sort this relatively short list by an efficient method like QuickSort. Then their maintenance program could merge this sorted list of new customers with the already sorted CustomerFile. What sorting key would they use? That depends, of course, on how they want to use the data. Sometimes companies sort their data on more than one key. For example, for a large national mailing list, the company might want to sort their customers by their zip code in order to take advantage of the lower rates for zipcoded bulk mail. In that case they might maintain one file sorted on the ZipCode field of the Customer record. If the company wanted to sort alphabetically on their customers' names, the file type and the comparison test would have to be modified as shown:

**procedure** Merge1and2on3(**var** F, G, H : CustomerFile);

and the simple comparison test for merging files of integers:

**if** F^ < G^ **then**

would have to be modified to:

**if** (F^.LastName < G^.Lastname) **or**
    ((F^.LastName = G^.LastName) **and** (F^.FirstName < G^.FirstName)) **then**

in order to merge the files by the lexicographic order of the customers'
last and first names.

Now we would like to develop an algorithm and procedure for sorting
an unsorted file. Is there any way to use the concept of merging two
sorted sequences to help solve this problem? Yes; it's called "natural
merge sort." Before we can describe this method, we have to define a
"maximal run" or, more briefly, a "run." A maximal run or a run is an
ordered subsequence of items in a sequence; we say that an ascending run
is "maximal" if the item in the sequence that precedes the run is
greater than the first item in the run and the item that succeeds the
run is less than the last item in the run; each item in the run is equal
to or less than its successor. In the following list of randomly chosen
numbers, we have marked the end of each run with a "*."

  C: 80* 68* 30  67  70* 21  62* 01  79* 75* 18  53* 29  65* 18  85* 68*

Notice that this sequence of numbers contains "natural runs." Since
we selected the numbers for the sequence from a random number table, the
runs are typically quite short, one or two items per run, although
there's one run, <30  67  70>, of three items. The fact that any
sequence of items (upon which there is defined some ordering relation)
has natural runs gives both the name and the basis to "natural merge
sort." The method of natural merge sort is quite simple: take the file
to be sorted (or better still a copy of the file--to protect the
original data) and distribute the natural runs alternately to two
auxiliary files, F and G. (We'll call the filecopy of the original file,
C.) Then merge the runs distributed onto F and G back onto C. The
merging process increases the length of the runs and decreases the
number of runs on C. Continue distributing and merging the runs on C
until there is only one run on C. At that point, the procedure has
completely sorted C. Each cycle (distribution plus merge) approximately
halves the number of runs on C.

The following example should help you to see how the process works.
(You can also use this sequence to trace or test the procedure we'll
develop.) We start with the above list of random numbers.

ORIGINAL SEQUENCE
  C: 80* 68* 30  67  70* 21  62* 01  79* 75* 18  53* 29  65* 19  85* 68*

DISTRIBUTE
  F: 80* 30  67  70* 01  79* 18  53* 19  85*
  G: 68* 21  62  75* 29  65  68*
MERGE
  C: 68  80* 21  30  62  67  70  75* 01  29  65  68  79* 18  53* 19  85*

DISTRIBUTE
  F: 68  80* 01  29  65  68  79* 19  85*
  G: 21  30  62  67  70  75* 18  53*
MERGE
  C: 21  30  62  67  68  70  75  80* 01  18  29  53  65  68  79* 19  85*

```
DISTRIBUTE
   F: 21  30  62  67  68  70  75  80* 19  85*
   G: 01  18  29  53  65  68  79*
MERGE
   C: 01  18  21  29  30  53  62  65  67  68  68  70  75  79  80* 19  85*

DISTRIBUTE
   F: 01  18  21  29  30  53  62  65  67  68  68  70  75  79  80*
   G: 19  85*
MERGE
   C: 01  18  19  21  29  30  53  62  65  67  68  68  70  75  79  80  85*
```

Four cycles of distributing and merging runs were sufficient to sort this random sequence of 17 integers. If N is the number of components in a file, then a natural merge sort will always sort the components in LogBase2(N) or fewer cycles (see page 152 for a discussion of LogBase2).

Before we develop a procedure for carrying out the natural merge sort, we should develop the data structure of the file parameter. We assume that the data structure is a file of records and that each record contains a key field and an arbitrary number of information or data fields. The data part can be another record if you wish. We also assume that the data type of the key is positive integers. Our sorting algorithm will be general except you might have to change the relational tests for item succession if your key has a different data type.

```
   type
      KeyPlusData =
         record
             Key  : 0..maxint;
             Data : {Whatever you wish}
         end;
      FileType = file of KeyPlusData;
   var
      C : FileType
```

We also assume the declaration of two auxiliary files F and G.
We can now describe the heart of the natural merge sort algorithm:

```
   repeat
       initialize C for reading and F and G for writing;
       distribute runs;
       initialize C for writing and F and G for reading;
       initialize NumberOfRuns;
       merge the runs
   until NumberOfRuns := 1
```

Note the termination criterion for this loop: the number of runs on C is <u>one</u>. Obviously, if there is only one run on C, all the components of C are in order. We must keep careful count of the number of runs we copy onto C during the merging process.

Onward to refinement of the top level. The refinement of the initialization of files for reading and writing is trivial. The first nontrivial top-level statement is "distribute runs." This process is straightforward, however; all we have to do is alternate the copying of runs between F and G. The actual copying of one run is best delegated to a subprocedure "CopyNextRun." The only slightly tricky part is the detection of the end of a run. In order to detect the end of a run we use the file buffer variable "to peek ahead." Here's the finished procedure, DistributeRuns:

```
procedure DistributeRuns; {from C onto F and G}

    procedure CopyNextRun(var {from} C, {to} ForG : Filetype);
        var
            Item : KeyPlusData;
        begin {CopyNextRun}
            repeat
                read(C, Item); {Same as: Item := C^; get(C)}
                write(ForG, Item); {ForG^ := Item; put(ForG)}
                if eof(C) then
                    EndOfRun := true
                else {Peek ahead at C^, the next item from C}
                    EndOfRun := C^.Key < Item.Key
            until EndOfRun
        end; {CopyNextRun}

    begin {DistributeRuns}
        repeat
            CopyNextRun({from} C, {to} F);
            if not eof(C) then
                CopyNextRun({from} C, {to} G)
        until eof(C)
    end {DistributeRuns}
```

Now we must refine the next nontrivial part of NaturalMergeSort: "merge the runs." This procedure will be somewhat more complex than "distribute runs"; however, we have an earlier procedure Merge1and2on3 to start our thinking. Our present problem differs from the earlier one in three ways:

1. each file may contain many runs
2. there may be an unequal number of runs on each file
3. we want to count the number of runs merged or copied onto C

It may suprise you to learn that the number of runs on F and G may differ considerably. This is because the alternate runs we copy from C onto F (or G) can collapse into one run. This happened twice on the first distribution of the 17 random numbers in our earlier example. Notice that runs <21  62> and <75> collapsed into one run on file G; so did <19  65> and <68>. Consequently, after the first distribution, F has five runs and G has only three runs. Thus, we may exhaust one file during the merging of runs and still have <u>several</u> runs on the other file. We must be careful to copy <u>all</u> these remaining runs from the other file onto the C file.

The necessary modifications to Merge1and2on3 are easy to make if we express some of the key statements as additional procedures. The result of the next step of refinement is:

```
procedure MergeRuns;

    begin {MergeRuns}
        while not eof(F) and not eof(G) do
            begin
                MergeTwoRuns;
                NumberOfRuns := NumberOfRuns +1
            end;

        while not eof(F) do
            begin
                CopyNextRun({from}F, {to} C);
                NumberOfRuns := NumberOfRuns + 1
            end;

        while not eof(G) do
            begin
                CopyNextRun({from}G, {to} C);
                NumberOfRuns := NumberOfRuns + 1
            end;
    end {MergeRuns}
```

Notice that we have to invoke CopyNextRun from MergeRuns. Because we didn't foresee this when we wrote DistributeRuns, we "hid" CopyNextRun inside DistributeRuns' block. Now we'll bring CopyNextRun out of hiding and declare it globally so that MergeRuns can call it.

Since we know how to program CopyNextRun, our next refinement task is MergeTwoRuns. This will bring back the detail that we suppressed in Merge1and2on3 when we wrote MergeRuns; however, we'll need additional code to account for problems 1 and 2 above. MergeTwoRuns must not only merge components from F and G, it must also watch for the ends of the current runs and upon detecting the end of one run of a pair, it must copy the rest of the other run. After copying a component from F or G onto C, there are three possible states:

1. StillMerging: there are components remaining in the current runs on both files. The appropriate action, of course, is to continue merging components from the two files onto C.

2. EndOfFile: the last get has exhausted one of the files. The appropriate action is to copy the rest of the current run from the other file onto C.

3. EndOfRun: the value of F^.Key (or G^.Key) is less than the Key of the Item just copied from F (or G). The appropriate action is to copy the rest of the current run from the other file, G (or F), onto C.

Here's the refinement of MergeTwoRuns based on these requirements:

```
procedure MergeTwoRuns;
   var
      Item  : KeyPlusData;
      State : (EndOfFile, EndOfRun, StillMerging);
   begin
      State := StillMerging;
      repeat
         if F^.Key < G^.Key then
            begin
               read(F, Item);
               write(C, Item);
               if eof(F) then
                  State := EndOfFile
               else if F^.Key < Item.Key then
                  State := EndOfRun;
               if (State = EndOfFile) or (State = EndOfRun) then
                  CopyRestOfRun({from} G, {to} C)
            end
         else {G^.Key <= F^.Key}
            begin
               read(G, Item);
               write(C, Item);
               if eof(G) then
                  State := EndOfFile
               else if G^.Key < Item.Key then
                  State := EndOfRun;
               if (State = EndOfFile) or (State = EndOfRun) then
                  CopyRestOfRun({from} F, {to} C)
            end
      until State <> StillMerging
   end {MergeTwoRuns}
```

(We could use a Boolean variable instead of the tri-valued variable State since the procedure takes the same action for two of State's values. We introduced the slightly more complex variable to clarify the procedure's actions.) There's one more line to refine in this procedure: "CopyRestOfRun...." The procedure CopyNextRun will copy the rest of a run because it copies one run starting from the current position in the file.

We're finished, having refined all English statements into Pascal code. Here's the complete procedure, preceded by the necessary global definitions.

```
type
   KeyPlusData =
      record
         Key  : 0..maxint;
         Data : {Whatever you wish}
      end;
   FileType = file of KeyPlusData;
var
   C : FileType

procedure NaturalMergeSort(var C : FileType);
   var
      F, G           : FileType;
      Item           : KeyPlusData; {Used in CopyNextRun and MergeTwoRuns}
      NumberOfRuns : 0..Maxint;

   procedure CopyNextRun(var {from} T, {to} U : Filetype);
      var
         EndOfRun : Boolean;
      begin {CopyNextRun}
         repeat
            read(T, Item); {Same as: Item := T^; get(T)}
            write(U, Item); {Same as: U^ := Item; put(U)}
            if eof(T) then
               EndOfRun := true
            else {Peek ahead at T^, the current item on T}
               EndOfRun := T^.Key < Item.Key
         until EndOfRun
      end; {CopyNextRun}

   procedure DistributeRuns; {from C onto F and G}
      begin {DistributeRuns}
         repeat
            CopyNextRun({from} C, {to} F);
            if not eof(C) then
               CopyNextRun({from} C, {to} G)
         until eof(C)
      end; {DistributeRuns}

   procedure MergeRuns;

      procedure MergeTwoRuns;
         var
            State : (EndOfFile, EndOfRun, StillMerging);
         begin {MergeTwoRuns}
            State := StillMerging;
```

```
          repeat
            if F^.Key < G^.Key then
                begin
                    read(F, Item);
                    write(C, Item);
                    if eof(F) then
                        State := EndOfFile
                    else if F^.Key < Item.Key then
                        State := EndOfRun;
                    if (State = EndOfFile) or (State = EndOfRun) then
                        CopyNextRun({from} G,{to} C) {Copy rest of run}
                end
            else {G^.Key <= F^.Key}
                begin
                    read(G, Item);
                    write(C, Item);
                    if eof(G) then
                        State := EndOfFile
                    else if G^.Key < Item.Key then
                        State := EndOfRun;
                    if (State = EndOfFile) or (State = EndOfRun) then
                        CopyNextRun({from} F,{to} C) {Copy rest of run}
                end
          until State <> StillMerging
        end; {MergeTwoRuns}

    begin {MergeRuns}
        while not eof(F) and not eof(G) do
            begin
                MergeTwoRuns;
                NumberOfRuns := NumberOfRuns + 1
            end;
        while not eof(F) do
            begin
                CopyNextRun({from}F, {to} C);
                NumberOfRuns := NumberOfRuns + 1
            end;
        while not eof(G) do
            begin
                CopyNextRun({from}G, {to} C);
                NumberOfRuns := NumberOfRuns + 1
            end;
    end; {MergeRuns}

begin {NaturalMergeSort}
    repeat
        reset(C);
        rewrite(F);
        rewrite(G);
        DistributeRuns;
```

```
        rewrite(C);
        reset(F);
        reset(G);
        NumberOfRuns := 0;
        MergeRuns;
    until NumberOfRuns = 1
end. {NaturalMergeSort}
```

EXERCISES

**1.** Write a program that counts the number of lines (or line markers) in a textfile F.

**2.** Write a program that finds the minimum, average, and maximum line lengths of a textfile F.

**3.** Write a procedure that copies the textfile F onto the textfile G, compressing multiple blanks as it copies. One scheme for compressing input blanks is to represent N blanks with #N for N greater than one. If # appears in the input text, you must choose some symbol other than #. Preserve the line markers in the file.

**4.** Now write a procedure that takes the file generated in the previous exercise and generates the original file, the one without compressed blanks.

**5.** Write a program that generates a textfile containing strings of multiple blanks, operates on this file with the procedure prepared in exercise 3, and finally creates the original textfile with the procedure prepared in exercise 4. In other words, write a program that tests the procedures you wrote in exercises 3 and 4.

**6.** Write and test a program that merges two ordered files of records into a single ordered file. Assume that the records have the form:

```
WordType =
    record
        Spelling   : packed array[1..12] of char;
        Definition : packed array[1..80]
    end
```

Assume that the files are ordered on the spelling of the word.

**7.** Write a program that copies Shakespearean sonnets from the input file to the output file. Assume that the text on the input file uses slashes (/s) for line separators. Copy the sonnets on the output file using line markers. Be sure that the output preserves the conventional typography of the sonnet--that is, indent the last couplet. Center the

number of the sonnet, a Roman numeral, on the first line; and leave one
blank line between the number of the sonnet and the first line.

**8.** Write a program that tests the procedure NaturalMergeSort.

**9.** Assume that text files F and G have the following structure: the
first twelve characters of each line make up an English word, left-hand
justified with trailing blanks if the word is less than twelve characters long; the remaining portion of each line contains the definition of
the word; the lines are alphabetically ordered on the field of the first
twelve  characters. Write a program that merges the two files into one
alphabetically ordered file.

**10.** The following program writes out the records of RecordFile, seven
fields of a record per line. Modify this program so that it prints out
the seven fields as they would appear on a mailing label or the address
on an envelope. Do not print out redundant trailing blanks.

```
program WriteRecords(RecordFile, output);
   type
      Records =
         record
            LastName  : packed array[1..15] of char;
            FirstName : packed array[1..11] of char;
            Title     : packed array[1..4]  of char;
            Street    : packed array[1..21] of char;
            City      : packed array[1..12] of char;
            State     : packed array[1..3]  of char;
            ZipCode   : packed array[1..5]  of char
         end;
   var
      RecordFile : file of Records;
begin
   reset(RecordFile);
   while not eof(RecordFile) do
      begin
         with RecordFile^ do
            begin
               write(LastName);
               write(FirstName);
               write(Title);
               write(Street);
               write(City);
               write(State);
               write(ZipCode)
            end {with};
         writeln;
         get(RecordFile)
      end {while
end.
```

# 11. Structured Data Type 4: The Set

In mathematics the term set denotes any collection of elements or objects that can be classed together. Pascal's definition is more restrictive because Pascal is strongly typed. In Pascal the collection of objects must all belong to the same base type. Furthermore, the base type must be an ordinal type. Here's an example of a set variable.

```
type
    Option  = (Air, FM, PwrBrks);
    Options = set of Option;
var
    MyCarsOptions, DesiredOptions, ThisCarsOptions : Options;
```

The base type for the set type Options is the enumerated type Option. What values (constants) are assignable to MyCarsOptions? All the subsets of the elements of Option. The collection of these subsets is called the powerset of the base type.  Here, then, are MyCarsOptions's possible values:

[Air, FM, PwrBrks], [Air, FM], [Air, PwrBrks],
  [FM, PwrBrks], [Air], [FM], [PwrBrks], [ ]

The order in which we list the elements is irrelevant; for sets are unordered collections. Thus:

[Air, FM, PwrBrks] = [FM, PwrBrks, Air] = [PwrBrks, Air, FM]  etc.

Note carefully the difference between the values of Option, an ordinal (enumerated) data type, and the values of Options, a set data type defined with Option as its base type. Option has three possible values; it can assume one and only one of these values at a time. Options has eight possible values; and, of course, it can assume one and only one of these values at a time. But some of the set type Options' values are actually collections of the values of Option. A variable whose values are actually collections of another variable's values can be very useful; for often we're interested in sets of a variable's values rather than the variable's individual values.

Here's another example:

```
type
   Letters      = 'A'..'Z';
   SetOfLetters = set of Letters;
var
   Vowels, Consonants : SetofLetters; {same as set of 'A'..'Z'}

begin
   Vowels := ['A', 'E', 'I', 'O', 'U'];
   Consonants := ['A'..'Z'] - Vowels;
```

Can you intuit the meaning the two assignment statements?


## CONSTRUCTING SETS


We construct set values by listing the elements between square brackets. If some of the values include a subrange of the base type, then we can use the notation X..Y. For example, the set [X..Y] denotes the set of all values of the base type on the closed interval X to Y. If X > Y, then [X..Y] denotes the empty set, usually denoted as [ ]. The empty set is useful. For example,

```
var
   StrippedCar, LoadedCar : Options;
begin
   StrippedCar := [ ]
   LoadedCar   := [Air..PwrBrks]
```

All the following expressions are equivalent ways of saying the same thing:

[1..5], [1, 2..5], [1, 2..4, 5], [1..4, 5], [1, 2, 3, 4, 5]

Use the expression that's the most readable (the first one); but they're all legal.

The elements of a set can be given as expressions. Of course, these expressions must yield values that belong to the base type of the set. Assume that CalledLetters has been declared as set of 'A'..'Z'.

MyCarsOptions := [Air, succ(Air)]

SetOfNumbers := [0, I..2*I]

CalledLetters := CalledLetters + [chr(ord('A') + Random)]
{Random must be a number between 0 and 25.}

TESTING FOR SET EQUALITY, SET INCLUSION, AND SET MEMBERSHIP


Among the useful things we do with sets are

1. to test two sets for equality or inequality;
2. to test a set for inclusion in another set;
3. to test an individual element for membership in a set.

For example, on page 111 we wrote the following test for the variable Z:

    **if** ((21 <= Z) **and** (Z <= 30)) **or** ((39 <= Z) **and** (Z <= 48)) **or**
       ((57 <= Z) **and** (Z <= 80)) **or** ((89 <= Z) **and** (Z <= 105)) **then**
       writeln('Element', Z:4, ' is a transition element.')

Now we can simplify this test for membership of Z to

    **if** Z **in** [21..30, 39..48, 57..80, 89..105] **then**
       writeln('Element', Z:4, ' is a transition element.')

The second statement is easier to write, easier to read, and faster
for the computer to process.
The relational and membership operators are:

| Operator | Operation | Examples |
|---|---|---|
| = | set equality | [5..4] = [ ] is true; |
| | | [Air] = [FM] is false |
| <> | set inequality | [1, 2..5] <> [2..5] is true; |
| | | [PwrBrks] <> [PwrBrks] is false |
| <= | set inclusion | [2..5] <= [1, 2..5] is true; |
| | | [1..3] <= [1, 3] is false |
| >= | set inclusion | [Air..PwrBrks] >= [FM] is true; |
| | | [1, 2] >= [1, 3] is false |
| **in** | set membership | 6 **in** [1..6] is true; |
| | | C **in** [A, E, I, O, U] is false |

**Notes: 1.** All the above operators produce a Boolean result. **2.** If X
and Y are set operands, X <= Y denotes the inclusion of X in Y; and X >=
Y denotes the inclusion of Y in X. **3.** The left operand of **in** must be an
individual ordinal value belonging to the base type T; the right operand
must be a set whose type is **set of** T. The operator **in** yields the value
true if the ordinal value is a member of the right-hand operand;
otherwise it yields the value false. **End of notes.**
    Note that

    [7] <= [1, 3..5, 7]

and this expression using the in operator,

   7 **in** [1, 3..5, 7]

are equivalent; but the latter is clearer and simpler.
   If we want to check for the membership of 1 <u>and</u> 7 simultaneously in
the second set, the set inclusion notation is more compact,

   [1, 7] <= [1, 3..5, 7]

compared to the set membership notation:

   (1 **in** [1, 3..5, 7]) **and** (7 **in** [1, 3..5, 7])


AN EXAMPLE OF LEXICAL ANALYSIS


   Pascal source programs consist of identifiers, numbers, and
operators. The compiler must recognize these symbols, analyze them,
represent them in some convenient internal form, optimize the program
they represent, and finally convert them into the object code (assembly
or machine language) of the computer.
   The part of the compiler that recognizes the symbols is sometimes
called the <u>lexical analyzer</u> and sometimes called the <u>scanner</u>. The
lexical analyzer scans the characters of the Pascal source program from
beginning to end and constructs the actual lexical units of the
program--the symbols for integers, identifiers, reserved words,
two-character symbols like <>, :=, <=, and .., and so on. The lexical
analyzer then passes these symbols on to the syntax and semantic
analyzer for the next stage of analysis. The lexical analyzer also
builds a symbol table for the identifiers and constants.
   The set notation we have just introduced is especially handy for the
character-by-character conversion of the Pascal source code into the
basic lexical units. To demonstrate this usefulness, we will show you a
portion of a lexical analyzer. The lexical analyzer reads one symbol
from the input stream each time it's called. The advantage of using <u>sets</u>
of characters for the various tests in the analyzer is that its code is
portable, i.e., independent of the computer's particular character set
(ASCII, EBCDIC, or whatever). Preceded by the required global
declarations, a portion of the procedure follows.

```
   var
      Symbol : (Number, Identifier, LeqOrIncludedIn, GeqOrIncludes,
            ReplaceWith)

      Ch : char;
      I  : integer;
```

```
Name =
    record
        J : 0..MaxJ;
        Spelling : array[1..MaxJ] of char;
    end

procedure LexicalAnalyzer;
    var
        Ch1, Ch2 : char;
    begin
        while Ch = ' ' do
            read(Ch);
        if Ch in ['0'..'9'] then
            begin
                Symbol := Number;
                I := 0;
                repeat
                    I := 10*I + ord(Ch) - ord('0');
                    read(Ch)
                until not (Ch in ['0'..'9'])
            end {Number}
        else if Ch in ['A'..'Z', 'a'..'z'] then
            with Name do
                begin
                    Symbol := Identifer;
                    J := 0;
                    repeat
                        if J < MaxJ then
                            begin
                                J := J + 1;
                                Spelling[J] := Ch
                            end;
                        read(Ch)
                    until not (Ch in ['A'..'Z', 'a'..'z', '0'..'9'])
                end {Identifer}
        else if Ch in [':', '<', '>'] then
            begin
                Ch1 := Ch;
                read(Ch2);
                if Ch2 = '=' then
                    begin
                        case Ch1 of
                            ':': Symbol := ReplaceWith;
                            '<': Symbol := LeqOrIncludedIn;
                            '>': Symbol := GeqOrIncludes
                        end;
                        read(Ch)
                    end
                else
                    ET CETERA;
    end {LexicalAnalyzer}
```

There's one point of syntax worth emphasizing here. You might be inclined to write

    **until** Ch **not in** ['0'..'9'] {INCORRECT SYNTAX}

because this construction is close to ordinary English syntax. Clear to the ear or not, it's incorrect syntax. The operator **not** must precede a Boolean variable, constant, function designator, or expression. "**in** ['0'..'9']" is none of these; it's <u>part</u> of a Boolean expression. The full Boolean expression is

    Ch **in** ['0'..'9']

and the correct negation of this expression is

    **not** (Ch **in** ['0'..'9'])


## PERFORMING ARITHMETIC ON SETS

There are three arithmetic operators for sets. They accept set operands and produce a set result. We used one arithmetic operation, set union, in the opening section of this chapter:

    CalledLetters := CalledLetters + [chr(ord('A') + Random)]

Here's a summary of the arithmetic operators for sets.

| Operator | Operation | Examples |
|---|---|---|
| + | set union | [3..5] + [1, 2] = [1..5] <br> [Air] + [FM] = [Air, FM] |
| - | set difference | LoadedCar - [PwrBrks] = [Air, FM] <br> [1..10] - [1..5] = [6..10] |
| * | set intersection | [1..5]*[6..10] = [ ] <br> LoadedCar*[Air, FM] = [Air, FM] |

**Notes: 1.** X + Y is the set of all values that are either in X, in Y, or in both X and Y. **2.** X - Y is the set of all values that are in X but not in Y. **3.** X*Y is the set of all values that are in X <u>and</u> in Y. **End of notes.**

The set union and difference operators are highly useful for adding or deleting a single element from a set. For example,

    PrimeNumbers := PrimeNumbers + [977]

If PrimeNumbers already contains 977, the operation has no effect. Similarly, the last statement below removes Revolver from Arsenal; if Arsenal does not contain Revolver, the statement has no effect.

```
type
    Weapon = (MachineGun, Carbine, Revolver, HandGrenade, Bazooka);
var
    Arsenal : set of Weapon;
begin
    Arsenal := Arsenal - [Revolver]
```

## SUBPROGRAMS FOR PROCESSING SETS

To illustrate operations on sets, we offer the following subprograms. The first accepts the following record as a parameter, returning the number of distinct letters in the word's spelling.

```
type
    Index = 1..MaxWordLength;
    WordType =
        record
            Length   : Index;
            Spelling : array[Index] of char
        end;

function NmbrOfDistinctLetters(Word : WordType) : Index;

    var
        J        : Index;
        Count    : 0..MaxWordLength;
        Counted  : set of char;
        Letters  : set of char;
    begin
        Letters := ['A'..'Z', 'a'..'z']; {count u.c. or l.c. letters}
        Counted := [ ]; {set of letters already counted}
        Count   := 0;
        for J := 1 to Word.Length do
            begin
                if (Word.Spelling[J] in Letters) and
                    not (Word.Spelling[J] in Counted) then
                    begin
                        Count := Count + 1;
                        Counted := Counted + [Word.Spelling[J]]
                    end
            end; {for loop}
        NmbrOfDistinctLetters := Count
    end {NmbrOfDistinctLetters}
```

Our next subprogram accepts a set of letters and a word (of the same data type as the first example); it returns true if all the letters in the set are contained in the word and false otherwise.

```
type
    SetOfChar = set of char;

function LettersInWord(Letters: SetOfChar; Word: WordType) : Boolean;
    var
        CharactersInWord : SetOfChar;
        J                : Index;
    begin
        CharactersInWord := [ ]; {make a set of the characters in word}
        for J := 1 to Word.Length do
            CharactersInWord := CharactersInWord + [Word.Spelling[J]];
        LettersInWord := Letters <= CharactersInWord
    end
```

The next subprogram returns the largest element of a set S of type set of 1..N. If the set is empty the function returns the value 0.

```
type
    Base = 1..N;
    ExtendedBase = 0..N;
    PowerSetOfBase = set of Base;

function MaxElement(S : PowerSetOfBase) : ExtendedBase;
    var
        Element : Base;
    begin
        if S = [ ] then
            MaxElement := 0
        else
            begin
                Element := N;
                while not (Element in S) do
                    Element := pred(Element);
                MaxElement := Element
            end
    end
```

The next subprogram returns the number of elements in a set S of type set of 1..N. The same global type definitions as above apply.

```
function NmbrOfElements(S : PowerSetOfBase) : ExtendedBase;
    var
        Count   : ExtendedBase;
        Element : Base;
```

```
    begin
       Count := 0;
       for Element := 1 to N do
           if Element in S then
               Count := Count + 1;
       NmbrOfElements := Count
    end {NmbrOfElements}
```

## LIMITATIONS OF PASCAL SETS

Pascal's set data type is elegant and useful. Nevertheless, this data type is practically unique to Pascal. Even the authors of the new programming language Ada--an enlargement and generalization of Pascal--have not deemed sets essential or convenient enough to include them in Pascal's larger offspring. It's regrettable to dispense with sets because alternative notation is often harder to write, harder to read, and slower to run.

Even Pascal's official attitude toward sets is somewhat dismissive. By limiting sets to elements of an ordinal base type, Pascal precludes some extremely useful data structures. For example, sets of strings would be _very_ useful in computer-aided instruction and natural language processing. On the other hand, Pascal is a compact general-purpose language, not an engorged all-purpose language. It compiles efficiently; even a small microcomputer can compile the full language. The language designer had to resist a never-ending accretion of "features."

Perhaps even more harmful to the usefulness of sets is Pascal's official tolerance of sets of small cardinality. Here's the relevant statement from the proposed BSI/ISO Pascal standard currently under review: "The largest and smallest values of integer type permitted as members of a value of a set type shall be implementation defined." In other words, the size of the set data type is up to the compiler writer. With this language it would be possible for a standard Pascal compiler to limit sets to eight elements. A limit this austere is unlikely; but it's not unlikely to find Pascal compilers that won't handle the following set definition,

```
    type
       ASCII = set of char
```

because the cardinality of its base, 95, is too large. Of the three Pascal compilers the author uses, one limits sets to 64 elements, one limits sets to 512 elements, and one limits sets to 2040 elements. Interestingly, the first one (64 elements) is written for a 16-bit machine and the second one (512 elements) runs on all the popular 8-bit machines. Obviously, implementation-defined limits can be rather arbitrary.

What all this means to you is this: Check your implementation-defined limits before you write an elegant program using a large set variable.

EXERCISES

1. Rewrite the following using set notation:

    a. ('A' <= Ch) **and** (Ch <= 'D')
    b. (I = 3) **and** (I = 5) **and** (I = 7)
    c. ('0' <= Ch) **and** (Ch <= '9') **or**
        ('A' <= Ch) **and** (Ch <= 'Z')

2. Assuming that **set of** char is possible on your implementation, write a program that reads three sentences and prints out all the characters that appear in both the first and second sentences and not in the third sentence.

3. Assume that a set is defined as

**type**
    Fruit = (Apple, Apricot, Banana, Blueberry, Cherry, Orange, Peach,
          Pear, Pineapple, Plum);
    Salad = **set of** Fruit

Write a procedure that prints the value of a variable of type Salad; i.e., if the members of the set are Apricot, Cherry, and Orange, print

[Apricot, Cherry, Orange]

4. What is the cardinality of the following sets:

    a. **set of** 1..3
    b. **set of** '0'..'9'
    c. **set of** 1..N

5. Write a program that reads a text of English prose and prints out the word with the largest number of _distinct_ characters.

6. Write a program that reads a text of English prose and prints out the word with the largest number of distinct vowels.

7. Assuming the following global definition:

**type**
    LexicalType = (LowercaseLetter, UppercaseLetter, Digit,
          WordSeparator, Punctuation, Other)

write a function which receives a character, determines its lexical category, and returns a value of type LexicalType. Blanks and line markers are word separators.

8. Write a function that returns a fruit missing from your salad. Any fruit not in your salad will do. See problem 3.

# Appendix A
# Backus-Naur Description of Pascal

"**metalanguage:** a language used to talk about another language"

The Backus-Naur Form (BNF) is a metalanguage. J. W. Backus developed it to describe the ALGOL programming language; and Peter Naur used it in his masterful report on ALGOL 60. BNF is useful for describing the syntax of artificial and natural languages. We shall use an extended form of BNF, called EBNF, to describe Pascal's syntax.

The extended Backus-Naur form has several meta-symbols for describing languages; these symbols belong to the metalanguage, not to Pascal.

::=   means "may be composed of"

|    means "or"

{X}   means zero or more repetitions of X

Angle brackets, < >, are used to enclose the syntactic categories of the decribed language. Some examples of the syntactic categories of English are <sentence>, <noun>, <verb>, and <adjective>. Examples of syntactic categories in Pascal are <program>, <program heading>, <block>, <variable declaration>, and <compound statement>.

We can verify whether the following Pascal statement is <u>syntactically</u> correct by determining whether we can generate it with the EBNF syntax rules.

```
for J := 1 to N - 1 do
   begin
      repeat
         read(Ch)
      until Ch <> ' ';
      write(Ch);
      readln
   end
```

This is obviously a for statement; so we start with the EBNF definition of a for statement:

```
<for statement> ::=
    for <control variable> := <for list> do
        <statement>
```

This EBNF statement is one of Pascal's syntax rules. You can find it on page 291 of this appendix. The syntax rules in this appendix have been arranged in alphabetical order for your convenience.

Now that we have a rule that offers promise of generating the statement in question, we start replacing each syntactic category on the right-hand side of the rule with its own defining rule, looking up the category in the seven-page section beginning on page 289. For example, the right-hand side of the above rule becomes

```
for <identifier> := <for list> do
    <statement>
```

because

```
<control variable> ::= <identifier>
```

and then becomes

```
for <letter> {<letter or digit>} := <for list> do
    <statement>
```

because of the defining rule for <identifier>. The above can be validly reduced to

```
for J := <for list> do
    <statement>
```

by substituting J for <letter> and using zero iterations of <letter or digit>.

Next, we try to produce "1 to N - 1" from <for list>. The definition of <for list> offers two alternatives; we choose the first, the one involving to.

```
for J := <initial value> to <final value> do
    <statement>
```

We make the following replacements for <initial value>, using one EBNF rule after another:

```
<initial value> => <expression> => <simple expression> =>
<sign> <term> => <sign> <factor> => <sign> <unsigned constant> => 1
```

In the above replacements we left { <adding operator> <term> } out of

the replacement for <simple expression> and { <multiplying operator> <factor> } out of the replacement for <term> because we foresaw that we would not need these syntactical entities.
    We make the following replacements for <final value>:

    <final value> => <expression> => <simple expression> =>
<sign> <term> <adding operator> <term> => <sign> <factor> <adding operator> <factor> => <variable> <adding operator> <factor> => N <adding operator> <factor> => N - <factor> => N - <unsigned constant> => N - 1

which produces

    **for** J := 1 **to** N - 1 **do**
        <statement>

    We must try to produce the particular compound statement in the sample code from the syntactical entity <statement>.

    <statement> => <unlabelled statement> => <structured statement> =>
<compound statement> => **begin** <statement> {; <statement> } **end** =>
**begin** <statement> ; <statement> ; <statement> **end**

We can replace the first <statement> in this compound statement by the following sequence of rules:

    <statement> => <unlabelled statement> => <structured statement> =>
<repetitive statement> => <repeat statement> =>
**repeat** <statement> **until** <expression> =>
**repeat** read(Ch) **until** <expression> =>
**repeat**
    read(Ch)
**until** <simple expression> <relational operator> <simple expression> =>
**repeat**
    read(Ch)
**until** Ch <> ' '

where we telescoped several replacements near the end of the production. We can finish generating the sample Pascal statement from <for statement> by the followng replacement:

    <statement> ; <statement> ::= write(Ch); readln

Thus we succeeded in generating the Pascal statement from the EBNF rules for Pascal. This generation assures us that the Pascal statement is syntactically correct.
    If the process seems tedious (even with some of the steps suppressed), don't be discouraged. You don't have to check every statement you write by this drawn out process. But when you're unsure of your syntactical footing, you can firm it up by reference to the latter part of this appendix. It's really useful to have a complete and

succinct--and alphabetized--set of syntax rules ready at hand. Try to get used to using them as you prepare and edit your code. It's possible--and desirable--to write your Pascal programs without syntax errors by keeping this appendix at your side while you're writing. Until I finished this book, I didn't have the syntax rules arranged in alphabetical order; and it wasn't always as fast and convenient as it is now to check the rules. Now I haven't--and you haven't--any excuse to try to compile a program with questionable syntax.

## EXTENDED BACKUS-NAUR DESCRIPTION OF PASCAL

<actual parameter> ::= <expression> | <variable> |
   <procedure identifier> | <function identifier>

<adding operator> ::= + | - | **or**

<array type> ::=
   **array**[<index type>{, <index type>}] **of** <component type>

<array variable> ::= <variable>

<assignment statement> ::= <variable> := <expression> |
   <function identifier> := <expression>

<base type> ::= <ordinial type>

<block> ::= <label declaration part> <constant definition part>
   <type definition part> <variable declaration part>
   <procedure and function declaration part> <statement part>

<Boolean expression> ::= <expression>

<case label> ::= <constant>

<case label list> ::= <case label>{, <case label>}

<case list element> ::= <case label list> : <statement> | <empty>

<case statement> ::= **case** <expression> **of**
                  <case list element>{; <case list element>}
         **end**

<character string> ::= '<character>{<character>}'

<component type> ::= <type>

<component variable> ::= <indexed variable> | <field designator> |
   <file buffer>

<compound statement> ::= **begin**
             <statement>{; <statement>}
         **end**

<conditional statement> ::= <if statement> | <case statement>

<constant> ::= <unsigned number> | <sign><unsigned number> |
   <constant identifier> | <sign><constant identifier> |
   <character string>

&lt;constant definition&gt; ::= &lt;identifier&gt; = &lt;constant&gt;

&lt;constant definition part&gt; ::=
   &lt;empty&gt; | **const** &lt;constant definition&gt;{; &lt;constant definition&gt;};

&lt;constant identifier&gt; ::= &lt;identifier&gt;

&lt;control variable&gt; ::= &lt;identifier&gt;

&lt;digit&gt; ::= 0|1|2|3|4|5|6|7|8|9

&lt;directive&gt; ::= &lt;letter&gt;{&lt;letter or digit&gt;}

&lt;element&gt; ::= &lt;expression&gt; | &lt;expression&gt;..&lt;expression&gt;

&lt;element list&gt; ::= &lt;element&gt; {, &lt;element&gt;} | &lt;empty&gt;

&lt;empty&gt; ::=

&lt;empty statement&gt; ::= &lt;empty&gt;

&lt;entire variable&gt; ::= &lt;variable identifier&gt;

&lt;enumerated type&gt; ::= (&lt;identifier list&gt;)
   Note: BSI/ISO Working Draft/3, 1978

&lt;expression&gt; ::= &lt;simple expression&gt; |
   &lt;simple expression&gt; &lt;relational operator&gt; &lt;simple expression&gt;

&lt;factor&gt; ::= &lt;variable&gt; | &lt;unsigned constant&gt; | (&lt;expression&gt;) |
   &lt;function designator&gt; | &lt;set&gt; | **not** &lt;factor&gt;

&lt;field designator&gt; ::= &lt;record variable&gt;.&lt;field identifier&gt;

&lt;field identifier&gt; ::= &lt;identifier&gt;

&lt;field list&gt; ::= &lt;fixed part&gt; | &lt;fixed part&gt;; &lt;variant part&gt; |
   &lt;variant part&gt;

&lt;file buffer&gt; ::= &lt;file variable&gt;^

&lt;file identifier&gt; ::= &lt;identifier&gt;

&lt;file type&gt; ::= **file of** &lt;type&gt;

&lt;file variable&gt; ::= &lt;variable&gt;

&lt;final value&gt; ::= &lt;expression&gt;

&lt;fixed part&gt; ::= &lt;record section&gt;{; &lt;record section&gt;}

```
<for list> ::= <initial value> to <final value> |
   <initial value> downto <final value>

<for statement> ::=
   for <control variable> := <for list> do
      <statement>

<formal parameter section> ::= <parameter group> |
   var <parameter group> | function <parameter group> |
   procedure <identifier> {, <identifier>}
   Note: Jensen & Wirth, 1974

<formal parameter section> ::= <parameter group> |
   var <parameter group> | <procedure heading> | <function heading>
   Note : BSI/ISO Working Draft/3, 1978

<function declaration> ::= <function heading>; <block> |
   <function heading>; <directive>

<function designator> ::= <function identifier> |
   <function identifier>(<actual parameter>{, <actual parameter>})

<function heading> ::= function <identifier> : <result type> |
   function <identifier>(<formal parameter section>
   {; <formal parameter section>}) : <result type>

<function identifier> ::= <identifier>

<goto statement> ::= goto <label>

<identifier> ::= <letter> {<letter or digit>}

<identifier list> ::= <identifier> {, <identifier>}

<if statement> ::=
   if <Boolean expression> then
      <statement> |
   if <Boolean expression> then
      <statement>
   else
      <statement>

<index type> ::= <ordinal type>

<indexed variable> ::= <array variable>[<expression>{, <expression>}]

<initial value> ::= <expression>

<label> ::= <unsigned integer>
```

‹label declaration part› ..- ‹empty› | **label** ‹label›{, ‹label›};

‹letter› ::= A| B| C| D| E| F| G| H| I| J| K| L| M| N| O| P| Q| R| S| T| U| V| W| X| Y| Z|

  a| b| c| d| e| f| g| h| i| j| k| l| m| n| o| p| q| r| s| t| u| v| w| x| y| z

‹letter or digit› ::= ‹letter› | ‹digit›

‹multiplying operator› ::= * | / | **div** | **mod** | **and**

‹ordinal type› ::=
  ‹enumerated type› | ‹subrange type› | ‹ordinal type identifier›

‹ordinal type identifier› ::= ‹type identifier›

‹parameter group› ::=
  ‹identifier›{, ‹identifier›} : ‹type identifier›

‹pointer type› ::= ^‹type identifier›

‹pointer variable› ::= ‹variable›

‹procedure and function declaration part› ::=
  {‹procedure or function declaration›;}

‹procedure declaration› ::= ‹procedure heading›; ‹block› |
  ‹procedure heading›; ‹directive›

‹procedure heading› ::= **procedure** ‹identifier› |
  **procedure** ‹identifier›(‹formal parameter section›
  {; ‹formal parameter section›})

‹procedure identifier› ::= ‹identifier›

‹procedure or function declaration› ::=
  ‹procedure declaration› | ‹function declaration›

‹program› ::= ‹program heading›; ‹block›.

‹program heading› ::=
  **program** ‹identifier›(‹file identifier›{, ‹file identifier›})

‹real type› ::= ‹real type identifier›

‹real type identifier› ::= ‹type identifier›

‹record section› ::=
  ‹field identifier›{, ‹field identifier›} : ‹type› | ‹empty›

```
<record type> ::=
   record
      <field list>
   end
```

`<record variable> ::= <variable>`

`<record variable list> ::= <record variable>{, <record variable>}`

`<referenced variable> ::= <pointer variable>^`

`<relational operator> ::=  = | <> | < | <= | >= | > | in`

```
<repeat statement> ::=
   repeat
      <statement>{; <statement>}
   until <Boolean expression>
```

```
<repetitive statement> ::=
   <while statement> | <repeat statement> | <for statement>
```

`<result type> ::= <simple type identifier>   <pointer type identifier>`

```
<scalar type> ::= (<identifier list>)
   Note: Jensen & Wirth, 1975 (same as <enumerated type>)
```

`<scale factor> ::= <unsigned integer> | <sign><unsigned integer>`

`<set> ::= [<element list>]`

`<set type> ::= set of <base type>`

`<sign> ::= + | - |`

`<signed integer> ::= <sign><unsigned integer>`

`<signed number> ::= <sign><unsigned number>`

`<simple expression> ::= <sign><term>{ <adding operator> <term>}`

```
<simple statement> ::= <assignment statement> | <procedure statement> |
   <goto statement> | <empty statement>
```

```
<simple type> ::= <ordinal type> | <real type>
   Note: BSI/ISO Working Draft/3, 1978
```

```
<simple type> ::= <scalar type> | <subrange type> | <type identifier>
   Note: Jensen & Wirth, 1974
```

`<simple type identifier> ::= <type identifier>`

⟨special symbol⟩ ::= + | - | * | / | = | ⟨ | ⟩ | [ | ] | . | , | : |

   ; | ^ | ⟨⟩ | ⟨= | ⟩= | := | .. | ⟨word symbol⟩

⟨statement⟩ ::= ⟨unlabelled statement⟩ |
   ⟨label⟩ : ⟨unlabelled statement⟩

⟨statement part⟩ ::= ⟨compound statement⟩

⟨string⟩ ::= '⟨character⟩{⟨character⟩}'

⟨string type⟩ ::= **packed array**[1..N] **of** char

⟨structured statement⟩ ::=
   ⟨compound statement⟩ | ⟨conditional statement⟩ |
   ⟨repetitive statement⟩ | ⟨with statement⟩

⟨structured type⟩ ::= ⟨unpacked structured type⟩ |
   **packed** ⟨unpacked structured type⟩ | ⟨structured type identifier⟩

⟨subrange type⟩ ::= ⟨constant⟩..⟨constant⟩

⟨tag field⟩ ::= ⟨field identifier⟩ : | ⟨empty⟩

⟨tag type⟩ ::= ⟨ordinal type identifier⟩

⟨term⟩ ::= ⟨factor⟩{⟨multiplying operator⟩⟨factor⟩}

⟨type⟩ ::= ⟨simple type⟩ | ⟨structured type⟩ | ⟨pointer type⟩

⟨type definition⟩ ::= ⟨identifier⟩ = ⟨type⟩

⟨type definition part⟩ ::=
   ⟨empty⟩ | **type** ⟨type definition⟩{; ⟨type definition⟩};

⟨type identifier⟩ ::= ⟨identifier⟩

⟨unlabelled statement⟩ ::= ⟨simple statement⟩ | ⟨structured statement⟩

⟨unpacked structured type⟩ ::=
   ⟨array type⟩ | ⟨record type⟩ | ⟨set type⟩ | ⟨file type⟩

⟨unsigned constant⟩ ::=
   ⟨unsigned number⟩ | ⟨string⟩ | ⟨constant identifier⟩ | **nil**

⟨unsigned integer⟩ ::= ⟨digit⟩{⟨digit⟩}

⟨unsigned number⟩ ::= ⟨unsigned integer⟩ | ⟨unsigned real⟩

```
<unsigned real> ::= <unsigned integer>.<digit>{<digit>} |
    <unsigned integer>.<digit>{<digit>}E<scale factor> |
    <unsigned integer>E<scale factor>

<variable> ::=
    <entire variable> | <component variable>  | <referenced variable>

<variable declaration> ::= <identifier list> : <type>

<variable declaration part> ::=
    <empty> | var <variable declaration>{; <variable declaration>};

<variable identifier> ::= <identifier>

<variant> ::= <case label list> : (<field list>) | <empty>

<variant part> ::=
    case <tag field> <type identifier> of
        <variant>{; <variant>}

<while statement> ::=
    while <Boolean expression> do
        <statement>

<with statement> ::=
    with <record variable list> do
        <statement>

<word symbol> ::= and | array | begin | case | const | div | downto |

    do | else | end | file | for | function | goto | if | in | label |

    mod | nil | not | of | or | packed | procedure | program | record |

    repeat | set | then | to | type | until | var | while | with
```

# Appendix B
# ASCII and EBCDIC Character Codes

The ASCII and EBCDIC character codes are the most frequently used character codes. The following tables give the decimal ordinal number for each character. The missing numbers are either unprintable control codes or undefined codes.

| | | | | | | | | | | | | |
|---|---|---|---|---|---|---|---|---|---|---|---|---|
| 32 | blank | 48 | 0 | 64 | @ | 80 | P | 96 | ` | 112 | p |
| 33 | ! | 49 | 1 | 65 | A | 81 | Q | 97 | a | 113 | q |
| 34 | " | 50 | 2 | 66 | B | 82 | R | 98 | b | 114 | r |
| 35 | # | 51 | 3 | 67 | C | 83 | S | 99 | c | 115 | s |
| 36 | $ | 52 | 4 | 68 | D | 84 | T | 100 | d | 116 | t |
| 37 | % | 53 | 5 | 69 | E | 85 | U | 101 | e | 117 | u |
| 38 | & | 54 | 6 | 70 | F | 86 | V | 102 | f | 118 | v |
| 39 | ' | 55 | 7 | 71 | G | 87 | W | 103 | g | 119 | w |
| 40 | ( | 56 | 8 | 72 | H | 88 | X | 104 | h | 120 | x |
| 41 | ) | 57 | 9 | 73 | I | 89 | Y | 105 | i | 121 | y |
| 42 | * | 58 | : | 74 | J | 90 | Z | 106 | j | 122 | z |
| 43 | + | 59 | ; | 75 | K | 91 | [ | 107 | k | 123 | { |
| 44 | , | 60 | < | 76 | L | 92 | \ | 108 | l | 124 | \| |
| 45 | - | 61 | = | 77 | M | 93 | ] | 109 | m | 125 | } |
| 46 | . | 62 | > | 78 | N | 94 | ^ | 110 | n | 126 | ~ |
| 47 | / | 63 | ? | 79 | O | 95 | _ | 111 | o | | |

**Figure B-1** The ASCII character code (decimal)

| 129 | a | 145 | j |     |   | 193 | A | 209 | J |     |   |
|-----|---|-----|---|-----|---|-----|---|-----|---|-----|---|
| 130 | b | 146 | k | 162 | s | 194 | B | 210 | K | 226 | S |
| 131 | c | 147 | l | 163 | t | 195 | C | 211 | L | 227 | T |
| 132 | d | 148 | m | 164 | u | 196 | D | 212 | M | 228 | U |
| 133 | e | 149 | n | 165 | v | 197 | E | 213 | N | 229 | V |
| 134 | f | 150 | o | 166 | w | 198 | F | 214 | O | 230 | W |
| 135 | g | 151 | p | 167 | x | 199 | G | 215 | P | 231 | X |
| 136 | h | 152 | q | 168 | y | 200 | H | 216 | Q | 232 | Y |
| 137 | i | 153 | r | 169 | z | 201 | I | 217 | R | 233 | Z |

| 240 | 0 | 64 | blank | 80 | & | 96  | −  |     |   |
|-----|---|----|-------|----|---|-----|----|-----|---|
| 241 | 1 |    |       |    |   | 97  | /  |     |   |
| 242 | 2 | 74 | c     | 90 | ! |     |    | 122 | : |
| 243 | 3 |    |       | 91 | $ | 107 | ,  | 123 | # |
| 244 | 4 | 76 | <     | 92 | * | 108 | %  | 124 | @ |
| 245 | 5 | 77 | (     | 93 | ) | 109 | _  | 125 | ` |
| 246 | 6 | 78 | +     | 94 | ; | 110 | >  | 126 | = |
| 247 | 7 | 79 | \|    | 95 | ¬ | 111 | ?  | 127 | " |
| 248 | 8 |    |       |    |   |     |    |     |   |
| 249 | 9 |    |       |    |   |     |    |     |   |

**Figure B-2**  EBCDIC character code (decimal)

# Appendix C
# How to Trace Programs

In this appendix we give some tips on tracing a program. By "tracing a program" we mean hand-checking it. Some compilers offer a trace mode; but the tips in this appendix apply to what you can do yourself with just the listing of your program and paper and pencil. It's a good idea to hand-check your program before you try to run it. It's more than a good idea--it's essential--to hand-check your program if it isn't doing what you intended.

When hand-checking a program it's essential that you interpret each statement exactly as the computer processor would. This means that you must temporarily set aside your intentions for the code. You want to make a literal interpretation. One reason that even literate authors who can spell well, write grammatically, and punctuate correctly submit to and even welcome copy editing is that they know they can't see their own mistakes because they're so involved with their intentions and experienced meaning. Thus, even better than hand-checking your own program is having someone else hand-check it--at least whenever you're simply baffled by the code's actual performance. On the other hand, by distancing yourself from your intentions and interpreting each statement in a literal way, you should be able to perform effective hand-checking of your own code.

It's important to hand-check programs for extreme and rare values as well as frequently occurring ones. For example, the value zero is often a special case; code that works for other values may fail for zero. Therefore, be sure to check the code for zero, end points, and other values that may require special action or treatment.

There are many ways to hand-trace a program. The one we'll show you here is one we like; it has the advantage of a certain amount of formality that precludes you from drawing inferences while you should be processing statements and evaluating expressions. In this method you set up a table with a column for each variable and for each anonymous Boolean expression and a row for each statement or partial statement that could change the value of one of the columns. The best way to explain the method is to illustrate it with an example. The example is a procedure for computing the quotient and remainder resulting from the division of one positive integer by another.

Here's the procedure followed by the trace table. Note that we have numbered the lines that change the values of the columns.

```
    procedure IntegerDivision(   Dividend, Divisor   : integer;
                             var Quotient, Remainder : integer);
       begin
{2}    if (Dividend > 0) and (Divisor > 0) then
          begin
{3}          Remainder := Dividend;
{4}          Quotient  := 0;
{5}          while Remainder >= Divisor do
                begin
{6}                Remainder := Remainder - Divisor;
{7}                Quotient  := Quotient + 1
                end
          end
       end
```

Assuming that the following statement invokes the procedure:

```
{1}    IntegerDivision(17, 5, Quotient, Remainder)
```

the trace table is:

| | Dividend | Divisor | Quotient | Remainder | Dividend>0 and Divisor>0 | Remainder>=Divisor |
|---|---|---|---|---|---|---|
| {1} | 17 | 5 | ? | ? | ? | ? |
| {2} | | | | | true | |
| {3} | | | | 17 | | |
| {4} | | | 0 | | | |
| {5} | | | | | | true |
| {6} | | | | 12 | | |
| {7} | | | 1 | | | |
| {5} | | | | | | true |
| {6} | | | | 7 | | |
| {7} | | | 2 | | | |
| {5} | | | | | | true |
| {6} | | | | 2 | | |
| {7} | | | 3 | | | |
| {5} | | | | | | false |

Return to caller with Quotient = 3, Remainder = 2

It's necessary to write a value in a column only when a row changes the corresponding variable. Be sure to start with ?s for all the undefined variables. Trying to compute with an undefined variable is a common

programming error; hand-checking a program can detect these initialization errors.

Hand-checking a recursive subprogram can be quite confusing if you
don't have a methodical approach. The approach we show you here avoids
confusion; but you have to draw a box for each invocation of the
subprogram. In this method, you handle the return address by explicitly
drawing arrows which link the different invocations together. Once
again, an illustration best explains the method. We'll trace the
following recursive function

```
function Power(X : real; N : integer) : real; {N >= 0}
   begin {Power}
      if N = 0 then
         Power := 1
      else
         Power := X*Power(X, N - 1)
   end {Power}
```

assuming that the main program invokes it with this statement:

```
Y := Power(2, 3)
```

The invocation from Main passes the actual parameters 2 and 3 to Power,
indicated by the top two arrows in Figure C-1 (a). Power cannot return a
value at this time; however, we draw the bottom arrow in Figure C-1 (a)
to indicate that this first call should return 2*Power(2, 2) as soon as
the next (recursive) call of Power can return a value for Power(2, 2).
In Figure C-1 (b) we indicate the next (recursive) call of Power. Power
invokes itself two times without returning a value: Figures C-1 (b) and
(c). On its third recursive call--Power(2, 0)--Power finally returns a
value, 1. This is illustrated in Figure C-1 (d). Thus the fourth call
returns 1; the third call returns 2; the second call returns 4; and the
first call returns 8, the correct answer.


EXERCISES


   1. Trace IntegerDivision for these calls:

      a. IntegerDivision(4, 5)
      b. IntegerDivision(12, 3)
      c. IntegerDivision(1, 1)

   2. Write a recursive function to find the Nth term in the Fibonacci
series. This is a very inefficient way to generate Fibonacci numbers;
however, it's an interesting example to check by hand.

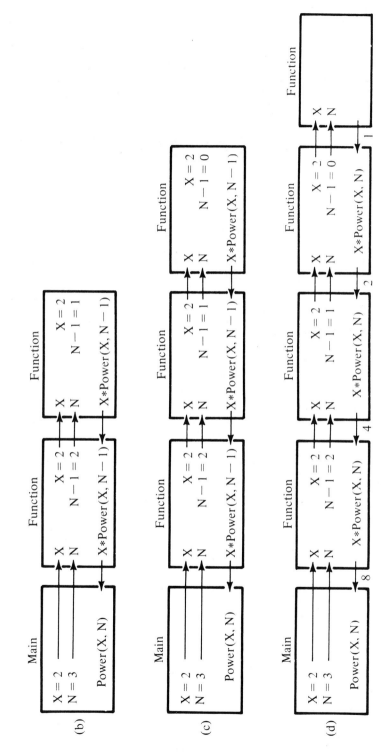

**Figure C.1** Recursive activation of Power

# Appendix D
# IBM 9-Unit System
# for Character Widths

| 3 Units | 4 Units | 5 Units | 6 Units | | 7 Units | 8 Units | | 9 Units |
|---------|---------|---------|---------|---|---------|---------|---|---------|
| i | f | a | b | P | B | w | V | m |
| j | r | c | d | S | C | A | X | M |
| l | s | e | h | * | E | D | Y | W |
| . | t | g | k | $ | F | G | & | |
| , | I | v | n | + | L | H | % | |
| ; | : | z | o | = | T | K | @ | |
| ' | ) | J | p | ] | Z | N | – | |
| ` | ( | ? | q | u | | O | | |
| | ! | [ | x | y | | Q | | |
| | / | | all | | | R | | |
| | | | numbers | | | U | | |

IBM "Selectric" Composer Character Unit Values

# Appendix E
# Summary of Data Types
# and Denotations of Variables

Figure E-1 gives a summary of Pascal's data types. Note that the simple data type has two subtypes, the <u>ordinal</u> data type and the <u>real</u> data type. The ordinal data type can be used as an array index, as a variant record tag type and case constant, and as a case index and case label. (The real data type cannot.) However, the integer data type cannot be directly used for these three entities; a subrange of the integer host type must be used--not the full integer range.

A variable denotation designates either an entire variable, a component of a variable, or a variable referenced by a pointer. In BNF notation

```
<variable> ::=
    <entire variable> | <component variable> | <referenced variable>
```

To describe these variables, we need some examples. Assume these definitions and declarations throughout this appendix:

```
type
    Pointer  = ^FullName;
    FullName =
        record
            Last       : packed array[1..15] of char;
            First      : packed array[1..12] of char;
            MiddleInit : char
        end;
var
    Ptr   : Pointer;
    Name  : FullName;
    Names : file of FullName;
    Done  : Boolean;
    Ch    : Char;
    I     : integer;
    X     : real;
    A     : array[1..100] of Name;
    M     : array[1..100, Boolean, Char] of real
```

## Entire Variables

An entire variable is an identifier that denotes a simple variable, a pointer variable, or an _entire_ structured (composite) variable. Examples are: Ptr, Name, Names, Done, Ch, I, X, A, M.

## Component Variables

A composite variable identifier followed by a selector denotes a _component_ of a composite variable. There are three kinds of composite data types and three associated forms of component selector.

    <composite type> ::= <array type> | <record type> | <file type>

    <component variable> ::=
       <indexed variable> | <field designator> | <file buffer>

## Indexed Variables

An indexed variable is a component of an array type. It's denoted as follows:

    <indexed variable> ::=
       <array variable> [ expression {, <expression> } ]

Each index expression must be an ordinal type compatible with the index type declared in the definition of the array type or the declaration of the array variable.

Examples:

    A[55]
    A[I div 2]
    A[ord(Ch)]
    A[trunc(X)]
    M[2*I, true, 'Q']
    M[12, Ch <> ' ', '1']

## Field Designators

A field designator denotes a component of a record type. Its form is

    <field designator> ::= <record variable> . <field identifier>

Examples:

    Name.Last
    Name.First
    Name.MiddleInit

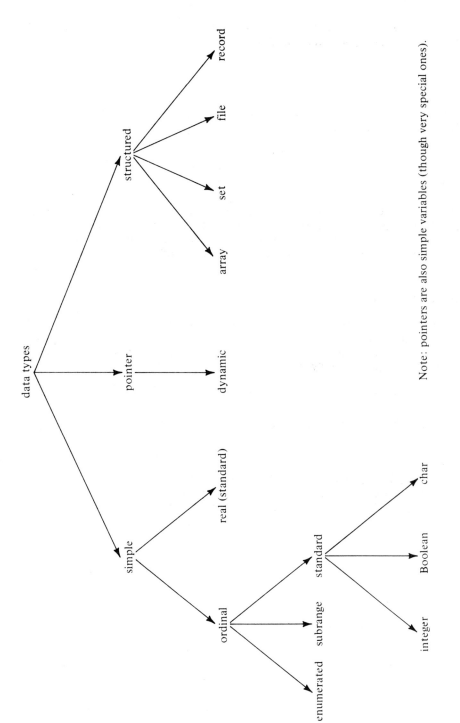

**Figure E.1** Pascal data types

## File Buffers

A file buffer, or buffer variable, denotes the currently accessible component of a file type. The following declaration

**var**
   F : **file of** T

automatically creates a file buffer variable of type T. This buffer variable is referred to by F^.

    &lt;file buffer&gt; ::= &lt;file variable&gt;^

Examples:

    Names^  {denoting the current whole record}
    Names^.MiddleInit  {denoting one field in the current record}
    Names^.Last[1]  {denoting the first character of the last name}
    Names^.First[N]  {denoting the Nth character of the first name}

## Referenced Variables

A referenced variable denotes the dynamic variable to which a pointer variable points. If P is a pointer variable defined to point at a dynamic variable of type T, then P denotes the pointer variable (or its value) and P^ denotes the dynamic variable to which P points.

    &lt;referenced variable&gt; ::= &lt;pointer variable&gt;^

It's an error to write "P^" if P's value is either **nil** or undefined.

Examples:

    Ptr^  {denotes a dynamic record of type FullName}
    Ptr^.Last  {denotes field Last of dynamic record}
    Ptr^.First[N]  {denotes Nth character of field First}

# Bibliography

BOOKS

In early 1980 there were one dozen books expounding Pascal or using Pascal as their main linguistic vehicle. From those dozen books, I have selected those I find most useful and durable. I place Professor Wirth's writing in a class by itself.

Jensen, K., & Wirth, N. <u>Pascal user manual and report</u> (2nd ed.). New York: Springer-Verlag, 1974. A durable gem that has been the <u>de facto</u> standard for Pascal. The present standardization effort for Pascal may finally overtake it. It's less than a textbook but more than a language manual. My biggest complaint is that the EBNF description is not alphabetized, making it hard to find a syntactic class quickly. Will there be a 3rd edition? We hope so.

Wirth, N. <u>Algorithms + data structures = programs</u>. Englewood Cliffs, NJ: Prentice-Hall, 1976. Wirth + Data Structures + Sorting + Recursive Algorithms + Dynamic Information Structures + Language Structures and Compilers + Pascal = a book that every serious student of computer science ought to read. Not an <u>introductory</u> book on programming or Pascal, this excellent book is <u>the</u> book to read after you've mastered an introductory course. Like Pascal, Wirth's writing is a nice balance of virtues.

Of all the other books on or in Pascal, I found the following three the most useful.

Welsh, J., & Elder, J. <u>Introduction to Pascal</u>. Englewood Cliffs, N. J.: Prentice-Hall International, 1979.

Grogono, P. <u>Programming in Pascal</u>. Reading, MA.: Addison-Wesley, 1978.

Findlay, W., & Watt, D.A. <u>Pascal: an introduction to methodical programming</u>. Potomac, MD.: Computer Science Press, 1978.

In case you think that Pascal is a phenomenon of the United States, the
above authors are Swiss, Irish, Canadian, and British.


MAGAZINES and JOURNALS


    Besides the above books there are important periodical sources of
articles about Pascal or Pascal programs. The first we'll mention is
unique--and a super bargain: <u>Pascal News</u>. <u>Pascal News</u> is a publication
of the Pascal User's Group (PUG); it publishes application programs,
software tools, articles, updates on Pascal standardization efforts,
implementation notes, and special features. For example, in issue 16,
October, 1979, <u>Pascal News</u> published a description of a Pascal
validation suite: "The validation suite provides program and procedures
whereby the correctness (or otherwise) of a Pascal processor may be
tested." <u>Pascal News</u> is an excellent source of <u>long</u> programs. Membership
in PUG is only $6.00 per year in the United States. (Membership brings
you all issues of <u>Pascal News</u> for one academic year.) See the
"All-Purpose Coupon" and information about ordering back issues on the
following pages.

<u>Software: Practice & Experience</u>, published monthly by John Wiley and
Sons, and <u>SIGPLAN Notices</u>, published monthly by the Special Interest
Group on Programming Languages of the Association for Computing
Machinery, also publish articles on Pascal and Pascal-based languages.
    In addition, the microcomputer and personal computer magazines
frequently publish articles on Pascal programming, compilers,
interpreters, and machines.

- - - - - - ALL-PURPOSE COUPON - - - - - -

Pascal Users' Group, c/o Rick Shaw
P.O. Box 888524
Atlanta, Georgia 30338 USA

**NOTE**

-- Membership is for an academic year (ending June 30th).
-- Membership fee and All-Purpose Coupon is sent to your Regional
-- Representative.
-- SEE THE POLICY SECTION ON THE REVERSE SIDE FOR PRICES AND ALTERNATE
   ADDRESS if you are located in the European or Australasian Regions.
-- Membership and Renewal are the same price.
-- The U.S. Postal Service does not forward Pascal News.
- - - - - - - - - - - - - - - - - - - - - - - - - - - - - - - - - - -

[ ] Enter me as a new member for:

[ ] Renew my subscription for:

[ ] 1 year  ending June 30, 1980

[ ] 2 years ending June 30, 1981

[ ] 3 years ending June 30, 1982

[ ] Send Back Issue(s)

[ ] My new/correct address/phone is listed below.

[ ] Enclosed please find a contribution, idea, article or opinion
    which is submitted for publication in the Pascal News.

[ ] Comments:_____

    _____

! ENCLOSED PLEASE FIND: A$   $

Name     _____

Address  _____

         _____

         _____

Phone    _____

Computer_____

Date     _____

JOINING PASCAL USERS' GROUP?


- Membership is open to anyone--particularly the Pascal user, teacher, maintainer, implementor, distributor, or just plain fan.
- Please enclose the proper prepayment (check payable to "Pascal Users' Group"); we will not bill you.
- Please do not send us purchase orders; we can't endure the paperwork!
- When you join PUG any time within an academic year, July 1 to June 30, you will receive all issues of Pascal News for that year.
- We produce Pascal News as a means toward the end of promoting Pascal and communicating news of events surrounding Pascal to persons interested in Pascal. We're simply interested in the news ourselves and prefer to share it through Pascal News. We desire to minimize paperwork because we have other work to do.

- American Region (North and South America): Send $10.00 per year to the address on the reverse side. International telephone: 1-404-252-2600.

- European Region (Europe, North Africa, Western and Central Asia): Join through PUG (UK). Send  5.00 per year to: Pascal Users' Group, c/o Computer Studies Group, Mathematics Department, The University, Southampton SO9 5NH, United Kingdom. International telephone: 44-703-559122 x700.

- Australasia Region (Australia, East Asia--including Japan): Join through PUG(AUS). Send $A10.00 per year to: Pascal Users' Group, c/o Arthur Sale, Department of Information Science, University of Tasmania, Boox 252C GPO, Hobart, Tasmania 7001, Australia. International telephone; 61-02-23 0561.

- PUG(USA) produces Pascal News and keeps all mailing addresses on a common list. Regional representative collect memberships from their regions as a sevice, and they reprint and distribute Pascal News using a proof copy and mailing labels sent from PUG(USA). Persons in the Australasian and European Regions must join through their regional representatives. People in other places can join through PUG(USA).

# Index